MERGERS AND ACQUISITIONS SIMULATIONS

Stacey L. Bowers

Associate Professor of the Practice of Law
University of Denver Sturm College of Law

BRIDGE TO PRACTICE®

WEST ACADEMIC PUBLISHING

Bridge to Practice Series is a trademark registered in the U.S. Patent and Trademark Office.

© 2019 LEG, Inc. d/b/a West Academic
    444 Cedar Street, Suite 700
    St. Paul, MN 55101
    1-877-888-1330

West, West Academic Publishing, and West Academic are trademarks of West Publishing Corporation, used under license.

Printed in the United States of America

ISBN: 978-1-68467-232-5

To Jeff, my staunch supporter.
I could not ask for a better partner in life.

ACKNOWLEDGMENTS

I am grateful to everyone who assisted me with this book and supported me through the process. Special thanks go to my acquisitions editors at West Academic, Jon Harkness and Louis Higgins, for their encouragement to work on this project and continuing support during its development and writing. I also want to extend my thanks to Michael P. Malloy at McGeorge School of Law for providing input and suggesting that I morph my Corporate Drafting: A Practical Approach into this Bridge to Practice Series. Additionally, thanks to my University of Denver Sturm College of Law colleagues for their support of this project.

Last, but certainly not least, I want to thank all my corporate drafting students through the years who offered insight into how to make many of these simulations better and more valuable. This book would not exist without their help.

INTRODUCTION

A critical skill for any aspiring transactional lawyer is the ability to draft documents that pertain to different types of deals and situations. One way for students to begin to develop and hone their drafting skills is to engage in a variety of simulations that help to lay a strong foundation as they move from law student to practicing attorney.

This book was developed and structured to be used as a stand-alone corporate drafting text book or in conjunction with a mergers and acquisitions course. The goal of the book is to create simulations for students that pertain to a merger and acquisition transaction starting with the formation of the client relationship and continuing through the merger transaction process and its ultimate closing. This book utilizes one cohesive scenario to form the basis of the underlying deal and asks students to draft a variety of documents, engage in negotiations, and assess legal issues relating to the merger transaction. The simulations in this book provide a wide range of discrete assignments that ultimately lead to a student drafting an entire merger and acquisition agreement along with many of the ancillary documents and filings that support a merger transaction.

Chapter One leads off with a brief overview of the main components of a merger and acquisition agreement and a stock purchase agreement. Chapter Two introduces students to the formation of the client relationship and the steps involved in that process. Chapter Three sets the groundwork for the potential merger transaction, including asking students to draft the confidentiality agreement, negotiate and draft the term sheet, and undertake a limited due diligence review. Chapters Four through Seven walk through the various provisions of the merger and acquisition agreement and include nine individual simulations that ultimately lead to students drafting the entire agreement. Chapter Eight introduces students to the various approvals required to effect a merger transaction and includes simulations requiring students to draft director and shareholder consent actions and a third-party consent. Chapter Nine presents two filings that often arise in the merger context—a Hart-Scott-Rodino Act filing and WARN Act notice—and asks students to analyze their applicability. Chapter Ten requires students to consider those ancillary documents that may be part of the merger transaction including the escrow, non-competition and non-solicitation, employment, and consulting agreements. Chapter Eleven familiarizes students with the closing process for a merger transaction and includes simulations pertaining to the preparation of a closing checklist and the various certificates that are required to close the transaction. Finally, Chapter Twelve wraps up by asking students to review and mark-up an indemnification provision and send the mark-up to the client under cover of an email communication, as well as prepare a press release announcing the merger.

The book contains 30 potential simulations of varying lengths and degrees of complexity, and allows professors to select the assignments they want to utilize during the course of the semester. While the chapters and simulations are designed to build upon one another, the book does not require the professor to utilize all of the simulations or in a particular order for it to function effectively.

The simulations in this book will introduce law students to the major components of a merger and acquisition, ask them to consider and draft the various documents that comprise a merger transaction, help them to understand the nuances of this type of large transaction, and ultimately prepare them to engage in this type of work early in their careers.

SUMMARY OF CONTENTS

TABLE OF CONTENTS

———————

MERGERS AND ACQUISITIONS SIMULATIONS

CHAPTER ONE

MERGERS AND ACQUISITIONS OVERVIEW

I. INTRODUCTION

The practice area of mergers and acquisitions is a staple for many transactional lawyers and runs the gamut from small to large dollar value transactions and involves companies of all types and sizes. Lawyers practicing in this field may participate in acquisitions that involve public companies, private companies, cross-border transactions, or private equity firms. This chapter introduces the basic structures of private mergers and acquisitions and the components of the merger and acquisition agreement and stock purchase agreement. In order to be a successful transactional lawyer, you must have a basic understanding of the contexts in which a private merger and acquisition takes place, as well as knowledge regarding the most effective deal structure for a particular merger transaction. The initial steps in that process are to understand the different structures employed in the context of private mergers and the types of agreements used for each structure. By understanding the structures and the agreements used to effect that structure, you are in a position to advise your client on the pros and cons of each and to discuss which structure may be the best fit for a particular transaction.

II. TYPES OF MERGER AND ACQUISITION STRUCTURES

A private merger and acquisition involves a transaction between two private companies and as a result, the securities law implications and complications that arise when a public company is involved do not exist in this scenario. That is not to say that there are not securities law related issues, but simply that the disclosure requirements imposed on public companies are not a consideration factor. The most common structures for these types of transactions generally take the form of a stock acquisition or merger.

A. STOCK ACQUISITION

A stock acquisition occurs when the buyer purchases the stock of the target company directly from the target company's selling shareholders. As a result, the buyer acquires all of the assets and rights of the target company and at the same time assumes all its liabilities and obligations. In essence, the ownership of the target company simply shifts from the selling shareholders of the target to the buyer, and to the outside world, the target continues to operate as it always has. This allows the buyer to acquire the target and easily continue to operate its business as a going concern. However, since the buyer also acquires the target company's liabilities and obligations, it must be cautious as that includes both known and unknown, as well as disclosed and undisclosed liabilities and ongoing obligations. There are a number of ways in which the buyer can attempt to protect itself from the target's liabilities, including operating the target as a wholly owned subsidiary of the buyer, as well as including indemnification and escrow protections in the stock purchase agreement.

A stock acquisition is often viewed as a more straightforward transaction, as opposed to a traditional merger. The parties (the buyer and the target's selling shareholders) enter into a stock purchase agreement for the sale of all of the issued and outstanding stock of the target and so the selling shareholders transfer the target stock to the buyer in exchange for the agreed upon consideration. Because the target continues to exist after the sale of the stock, this type of structure does not generally trigger third-party consents or contract assignment provisions. However, the buyer should be cognizant of any change of control provisions in the target's contracts as this transaction structure results in a change of control of the target. Additionally, provided the stock purchase agreement is solely entered into between the buyer and all of the target's selling shareholders, generally the necessary approvals of the target company's board of directors and selling shareholders can be accomplished through written consent actions. Finally, only the buyer's board of directors needs to approve the acquisition unless it is deemed material, and then, the buyer would also have to seek approval of its shareholders.

While straightforward, this structure is often not feasible when the target has a significant number of shareholders as the potential for certain shareholders to be holdouts or demand greater consideration is more likely to occur. In the case where the buyer can acquire 90% or more of the target's stock, the buyer may move forward with the stock acquisition and after the initial transaction closes, undertake a short form merger to acquire the interests of the remaining minority shareholders who were holdouts. A short form merger permits the buyer to acquire the minority shareholder interests without a vote and thus ultimately own 100% of the target's issued and outstanding stock through the two-step process, stock purchase followed by short form merger.

In the case where the buyer can acquire more than 50% of the target's stock, but less than the requisite 90% for a short form merger, and moves forward with the stock purchase, the buyer will have to contend with the remaining shareholders who do not participate in the stock acquisition and many times are disgruntled. Because that may be undesirable, the buyer should consider whether a traditional merger is the better option to utilize in acquiring the target in this circumstance.

All told, if the target has a limited number of shareholders who are all willing to agree to the same terms with limited negotiations, the stock purchase can be a simple and efficient way for the buyer to effect the acquisition of the target.

B. MERGERS

A merger transaction is one in which two companies are combined into a single entity with the surviving company assuming all of the assets and rights, and the liabilities and obligations of the target. Each state has a set of statutory requirements that govern a merger transaction that the lawyer must examine and follow to effect the transaction in compliance with the relevant laws. There are three primary ways to structures a merger transaction, a forward merger, a forward triangular merger, and a reverse triangular merger. While each structure has its own benefits and drawbacks, all three structure result in a change of control of the ownership of the target and the buyer should be aware of those implications.

1. Forward Merger

In a forward merger, the target merges with and into the buyer and thus ceases to exist as a separate entity and is subsumed into the buyer and its operations. Due to the fact that the target is merged into the buyer, the buyer cannot shield itself from the liabilities of the target. Because the target entity will cease to exist and the buyer will directly assume the target's obligations, third-party consent rights are generally triggered, which will require the buyer to obtain the consent of third parties to assign their contracts with the target to the buyer. A forward merger requires the approval of the buyer's board of directors, the target's board of directors, and at least a simple majority of the target's stockholders. Additionally, in most states the buyer must also secure the consent of at least a simple majority of its stockholders unless (i) the forward merger does not result in any changes to the buyer's articles of incorporation; (ii) the buyer's stock and its corresponding rights pre and post the forward merger remain the same; and (iii) no additional shares of buyer's stock are issued in connection with the forward merger.

2. Forward Triangular Merger

In a forward triangular merger, the target merges with and into a subsidiary of the buyer and thus ceases to exist as a separate entity and is subsumed into the subsidiary of the buyer. Since the target is merged into a subsidiary of the buyer, the buyer is able to shield itself from the liabilities of the target. Similar to the forward merger, because the target entity will cease to exist and the buyer's subsidiary will be the surviving corporation and assume the target's obligations, third-party consent rights are generally triggered, which will require the buyer to obtain the consent of third parties to assign their contracts with the target to the subsidiary of the buyer. A forward triangular merger requires the approval of the buyer's board of directors, the buyer's subsidiary's board of directors, and at least a simple majority of the subsidiary's shareholders, as well as the target's board of directors and at least a simple majority of the target's stockholders.

3. Reverse Triangular Merger

In a reverse triangular merger, the buyer's subsidiary merges with and into the target and thus the target is the surviving entity and continues to exist as a subsidiary of the buyer. Since the target becomes a subsidiary of the buyer, the buyer is able to shield itself from the liabilities of the target. Different from the forward and forward triangular merger, as the target continues to exist as a stand-alone subsidiary of the buyer, third party consent rights are not generally triggered. A reverse triangular merger requires the approval of the buyer's board of directors, the buyer's subsidiary's board of directors, at least a simple majority of the subsidiary's shareholders, as well as the target's board of directors and at least a simple majority of the target's stockholders.

C. REGULATORY APPROVALS

In addition to the corporate approvals delineated above in regard to each merger structure, the buyer must also determine whether the proposed merger transaction triggers other regulatory approvals. These other approvals may arise as a result of the specific industry in which the target operates or due to federal antitrust laws.

D. TAX CONSEQUENCES

Each of the discussed merger and acquisition structures have unique tax consequences, which should be carefully researched and understood so that each party is aware of the potential tax impacts. The tax consequences will differ depending on the party, buyer, target, or target's selling shareholders, and the parties may find themselves at odds over the best structure due to the various tax implications. Additionally, the type of consideration—cash, a promissory note, or buyer's stock—that is used may impact the tax consequences.

III. TYPES OF MERGER AND ACQUISITION AGREEMENTS

As discussed above, mergers and acquisitions come in all shapes and sizes. While each transaction will have its own specific terms and characteristics, every transaction requires an extensively negotiated and tailored agreement. In most mergers and acquisitions, the buyer's legal counsel will prepare the initial draft of the relevant agreement, which will incorporate the business terms the parties have agreed to, as well as likely favor the buyer. The agreement will undergo a number of rounds of revisions as the legal counsel for the parties negotiate various terms and provisions in an attempt to secure the best deal for their respective client within the bounds of what the business people have previously agreed to.

In most cases, the parties enter into the merger and acquisition agreement prior to the closing of the actual transaction. As a result, the agreement will contain a number of provisions regarding what the parties (mostly the target and the target's selling shareholders) can and cannot do during the period of time that commences with the execution of the merger and acquisition agreement and ends on the date of closing (the "gap period"). In the circumstance where execution of the agreement and closing of the transaction are simultaneous (which is rare), those particular provisions will be excluded from the merger and acquisition agreement.

Since you now have a basic understanding of the types of merger and acquisition structures, the next step is to examine and familiarize yourself with the various components of the related agreement. The most common agreements are the merger and acquisition agreement and stock purchase agreement.

A. MERGER AND ACQUISITION AGREEMENT

The merger and acquisition agreement will set forth all the details of the proposed merger transaction and will vary in length depending upon the size of the parties, the complexity of the transaction, and other details specific to that particular merger. The next sections briefly discuss each of the pertinent provisions of a merger and acquisition agreement.

1. Agreement Title

Most agreements contain some type of title at the top of the first page or on a stand-alone cover sheet that indicates the type of contract the document reflects. In order for a title to have value and meaning, it cannot simply be something generic such as "Agreement." While it is true that the document is an "agreement" that moniker does not provide the reader with any insight as to the content of the contract. The title should clearly indicate what this particular agreement addresses. In regard to a merger transaction, the title of the agreement might be any of the following: Merger Agreement; Merger Agreement and Plan of Merger; Merger and Acquisition Agreement; or another adequately descriptive title.

2. Introductory Paragraph or Preamble

The introductory paragraph, or preamble, generally restates the type of agreement being entered into, identifies all the parties to the transaction, indicates each party's state of incorporation or organization (when a business entity), and stipulates the date of the contract. The contract date may be the date of execution or another specified effective date and should include language that makes the date reference clear. In many cases, the introductory paragraph also sets forth the defined terms to be used within the agreement to identify the parties.

The parties to the agreement include the buyer, buyer's newly formed subsidiary (if a triangular merger), the selling company, and the stockholder representative for the selling company's shareholders. Though, in the case where there are only a few selling company shareholders, those individuals may be parties to the agreement. In the case of a triangular merger structure, the buyer is generally referred to as the "parent", the newly created subsidiary of the buyer is referred to as the "merger sub", the company being purchased is referred to as the "target", and the representative for the target's selling shareholders is referred to as the "stockholder representative." If the target's shareholders are parties to the agreement, they are collectively referred to as the "selling shareholders."

3. Recitals and Lead-in

After the introductory paragraph, it is commonplace to include a list of recitals that may begin with the term "whereas" or may be numbered or lettered. These recitals set forth the background information and provide context for the transaction. The recitals often help to clarify the parties' intentions for entering into the agreement and can provide guidance as to the contract's underlying purpose.

Some common recitals in a merger and acquisition agreement include: (i) statements regarding the nature of the transaction and why the parties are entering into the transaction; (ii) a stipulation that the board of directors of each company believes that the merger is fair and in the best interests of their respective shareholders; (iii) a stipulation that the respective boards of directors have voted in favor of the merger; (iv) a statement that the merger meets certain tax requirements; and (v) a statement that the parties desire to make certain representations, warranties, and covenants in connection with the merger. Other information that might be referenced in the recitals are the parties' intent to enter into certain employment or non-compete agreements with key persons or shareholders, or that a portion of the cash consideration is being placed in escrow.

Immediately after the recitals, there is a lead-in sentence that indicates that the parties agree to be bound by the terms that are set forth next, meaning the substantive body of the agreement.

4. Definitions

Generally, the first provision of the merger and acquisition agreement contains all the relevant defined terms. Though, in some cases, the definitions may be the last provision of or attached as an appendix to the agreement. This section will list all of the defined terms used throughout the agreement, whether defined in this particular provision or with a cross-reference to the specific section where such term is defined in the body of the agreement. Definitions should not be treated as boilerplate and each definition should be drafted and reviewed carefully to make certain it fits the context of the particular merger transaction. Additionally, definitions should be used consistently throughout the agreement and every capitalized term used in the agreement (with the exception of proper nouns) should be listed in the definition provision.

5. The Merger and Merger Consideration

One of the most important components of the merger and acquisition agreement is the merger and merger consideration provision. This provision sets forth exactly how the merger will be effectuated between the parties. It also indicates the underlying structure of the merger; meaning that it indicates whether the structure is a forward (or direct) merger, a forward triangular merger, or a reverse triangular merger.

The merger and merger consideration provision covers a significant amount of content that is incredibly important to the buyer, target, and target's selling shareholders. Some of the main components of this provision include the particulars regarding closing; the items that each party must deliver at closing; the effective time of the merger, which ties into the filing of the certificate of merger with the applicable states; the effects of the merger on the target; the governing documents for and the officers and directors of the surviving entity; the effects of the merger in regard to the target's stock, including the impact to the target's stock option plans, warrants, or convertible shares; how dissenting shares will be managed; how the target's selling shareholders will surrender their shares and receive payment of the merger consideration; details regarding the escrow of merger consideration (if any); details regarding post-closing adjustments such as a net working capital adjustment (if any); and details regarding any additional merger consideration payments such as earn-outs (if any).

6. Representations and Warranties of the Target

The merger and acquisition agreement will contain a provision that covers all the representations and warranties of the target, which will be supplemented by disclosure schedules that contain exceptions to or additional information regarding the particular representation and warranty. In some merger transactions, particularly if the target is a closely held entity with very few shareholders, the target's selling shareholders may also be required to make certain representations and warranties. The representations and warranties are meant to act as a device to protect the parent and merger sub and establish the parameters that allow the parent to terminate the agreement or seek indemnification.

Typical target representations and warranties include: (i) organization and corporate existence; (ii) authority; (iii) consents and approvals of third parties; (iv) capitalization; (v) financial statements; (vi) no undisclosed liabilities or litigation; (vii) absence of changes; (viii) material contracts; (ix) title to and condition of assets; (x) compliance with applicable laws and governmental regulations; (xi) employment and labor matters; (xii) environmental matters; (xiii) tax matters; (xiv) title to property; (xv) intellectual property; and (xvi) other relevant representations and warranties.

7.   Representations and Warranties of the Parent and Merger Sub

Both the parent and merger sub (if applicable), also make certain representations and warranties though these often seem minimal when compared to those made by the target. These representations and warranties generally serve the purpose of providing the necessary assurances to the target and the target's shareholders that the parent has the requisite power to enter into the transaction and has adequate stock or cash to carry through with the payment of the merger consideration at closing.

Typical parent and merger sub representations and warranties include: (i) organization and corporate existence; (ii) authority; (iii) consents; (iv) compliance with applicable laws; (v) no conflicts; (vi) availability and ownership of shares (if a portion of the merger consideration is paid in stock); (vii) availability of adequate funds; and (viii) other relevant representations and warranties.

8.   Covenants

The merger and acquisition agreement will contain a covenants provision that addresses the requirements of the parties during the gap period, which provision sets out those actions the parties must undertake to get to closing. Each party to the merger and acquisition agreement will have covenants pertaining to it, such as actions the party must take (or refrain from taking) before the transaction can be closed. However, a majority of the covenants are meant to protect the parent and include covenants such as the following: (i) target will continue to conduct its business as it has done in the past and will not make any material changes to the manner in which it conducts the business; (ii) target agrees to allow parent access to books, records, and other information regarding the target's business or its assets; (iii) target agrees to notify parent of any material changes; (iv) target agrees to take whatever continuing actions need to be taken to ensure that the merger takes place, such as obtaining shareholder consent, regulatory approvals, or third party consents; (v) target agrees not to solicit other buyers; (vi) target or its high level employees often agree not to compete with parent after the closing of the merger; and (viii) other pertinent covenants that the parties agree to include. There is often a separate provision that deals only with tax related covenants.

9.   Closing Conditions

Most merger and acquisition agreements include a provision that addresses the various parties' obligations in regard to closing (unless the execution of the merger and acquisition agreement and closing of the transaction occur simultaneously). The target, as well as the parent and merger sub (if applicable), must meet certain conditions before the other side is obligated to close the deal.

The parent generally requires that the following target conditions be met prior to or as of the closing date: (i) that all the representations and warranties of the target remain true and accurate; (ii) that all the covenants of the target have been met; (iii) that no orders or decrees exist that prevent the completion of the merger; (iv) that target has secured all necessary consents and waivers; (iv) that target has secured the release of all liens on its personal or real property; and (v) that target has delivered specific documents such as the certificate of merger, employee releases, legal counsel's opinion, officer's certificates, as well as other required documents.

Generally the target requires the following parent and merger sub conditions to be met prior to or as of the closing date: (i) that all the representations and warranties of the parent and its merger sub remain true and accurate; (ii) that all the covenants of the parent and its merger sub have been met; (iii) that no orders or decrees exist that prevent the completion of the merger; and (iv) that parent and its merger sub will have delivered specific documents such as employment agreements, officers' certificates, as well as other required documents.

10. Indemnification

The indemnification provision addresses each party's obligation to indemnify the other parties to the merger transaction. Each deal is unique as to the content in the indemnification provision, but the main areas of coverage include indemnification for the misrepresentation or breach of a representation or warranty, breach of a covenant, or liabilities that arise as a result of third-party claims or lawsuits.

11. Termination

The termination provision addresses the circumstances that allow for the merger to be terminated by the parties, whether mutual or unilateral, the effects of a termination, any fees associated with a termination, and which party bears the costs associated with a termination.

12. Miscellaneous

As with any contract, there is a catchall provision that covers all the miscellaneous and relevant contract details that are not included in their own stand-alone sections. Some typical miscellaneous provisions are: (i) entire agreement; (ii) successors and assigns; (iii) notices; (iv) governing law and jurisdiction; (v) amendment and modification; (vi) waiver rights; (vii) headings; (viii) counterparts; (ix) severability; (x) waiver of jury trial; and more.

13. Exhibits

Most merger and acquisition agreements will contain a number of exhibits. These may include net working capital calculations, ancillary agreements to the transaction, forms of the certificates of merger, forms of third party consents, officers' certificates, and other related information. Each deal is unique as to the exhibits that may be attached to the merger and acquisition agreement.

14. Disclosure Schedules

Merger and acquisition agreements will also contain a set of disclosure schedules for each party that list exceptions to and supplemental information regarding the respective party's representations and warranties. If information is contained in a disclosure schedule, the relevant representation and warranty provision will reference the disclosure schedule. While disclosure schedules often include exceptions to the actual representations and warranties, they may simply list supplemental information that the parties did not desire to include in the main body of the merger and acquisition agreement (e.g. a list of all material contracts).

B. STOCK PURCHASE AGREEMENT

The stock purchase agreement will set forth all the details of the proposed stock acquisition and will vary in length depending upon the size of the parties, the complexity of the transaction, and other details specific to that particular transaction. The next sections briefly discuss the pertinent provisions of a stock purchase agreement. In the case where the provisions of the stock purchase agreement are essentially the same or very similar to a merger and acquisition agreement, the text will reference the discussion under "III(A) Merger and Acquisition Agreement" discussed above.

In the context of a stock acquisition, the parent and target's selling shareholders will enter into a stock purchase agreement. Generally the target itself is not a party to the agreement though in some circumstances the parties may require the target company to be a party to the agreement.

1. Agreement Title

See discussion above in III(A)(1).

2. Introductory Paragraph or Preamble

In the context of a stock acquisition, the parties to the agreement include the buyer and the selling company's shareholders. Generally the selling company is not a party to the agreement though in some circumstances the parties may require the selling company be a party. The buyer is generally referred to as the "buyer", the selling company's shareholders are collectively referred to as the "seller" or "selling shareholders," and if the selling company is a party, it is referred to as the "target."

3. Recitals and Lead-in

See discussion above in III(A)(3).

4. Definitions

See discussion above in III(A)(4).

5. Purchase and Sale

One of the most important components of the stock purchase agreement is the purchase and sale provision. This section sets forth the amount of consideration that the buyer will pay the selling shareholders at closing and how that consideration will be allocated among the selling shareholders, if more than one.

The purchase and sale provision covers a significant amount of content that is incredibly important to the buyer and selling shareholders. Some of the main components of this provision include the particulars regarding closing; the items that each party must deliver at closing; details regarding the escrow of the stock purchase consideration (if any); details regarding post-closing adjustments such as a net working capital adjustment (if any); and details regarding any additional stock purchase consideration payments such as earn-outs (if any).

6. Representations and Warranties of the Selling Shareholders

The stock purchase agreement will contain a provision that covers all the representations and warranties of the selling shareholders (many of which will pertain to the target) that will be supplemented by disclosure schedules that contain exceptions to or additional information regarding the particular representation and warranty. The representations and warranties are meant to act as a device to protect the buyer and establish the parameters that allow the buyer to terminate the agreement or seek indemnification.

Typical selling shareholder representations and warranties include: (i) organization and corporate existence of the selling shareholders (if entities) and the target; (ii) authority; (iii) consents and approvals of third parties; (iv) capitalization; (v) financial statements; (vi) no undisclosed liabilities or litigation; (vii) absence of changes; (viii) material contracts; (ix) title to and condition of assets; (x) compliance with applicable laws and governmental regulations; (xi) employment and labor matters; (xii) environmental matters; (xiii) tax matters; (xiv) title to property; (xv) intellectual property; and (xvi) other relevant representations and warranties.

7. Representations and Warranties of the Buyer

The buyer will also make certain representations and warranties though these often seem minimal when compared to those made by the selling shareholders. These representations and warranties generally serve the purpose of providing the necessary assurances to the selling shareholders that the buyer has the requisite power to enter into the transaction and has adequate stock or cash to carry through with the payment of the consideration at closing.

Typical buyer representations and warranties include: (i) organization and corporate existence; (ii) authority; (iii) consents; (iv) compliance with applicable laws; (v) no conflicts; (vi) availability and ownership of shares (if a portion of the consideration is paid in stock); (vii) availability of adequate funds; and (viii) other relevant representations and warranties.

8. Covenants

See discussion above in III(A)(8).

9. Closing Conditions

See discussion above in II(A)(9).

10. Indemnification

See discussion above in III(A)(10).

11. Termination

See discussion above in III(A)(11).

12. Miscellaneous

See discussion above in III(A)(12).

13. Exhibits

See discussion above in III(A)(13).

14. Disclosure Schedules

See discussion above in III(A)(14).

IV. WHICH STRUCTURE MAKES THE MOST SENSE AND WHY?[1]

For purposes of this simulation, you are a junior associate in a law firm. One of the partners asks you to sit in on a meeting with a new client of the firm, Axiom, Inc., which is currently in talks with a larger company in the same general industry regarding an acquisition. The partner asks you to pay close attention to the conversation with the client as she would like you to assess which merger and acquisition structure you think might best meet the needs of this new client. During the course of the meeting with the new client, you learn the following particulars:

---

[1] Note that this is the only stand-alone simulation. All other simulations will build on the same companies (Tree Services, Inc. and Dutch Elm Company) and the fact scenario.

- Axiom, Inc., has been in business for approximately 4 years and operates in a discrete subset of the technology industry.

- The potential buyer, Alpha Corporation, is a large technology company that wants to expand its operations into this particular part of the industry through a variety of acquisitions and is currently exploring several potential acquisition targets.

- Axiom has 5 primary shareholders who own 78% of the issued and outstanding common stock, with the remaining 22% owned by 14 employees (mainly through exercises of stock option grants), and 10 friends and family who were early investors.

- The 5 primary shareholders are all in favor of proceeding forward with the sale of Axiom, but have not yet begun conversations with the employees or friends and family shareholders to gauge their interest as the acquisition discussions with Alpha are still preliminary.

- Axiom generates the bulk of its revenues and profits through sales of its core products that it develops and designs internally, many of which are patented.

- Axiom has long-term debt in the form of a revolving credit facility with a commercial lender, which credit facility contains anti-assignment and change of control provisions.

- Axiom currently employs 28 people, including the 5 primary shareholders (who are the company's founders and executive officers).

- The 5 primary shareholders are most interested in selling their stock (and the company) for cash consideration and aren't really interested in taking any stock consideration in Alpha.

- Axiom, Inc. and the buyer are both Delaware companies.

Part A: Based on the information that you learned during the client meeting as set forth above, assess the pros and cons of each of the discussed merger and acquisition structures (ignore tax consequences). In addition, attempt to note any additional information you might need to make a more thorough evaluation.

Part B: Assume that Alpha Corporation has proposed a $350 million cash purchase. Using all the information you have, compare and contrast the Merger and Merger Consideration provision for a reverse triangular merger structure and the Purchase and Sale provision for a stock acquisition merger (ignore tax consequences).

CHAPTER TWO

ESTABLISHING THE CLIENT RELATIONSHIP

I. INTRODUCTION

One of the first steps in the legal representation process is the formation of the relationship between the law firm (and its lawyers) and the potential client. Generally, the attorney and potential client will have an initial phone or in-person consultation so that both parties can discuss the circumstances of the proposed transaction and relationship in order to determine whether to proceed with a formalized engagement. The client must decide whether the law firm and its lawyers are the best fit for its needs and the transaction at hand. At the same time, the law firm and its lawyers must make a decision as to whether the firm desires to represent the client and if the lawyers have the requisite skill set to do so. If both parties decide to move forward with the relationship, the next step will be to enter into an attorney-client engagement letter that forms the basis of the representation.

II. THE CLIENT INTERVIEW

For purposes of this simulation, you are a junior associate at the law firm of Williams & Rader, LLC. Sasha Williams, one of the named partners, has scheduled an initial consultation with a potential new client, Tree Services, Inc. (see Appendix A for details regarding this potential new client) in regard to a potential sale of the company to a large national competitor. Ms. Williams has asked you to put together a list of pertinent information she should gather in the initial client meeting in order for the firm to be in a position to possibly move forward with this client relationship.

Prepare a brief memo for Ms. Williams that sets forth the information you believe she should gather so that she, and the firm, can assess whether the firm should represent Tree Services, Inc.

III. THE ATTORNEY-CLIENT ENGAGEMENT LETTER

The attorney-client engagement letter, which may also be referred to as a retainer agreement or fee agreement, is a contractual arrangement that sets forth the terms of the relationship between the client and the law firm. The engagement letter helps ensure that the parties are in agreement as to the scope of the services that the law firm is being engaged to provide and the costs of those services, as well as the responsibilities of each of the parties.

The American Bar Association's Model Rules of Professional Conduct ("Model Rules") govern the matters that the law firm must include in an engagement letter. In particular, the law firm must disclose to the potential client the firm's rates for billable hours and the other fees and expenses for which it charges the client. This requirement prevents any misunderstanding between the parties as to the costs of the services that the firm will provide. In addition to reviewing the Model Rules, it is critical to review the specific state's rules of professional conduct in regard to engagement letters as many states have added specific requirements regarding what a law firm must include in the engagement letter. For instance, some states require a written contract or additional disclosures if the work is contingency fee based. The next sections discuss many, but not all, of the main components of the engagement letter.

A. IDENTIFICATION OF THE CLIENT

The engagement letter should set forth the identity of the client or clients, if there is more than one. In those circumstances where the client is an entity, it should be clear whether the law firm is only representing one particular entity or if it is also representing related entities, such as a subsidiary or affiliate. Additionally, both the client and law firm will want it to be clear which individuals have the right to speak for the entity. In those circumstances where the client is an individual, it should be clear in what capacity the law firm is representing the individual. For example, is the law firm representing the individual in their capacity as a majority shareholder, an officer, a director, an individual, or in both an official and individual capacity.

In those situations where the law firm is representing more than one client, the engagement letter should address what will happen in the event that a conflict of interest arises between the jointly represented parties. The letter should indicate what circumstances may result in the law firm withdrawing from the representation, whether as a whole or just in regard to some of the clients. For example, a law firm representing both the company and majority stockholders in a transaction may indicate that if a conflict arises it will continue to represent the company and the majority stockholders will have to seek other counsel.

In some circumstances, it can also be important to indicate those individuals or entities that do not fall within the definition of the client so there is no confusion as to whether the firm represents a particular party. For example, the firm may want to make it clear that it only represents the entity in a merger transaction and not the selling shareholders, if that is the case.

B. SCOPE OF THE REPRESENTATION

The engagement letter should specifically detail those matters for which the law firm is representing the client. It is generally in the best interests of both parties for the scope to be as concise and narrow as possible so that no misunderstandings arise as to the firm's obligations or the client's expectations. Additionally, the length of the representation should be noted, and in the case of a transaction, it may simply be stated that the representation ends upon completion of the transaction. Lastly, if the firm will not represent the client in regard to specific matters (e.g. tax, employment, or intellectual property), it is wise for that to also be set forth as a limitation to the scope of representation.

C. FEES, EXPENSES, AND BILLING PROCEDURES

Pursuant to the Model Rules, the fees that the law firm charges a client must be reasonable given the particular circumstances of the representation.[1] While fees must be reasonable, there is no set requirement as to how a law firm bills a client for its work. There are many different manners in which a law firm may charge the client ranging from the traditional billable hour plus actual expenses to a flat fee arrangement to a contingency fee arrangement. No matter the type of fee arrangement that the firm and client agree to, it should be clearly stipulated in the engagement letter and include relevant explanatory language so that the client has a clear understanding of how it will be charged for the services provided.

In addition to billing for the actual services performed, many firms also pass through a variety of expenses to the client, including printing, postage, legal research, filing fees, travel, and more. Just like the charges for actual work, the engagement letter should detail those expenses that the client will be responsible for paying.

In conjunction with the fees and expenses, the engagement letter should indicate how frequently the law firm will submit a bill to the client, as well as the firm's expectations regarding payment.

---

[1]   Model Rules of Prof'l Conduct R. 1.5 (2018).

The letter should indicate when payments are due, any penalty for a late payment, the process for objecting to a listed charge, and the methods of acceptable payment (e.g. check or wire transfer).

D. RETAINER

The engagement letter should also address whether the law firm requires a retainer from the client in conjunction with the representation. Generally, if it is a new client of the firm, the firm will require that the client submit a retainer in order to ensure that it can cover the fees and expenses of the representation. On the other hand, if it is a client that the firm has previously worked with and the client has established its ability to meet the fees and expenses (and has a track record of paying its bills on time), the firm may not require a retainer deposit.

In the event that a retainer is required, the letter should indicate how the retainer will be handled in regard to the client's bills. There are a variety of ways that the retainer arrangement may be structured—the law firm may (i) maintain the retainer deposit until the end of the engagement; (ii) apply the retainer to each successive invoice until it is depleted and then require the client to replenish the retainer; or (iii) apply the retainer to each successive invoice until it is depleted and then require the client to simply pay its bills. In any instance, it should be clear how the retainer will be managed and the process for the refund of any unearned retainer deposit at the end of the representation.

E. COMMUNICATION AND COOPERATION

Many engagement letters include provisions regarding communication and cooperation between the client and the law firm. This provision may indicate the level and frequency of communication from the law firm to the client, as well as the law firm's expectations about how the client will communicate relevant information and decisions regarding the representation to the law firm. In addition to discussing the importance of communication in general, this provision will often address the risks of electronic communication, whether email, text, phone, or other related type of electronic communication, and specifically require the client to acknowledge those ways in which it is willing to receive communications from the firm.

In regard to cooperation, the letter generally requires the client to commit that it will cooperate with the law firm in regard to the representation and that the client will be available to discuss matters that arise, review drafted documents, participate in phone calls, and more.

F. TERMINATION AND CLIENT'S FILE

The engagement letter should contain a provision that discusses how the relationship can be terminated, as well as what happens upon termination. Most letters give the client the unilateral right to terminate the representation at any time and for any reason upon the client's written notice to that effect to the specified party at the law firm. The law firm can generally terminate the representation for "good cause."[2] Other circumstances where the law firm can terminate the representation that may be included in the letter are if the (i) client does not honor the terms of the representation, (ii) client does not pay its fees and expenses in a timely manner; (iii) client fails to cooperate; or (iv) law firm's representation becomes illegal or unethical.

This provision should also address how the client's file is handled upon termination of the representation. In most engagement letters, the law firm will reserve the right to place a lien on the client's file in the event that the client has not paid the firm in full for its fees and expenses.

In the circumstance where termination occurs as a result of the completion of the representation, meaning the terms of the representation have come to a natural end, the provision should address

---

[2] Model Rules of Prof'l Conduct R. 1.6(b) (2018).

retention of the client's file. Generally, the letter will stipulate that the client can request that its file be returned to it, but that if it does not do so the law firm will maintain the file for a set number of years at which point in time the file will be destroyed.

G. DISPUTE RESOLUTION PROCESS

The engagement letter should include details regarding how a dispute between the parties will be handled. Like any contract, the parties can determine how they would like to manage the dispute process. Many times the parties will agree to arbitration, and in that case, the engagement letter should set forth a particular arbitrator or arbitral body. In some states, the bar association offers an arbitration process that the parties can utilize to resolve conflicts. No matter what the parties decide, the law firm should review its state's ethical rules to make sure the selected dispute resolution process complies with its legal and ethical obligations.

H. ATTORNEY-CLIENT PRIVILEGE

The engagement letter should contain a provision that discusses the concept of attorney-client privilege. The letter should explain those circumstances where communications may not be privileged, such as the law firm is compelled to disclose client communications by a court order. In those situations where the client is an entity, the letter should indicate those parties who can speak on behalf of the client and thus fall within the privilege—for example the executive officers, directors, or managers.

IV. ENTERING INTO THE CLIENT ENGAGEMENT

For purposes of this simulation you are a junior associate at the law firm of Williams & Rader, LLC. The initial client meeting that Sasha Williams had with Tree Services, Inc. went well and both parties desire to enter into an attorney-client relationship where your firm will represent Tree Services, Inc. in the potential sale of its business and all related aspects with the exception of any intellectual property matters.

Ms. Williams has asked you to draft the engagement letter for her review and that the letter should include all standard and relevant provisions for a transaction of this type. She has provided you with the following specific information:

- The firm has agreed to represent the entity, Tree Services, Inc., and the three primary shareholders, Melissa Green, Thomas Shrub, and Susan Brown.

- The firm requires an initial retainer of $150,000 and the retainer is due within three days of TSI's execution of the engagement letter. After the initial retainer is used, TSI will pay its bills when due. However, if TSI makes two or more late payments, the firm will require an additional $100,000 retainer to continue its representation.

- The firm will bill TSI hourly at the rates set forth below, which are adjusted at the beginning of each calendar year:

	Billing Rate Ranges
Partners	$385–$425/hour
Senior Associates	$315–$375/hour
Junior Associates	$225–$295/hour
Paralegals	$85–$105/hour
Law Clerks	$60–$80/hour

- The firm will require TSI to pay the following expenses: photocopying, filing fees, legal research, and travel and travel related costs. ✓

- The firm invoices at the beginning of each calendar month for the prior month's work and invoices are due within 20 days of their date. Late payments accrue interest at the rate of 8% per annum. Clients have 7 days to dispute an invoice charge.

- The client may elect to pursue binding arbitration regarding disputes.

CHAPTER THREE

LAYING THE GROUNDWORK FOR THE MERGER AND ACQUISITION

I. INTRODUCTION

Before the parties can enter into official discussions regarding a merger and acquisition or start the process of drafting the definitive merger and acquisition agreement, a number of initial steps should take place. While these steps help to lay the groundwork for the actual merger and acquisition, they also act as protective devices for the parties to the transaction. In essence, they allow the parties to commence the merger and acquisition process and discover whether the transaction is in the parties' best interests before traveling too far down the path of a transaction that turns out not to be suitable for any number of reasons. The three main initial steps to lay the groundwork for the transaction may include entering into a confidentiality agreement, agreeing to and setting forth the preliminary terms of the merger and acquisition in a term sheet or letter of intent, and initiating the due diligence review process. While the parties may pick and choose among the three preliminary steps, it is fairly typical for all three to occur as part of any merger and acquisition.

II. CONFIDENTIALITY AGREEMENT

Prior to commencing detailed negotiations of the potential merger and acquisition and the target entity sharing information regarding its business operations and financial condition with the potential buyer, the parties to the transaction should enter into a confidentiality agreement. This agreement protects the target entity and allows it to share sensitive and confidential information with the buyer, while at the same time restricting the buyer from sharing that information with non-affiliated third parties. The confidentiality agreement should also prevent the potential buyer from using the information for a purpose other than evaluating the potential merger and acquisition, such as gaining access to trade secrets of the target, poaching key employees of the target, or using it to gain control of the target in a different manner.

The next sections discuss the most critical components of the confidentiality agreement.

A. DEFINITION OF CONFIDENTIAL INFORMATION

The definition of what is, or is not, included in confidential information is of utmost importance to the target, as this is how the target protects itself as the buyer will be prevented from disclosing any material that falls within this definition, with limited exceptions. Because of this, the target wants this definition to be as broad as possible and cover all the material that the target shares with the potential buyer and its representatives, as well as any materials that the buyer prepares or derives based on the provided confidential information. General exceptions include information received by the potential buyer from third parties when the buyer had no reason to believe the third party was subject to a confidentiality restriction and information that becomes public through no fault of the potential buyer or its representatives.

B. PERMITTED USE OF THE CONFIDENTIAL INFORMATION

This is the provision that requires the potential buyer to keep the target's confidential information confidential, with the exception of sharing it with those permitted representatives of the buyer, such as its accountants, financial advisors, and legal counsel. The target should ensure that the buyer is responsible for notifying its permitted representatives of the confidentiality obligations and is also responsible for breaches by those third-parties who are permitted representatives (which the potential buyer is likely to push back on). This provision should also make it clear in what ways the potential buyer can use the confidential information—meaning simply to evaluate, negotiate, and finalize the transaction and for no other purpose (e.g. a hostile acquisition or soliciting target's key employees).

C. RETURN OR DESTRUCTION OF THE CONFIDENTIAL INFORMATION

While this provision loses its significance when the merger and acquisition transaction closes, it is essential in those circumstances where the transaction is not finalized. This provision should require the potential buyer to either return or destroy all confidential information (and derived works) at the target's request, as well as certify to the return or destruction of all confidential information.

D. OTHER PERTINENT PROVISIONS

In addition to the three critical components discussed above, the confidentiality agreement may contain other essential provisions dependent upon the nature of the transaction and the respective parties' bargaining power. Such provisions might include:

(i)   a non-solicitation provision that prevents the potential buyer from hiring the target's employees during the course of negotiations and for a set period of time if the transaction fails to close;

(ii)   a standstill provision that prevents the buyer from a hostile takeover if the parties fail to complete a mutually agreed upon merger and acquisition, which provision is crucial when the target is a publicly-traded company;

(iii) an exclusivity or no-shop provision that requires the target to negotiate exclusively with the potential buyer for a set period of time;

(iv) a no further obligations provision to ensure that the parties are not bound to move forward with the merger and acquisition just by entering into the confidentiality agreement; and

(v) other standard miscellaneous provisions including term, remedies, disclaimer of representations and warranties, duty to inform of unauthorized disclosures, public announcements, governing law, assignment, waivers, severability, entire agreement, and notices.

III. ENTERING INTO THE CONFIDENTIALITY AGREEMENT

For purposes of this simulation you are a junior associate at the law firm of Williams & Rader, LLC. Sasha Williams has told you that Tree Services, Inc. and its primary selling shareholders indicated that they want to move forward with formal negotiations with Dutch Elm Company regarding its potential acquisition of Tree Services, Inc. Ms. Williams has requested that you draft a standard unilateral confidentiality agreement that contains all those provisions and terms that you deem relevant and forward it to her for review. She provided you with the following additional information to take into account when drafting the agreement:

- Tree Services, Inc. and its primary shareholders feel strongly about protecting all of the company's business and related information. — 1(b) eval material

- The company and its primary shareholders believe that they can reach an agreement with Dutch Elm Company and close the merger and acquisition within the next 6–9 months and may be willing to re-evaluate if the transaction is not closed in that amount of time. — term of 2+ years

- The company and its primary shareholders desire to protect the key employees during *8, Non Solicitation* merger talks and also in the event the transaction does not come to fruition.

- The company and its primary shareholders are willing to agree to refrain from talking with other potential buyers (other than Dutch Elm Company) for a limited amount of time.

- The company and its primary shareholders would like to place strict limitations on those representatives that Dutch Elm Company can share TSI's confidential information with. *— Affiliate, Person, Representative*

IV. TERM SHEET

The term sheet, which may also be referred to as a letter of intent or memorandum of understanding, is the agreement between the parties that sets forth the major terms of the proposed merger and acquisition transaction. The term sheet is typically non-binding (with the exception of certain select provisions) meaning that while it includes the important terms regarding the proposed merger and acquisition, it does not obligate the parties to consummate the transaction or bind them to the proposed merger terms. However, the term sheet serves important purposes, including that it often signifies the parties' strong intent and commitment to move forward with the transaction, can highlight potential significant deal issues or deal breakers, can compel the parties to focus on negotiations, and can help to avoid potential misunderstandings regarding the terms of the deal.

The next sections discuss the most critical components of the term sheet.

A. TERMS OF THE PROPOSED TRANSACTION

This provision sets forth the proposed terms of the transaction that the parties have tentatively agreed to and is generally the most important for the business people involved in the transaction. It should set forth the underlying structure of the transaction and what the buyer is purchasing for the consideration it is providing. The provision should specify the consideration, whether all cash, all buyer stock, or a combination of both, as well as when, how, and in what proportion the consideration will be paid such as all at closing or some held back or placed in an escrow for the established purposes (e.g. indemnification escrow, purchase price adjustment, or earn-out escrow). This provision should also address the details of any purchase price adjustments (e.g. net working capital adjustment) or additional consideration (e.g. earn-out consideration) and potentially related escrows.

B. CONDITIONS OF BUYER *→ what needs to happen between LOI & sign of document*

This provision will set forth those major conditions that must be met in order for buyer to be compelled to close the transaction with a reference to the fact that the definitive agreement will contain all customary closing conditions for a transaction of this type. In particular, this provision will generally reference buyer's satisfactory completion of its due diligence of the target, buyer's receipt of its financing commitment letters (if necessary), the receipt of board of director and shareholder approvals (of all necessary parties), the receipt of required regulatory approvals (e.g. Hart-Scott-Rodino antitrust approval), the retention of any key employees, and the finalization and execution of a definitive merger and acquisition agreement.

C. COVENANTS OF TARGET

This provision will specify how the target must run its business and operations starting on the date the term sheet is executed through the date the definitive agreement is executed. In essence, the buyer wants to ensure that the target continues to operate in the ordinary course of its business, maintains its assets and equipment, and maintains its key employees and customers.

D. EXCLUSIVITY

This provision is going to require the target to deal exclusively with the buyer regarding a potential acquisition commencing on the date of execution of the term sheet and continuing until the term sheet has terminated or a specified date. This acts as incentive for the potential buyer to begin the process of due diligence and drafting the definitive agreement, which can be costly obligations. The provision should make it clear the length of the exclusivity period and what occurs upon its expiration including whether it can be mutually extended or whether one party owes the other any payment to cover expenses. While primarily meant to protect the potential buyer, the target should ensure that the provision does not prevent it from meeting its fiduciary obligations if an unsolicited offer is presented from another party or tie its hands for too long of a period of time.

E. TERMINATION

This provision sets forth the circumstances under which the term sheet automatically terminates, meaning upon execution of a definitive agreement, by mutual agreement, or by a certain date and time. This provision should also reference the other provisions of the term sheet that survive termination such as expense reimbursements, governing law, and confidentiality.

F. OTHER PERTINENT PROVISIONS

In addition to the components discussed above, the term sheet may contain other provisions such as definitive agreement, due diligence, employment agreements, offer's expiration date, and standard miscellaneous clauses.

V. NEGOTIATING AND DRAFTING THE TERM SHEET

There are two parts to this simulation—the first involves negotiation of the terms of the potential transaction between Dutch Elm Company and Tree Services, Inc. and the second involves preparing a draft of the term sheet based upon the negotiated terms.

Part A: For purposes of this simulation, divide the class into two groups with one group acting as the junior associates at Williams & Rader, LLC, the firm that represents Tree Services, Inc. and the primary shareholders, and the other group acting as the junior associates at McClelland, Springer & Combelic, PC the firm that represents Dutch Elm Company.

Each group should review the respective information regarding their assigned client contained in Appendix A (Tree Services, Inc.) or Appendix B (Dutch Elm Company) in order to prepare and generate a list of questions for a meeting with their respective client. After meeting with their client, each group should reconvene and formulate a strategy to negotiate the terms of the term sheet based upon the information each group learned from their respective client, as well as their knowledge of the components of a term sheet. The groups should focus on their negotiation strategies regarding the structure of the merger; the consideration, including any escrow, adjustments, or additional consideration; any significant required conditions or covenants; and any other significant terms that the client or your group deems relevant.

After the groups have prepared their strategies, the groups will participate in a negotiation session where each group negotiates the terms of term sheet for their respective client.

Part B: For purposes of this simulation, you are a junior associate at the law firm that represents your assigned client for the term sheet negotiation in Part A above (Williams & Rader, LLC for TSI or McClelland, Springer & Combelic, PC for DEC). The partner handling the matter for your respective firm (Ms. Williams for TSI or Mr. Combelic for DEC) has tasked you with drafting the term sheet that addresses the negotiated terms and contains all the provisions and other related terms you deem relevant and based on your client's best interests.[1]

VI. DUE DILIGENCE

When the potential buyer and target have reached the stage in the merger and acquisition process where both parties are in a position to commit and desire to move forward with the transaction, the due diligence process generally begins. As noted in the discussion regarding confidentiality agreements, the target should ensure that the confidentiality agreement is in place prior to sharing confidential information with the potential buyer. Due diligence is the process that the buyer undertakes to investigate and understand the target and its business, and that it uses to determine whether it should proceed with the transaction. While the main components of the due diligence review are to identify and assess business concerns, legal risks, and required actions to effect the transaction, the process also enables the buyer to learn more about the potential opportunities that may result from the acquisition.

Due diligence is an on-going investigative process that takes place over the course of weeks or months, depending on the type, size, and timing of the potential transaction. While it is often commenced early in the process of the merger and acquisition, it is not unusual for drafting of the definitive agreement to be under way while the due diligence process continues. The buyer's goal is to learn as much as it can about the target it is acquiring in order to prepare a definitive agreement that addresses any potential issues or areas of concern (e.g. an indemnification escrow, purchase price adjustment, or additional closing conditions). No two due diligence processes unfold the same way as each is unique to the specific circumstances of the transaction.

The buyer's counsel will initiate the due diligence process by sending a due diligence request to the target and its legal counsel that lists all the material that the buyer desires to review. Some of the major categories of information that buyer will review include: (i) target's organizational documents; (ii) contracts of all types (e.g. employee, customer, supplier, licenses, and commercial loan agreements); (iii) financial and tax related information; (iv) pending and threatened litigation information; (v) intellectual property materials; and (vi) employee benefits information. Generally, the target will upload the requested information (typically in the form of documents) to an electronic or virtual data room for the buyer and its counsel to review. Buyer's counsel will review the provided information, make any necessary follow-up requests, and prepare a summary of its findings in the form requested by the buyer (e.g. a traditional memorandum, summary tables or spreadsheets, or another agreed upon format). The due diligence report's length generally correlates to the breadth and depth of the due diligence investigation, but more often than not can be quite lengthy. A good due diligence report should be as concise as possible and allow the buyer to easily spot issues, concerns, and required actions.

VII. UNDERTAKING DUE DILIGENCE

For purposes of this assignment you are a junior associate at the law firm of McClelland, Springer & Combelic, PC. Dutch Elm Company has asked Greg Combelic to commence the due diligence investigation of Tree Services, Inc. in regard to DEC's potential acquisition of TSI and Mr. Combelic submitted the initial due diligence request to TSI's legal counsel. Mr. Combelic has asked you to review the five documents listed below that TSI uploaded to the virtual data room and prepare a due diligence summary. Your summary should address any potential areas of concern or risks and

---

[1] If the students did not undertake the negotiation simulation in Part A, provide them with the specifics of the merger transaction included in the teacher's manual to complete this simulation and those in the following chapters.

list any required next steps or open action items, as well as include any other information you deem pertinent.

The five contracts (included in Appendix C) that you have been asked to review are as follows:

1.   Industrial Lease Agreement between Tree Services, Inc. and Giant Real Estate Company dated April 1, 2014.

2.   Loan Agreement between Tree Services, Inc. and Big Bank of Colorado dated June 15, 2018.

3.   Executive Employment Agreement between Tree Services, Inc. and Melissa Green dated February 1, 2008.

4.   Tree Services, Inc. 2013 Equity Incentive Plan.

5.   Customer Relationship Management Software License Agreement between Tree Services, Inc. and CRM Suiteware, Inc. dated June 10, 2017.

CHAPTER FOUR

THE MERGER AND ACQUISITION AGREEMENT—PART I

I. INTRODUCTION

As discussed in Chapter One, mergers occur in all types of ways depending upon such matters as whether the companies are small or large, privately owned or publicly traded, financially sound or distressed, in the same or different industries, as well as a plethora of other factors. Notwithstanding the manner of the merger and acquisition, the provisions that comprise the over-arching agreement are fairly similar from deal to deal. Chapters Four through Seven will examine all the main provisions in a merger and acquisition agreement.

Before diving into what many think of as the heart of the merger and acquisition agreement, the attorney drafting the agreement must set out the front matter meaning the cover page, table of contents, introductory paragraph, recitals, and lead-in. Once those initial matters have been covered, the next provision of the agreement is generally the pertinent definitions. While the inclination may be to treat the definitions as simply a boilerplate section of the agreement, they are anything but boilerplate. While many terms will be defined in the same way with the exact same words from one merger and acquisition agreement to the next, many terms will be defined in such a way as to be unique to the deal at hand.

II. THE FRONT MATTER

The front matter consists of the cover page, table of contents, introductory paragraph, recitals, and lead-in. Both the cover page and introductory paragraph should set forth the names of the parties to the agreement, as well as the state of incorporation if the party is a business entity. The introductory paragraph should also create a defined term for each party and the defined term should make it clear what role that particular party plays in the transaction. For instance the company making the acquisition is often defined as the "buyer" or "parent," if there is a subsidiary that will merge with the selling company, it is generally defined as the "merger sub," and the company being acquired is defined as the "target" or "seller." If individual shareholders are parties to the agreement, they are typically referred to as the "selling shareholders" and if there is a representative acting on behalf of all the selling shareholders that party is often referred to as the "stockholder representative."

Unless there are only a few shareholders, it is generally too much of a burden to require each shareholder to be a party to the merger and acquisition agreement. As a result, there is a stockholder representative that acts on behalf of all the selling shareholders. Whether the selling shareholders are parties or the stockholder representative is the sole party on their behalf, from the buyer's perspective it is important that those parties are bound as it is the selling shareholders, meaning those persons who receive the merger consideration, that will be responsible for satisfying any post-closing obligations on behalf of the target.

The next front matter content is the recitals. While recitals are not required in any agreement, they are helpful in that they provide background and context for the merger transaction. Additionally, the recitals provide an opportunity to call out important aspects of the transaction, such as the fact that certain key employees of the target will remain as employees after the closing or that a portion of the merger consideration will be held in escrow.

The last component of the front matter is the lead-in sentence to the substance of the merger and acquisition agreement. This sentence serves as the transition into the body of the agreement and makes it clear that all the parties identified in the introductory paragraph agree to be bound to all of the terms that are set forth.

III. DEFINITIONS

The majority of merger and acquisition agreements warrant a stand-alone definition provision that sets forth all the defined terms used within the agreement, whether defined in that provision or with a cross-reference to where the term is defined in the body of the agreement. As previously discussed, the definitions should never be viewed as simply boilerplate and copied from one agreement to the next without careful consideration. While many defined terms in a merger and acquisition context may be viewed as standard and often do not change, each defined term should be closely reviewed or drafted to ensure that it meets the requirements of the current transaction. In the context of a merger and acquisition agreement, it is not unusual for there to be more than one hundred defined terms, many of which are uniquely negotiated and phrased for a particular transaction. For instance, a defined term may be customized to exclude certain items from the definition of "current liabilities" or to limit the definition of "knowledge" to a smaller subset of the target company's officers. So, while it is a time consuming endeavor to carefully read and draft each defined term for a merger transaction, it is also a critical task to ensure that the defined terms accurately represent the specifics of the current deal, because the definitions play a critical role in the interpretation and meaning of the agreement and its provisions.

IV. DRAFTING THE FRONT MATTER AND DEFINITIONS

For the purposes of this simulation, you are a junior associate at the law firm of McClelland, Springer & Combelic, PC. Dutch Elm Company has asked the firm to prepare the initial draft of the merger and acquisition agreement based on the information set forth in the term sheet prepared in Chapter Three.

Mr. Combelic has asked you to draft the introductory paragraph, recitals, and lead-in sections. In addition, he has asked that you create definitions (or set forth accurate cross-references) for the terms or categories of terms set forth below based on the specifics of the deal[1]:

- Any terms defined in the introductory paragraph or recitals
- Business Day
- Dollars
- GAAP
- Governmental Authority
- Governmental Order
- Knowledge
- Law
- Person
- Representative

---

[1]   As you move through the various provisions of the merger and acquisition agreement you will add to your definition section so that most terms can be defined in conjunction with the relevant provisions.

CHAPTER FIVE

THE MERGER AND ACQUISITION AGREEMENT—PART II

I. INTRODUCTION

Now that the front matter portions of the merger and acquisition agreement have been completed, the next step is to draft the merger provision, which sets forth all the specifics regarding the mechanics of the transaction. This provision establishes the structure of the merger and acquisition—a forward merger, a forward triangular merger, or a reverse triangular merger, which helps to set the stage for the manner in which the provisions that follow will be drafted.[1] The merger provision also addresses the logistics regarding the closing of the transaction; what each of the parties must deliver at or before the closing; the effective time of the merger, as well as the effects of the merger to the various entities involved, their corporate governance documents, their stock and stock options (if any), and their constituents; the dissenting shareholder process; the surrender of and payment for stock (whether in cash, stock, or some combination); the details regarding any escrowed funds; the details regarding any purchase price adjustments, such as a net working capital adjustment or earn-out; and ancillary and related miscellaneous provisions.

II. THE MERGER PROVISION

The merger and merger consideration provisions may be two separate provisions of the merger and acquisition agreement or combined into one overarching provision. The next sections discuss the main, but not all of, the components of the merger provision.

A. THE MERGER

The merger section simply lays out the mechanics, or structure, of the merger transaction. In essence, this is the section that makes it clear whether the merger is a forward merger, a reverse triangular merger, or a forward triangular merger. As a result, it is the structure of the particular transaction that will dictate the terms set forth in this mechanical provision.

B. THE CLOSING AND CLOSING DELIVERABLES

The closing section provides the specifics regarding when and where the merger transaction will close. As opposed to setting a date specific, most mergers establish that the closing will take place on a business day that is so many days after the parties have met or waived all the requisite conditions of the merger. Additionally, while a physical location for closing is generally listed, in current times many closings happen virtually in that the respective parties execute the signature pages and email the executed pages to the law firm that is managing the closing process.

The closing deliverables section sets out those documents or items that each party must deliver either prior to, or at, the closing. Those items might include the delivery of executed ancillary documents (e.g. escrow agreement or employment agreement); officer and director resignations; officers' certificates; good standing certificates; transaction expenses or indebtedness certificates; estimated closing net working capital; wire transfer instructions; and other related documents.

---

[1] As a reminder, there are different tax implications associated with different merger structures and payment consideration options that the parties should critically consider before finalizing the particular structure of the merger. This text does not examine the tax implications of the various merger transaction structures.

C. THE EFFECTIVE TIME AND EFFECTS OF THE MERGER

The effective time section sets forth the manner in which and the documents that must be filed with the relevant states to ensure that the merger transaction is effective (i.e. the certificates of merger), as well as the effective time of the merger.

There are generally multiple provisions governing the various effects of the merger and these sections address such matters as (i) the vesting of rights and privileges and the assumption of liabilities and obligations; (ii) which certificate or articles of incorporation and bylaws will remain in effect after the closing; (iii) the directors and officers that will remain in office after the closing; (iv) the effect on the stock of the various entities (e.g. conversion of the target company's stock into the right to receive the consideration or conversion of the merger subsidiary's stock into the surviving entity's stock); and (v) the manner in which unexercised stock options will be handled.

D. DISSENTING SHARES

This section addresses the manner in which dissenting shares will be managed, meaning the shares held by those shareholders who did not vote in favor of the merger and exercised their right to seek an appraisal. In the situation where the target entity only has a few common shareholders, there may be no need for a dissenting shares provision as the transaction may require all the shareholders to sell their shares in order to move forward. However, in a merger transaction where there are a significant number of common shareholders, the agreement will need to set forth the process regarding dissenting shares.

E. SURRENDER AND PAYMENT OF CONSIDERATION

This section describes the various processes for the surrender of stock certificates and receipt of the merger consideration. In particular, it addresses how each shareholder of the target entity must surrender their stock in order to receive the agreed upon merger consideration, whether cash or stock. In the circumstance where there are only a few common shareholders, surrender of and payment for their shares generally occurs at closing and would be included as part of the closing deliverables. However, in a merger transaction where there are a significant number of common shareholders, an exchange agent is often appointed to manage the process of surrendering stock certificates and distributing the merger consideration, both the consideration paid at closing and any consideration the shareholders may receive if escrow funds remain at the expiration of the escrow period. This section will also address what happens to any merger consideration that remains unclaimed after a certain amount of time has lapsed.

F. ESCROW

This section will address any funds that are being placed in escrow as part of the merger transaction. It may include sections providing for escrows for indemnification purposes, purchase price adjustments, and stockholder representative expenses.

G. PURCHASE PRICE ADJUSTMENTS

This section will address any purchase price adjustments that were negotiated as part of the merger transaction, including the processes for determining, objecting, and disputing such purchase price adjustments, the payment of the purchase price adjustments, and any related provisions. For instance, the parties may have agreed to a net working capital adjustment to account for an increase or decrease in actual working capital at closing as compared to the amount of target working capital the buyer required as of closing or the parties may have agreed to a future earn-out payment based on some type of established financial metric being met at a specified point of time in the future.

III. DRAFTING THE MERGER PROVISION

For the purposes of this simulation, you are a junior associate at the law firm of McClelland, Springer & Combelic, PC. Dutch Elm Company has asked the firm to prepare the initial draft of the merger and acquisition agreement based on the information set forth in the term sheet prepared in Chapter Three.

Mr. Combelic has asked you to draft the merger provision sections of the merger and acquisition agreement, including adding all relevant defined terms to the definition section that you started as part of the exercise in Chapter Four. If you are missing any necessary information or it was not included in the term sheet, you can make reasonable assumptions regarding the missing information but should bracket any areas where you have made assumptions or require additional information to complete the provision.

CHAPTER SIX

THE MERGER AND ACQUISITION AGREEMENT—PART III

I. INTRODUCTION

Now that the merger provision sections have been completed, the next step is to draft those provisions that protect the buyer and ensure that the buyer is receiving the benefit of the bargain that was struck between the parties, that the target entity continues to be operated in the ordinary course of business from the time the merger and acquisition agreement is executed until the point in time when the merger transaction closes, and that the target meets all the required conditions so that the transaction can be closed. These provisions also protect the target entity and ensure the target (and the target's shareholders) that the buyer is in a position to meet its obligations as they pertain to the merger transaction and ensure that the buyer meets all of its required conditions so that the transaction can be closed.

II. REPRESENTATIONS AND WARRANTIES OF THE TARGET AND SELLING SHAREHOLDERS

The representations and warranties of the target act as mechanisms to protect the buyer and the merger subsidiary by requiring the target to make a significant number of representations and warranties regarding such things as its structure and existence, its authority to enter into the transaction, its financial condition, the ownership and status of its assets, its obligations and liabilities, its compliance with all types of laws ranging from governmental regulations to employment laws to environmental laws, as well as many other matters. In the event that a representation and warranty turns out to be false (either as a result of the target making an outright misrepresentation regarding a particular matter or as a result of the target failing to disclose an exception to the representation or warranty on the appropriate disclosure schedule), the target has breached the contract and the buyer and merger subsidiary can seek remedies for that breach.

The target company will want to limit the scope of its representations and warranties as much as feasible to curtail those situations where it may find itself in breach and thus provide the buyer with the right to terminate the merger transaction. At the same time, the buyer will want the target's representations and warranties to be as broad as possible to ensure it has the utmost protection and ability to terminate the merger if needed.

There are a number of ways in which the target can attempt to limit the breadth of its representations and warranties. The first way to protect itself is to ensure that it lists all exceptions (or carve outs) to the representations and warranties on the applicable disclosure schedules. Two other ways to protect itself are to incorporate materiality thresholds or to establish what constitutes a material adverse effect, or to add knowledge qualifiers. Lastly, the target can protect itself by establishing time parameters meaning that the representations and warranties are true and accurate from a date certain or from a trigger date such as the prior fiscal year's end. While the buyer may be unwilling to accept materiality or knowledge qualifiers in regard to some representations and warranties, it is commonplace for those qualifiers to be included in many instances.

In the circumstance where the target company is closely held and there are only a few selling shareholders, the buyer may also attempt to require the selling shareholders to represent and warrant to all of the same representations and warranties as provided by the target as the shareholders, especially in the situation where they are also the officers and directors of the target, are viewed as the target or the parties that have the necessary knowledge to ensure that the target's representations and warranties are true. In the situation, where the selling shareholders are not also the officers and directors of the target, the buyer may still require each selling shareholder to make limited representations and warranties and particularly if all are required to sell their shares in order to complete the merger transaction.

III. REPRESENTATIONS AND WARRANTIES OF THE BUYER AND MERGER SUBSIDIARY

The representations and warranties of the buyer and merger subsidiary also act as protective mechanisms for the target (and the selling shareholders), but in a slightly different manner. The buyer and merger subsidiary's representations and warranties address the abilities of both parties to enter into and consummate the merger transaction, as well as ensure that the parties have adequate financial capacity to pay the consideration at the closing of the transaction.

The buyer and merger subsidiary will attempt to limit the number of representations and warranties required to keep them to a minimum and address only those matters that are essential to their ability to finalize the merger transaction.

IV. DRAFTING REPRESENTATIONS AND WARRANTIES

For the purposes of this simulation, you are a junior associate at the law firm of McClelland, Springer & Combelic, PC. Dutch Elm Company has asked the firm to prepare the initial draft of the merger and acquisition agreement based on the information set forth in the term sheet prepared in Chapter Three.

Mr. Combelic has asked you to draft the target, buyer, and merger subsidiary's representations and warranties provisions of the merger and acquisition agreement, including the relevant disclosure schedules. In addition, you should add any relevant defined terms to the definition section that you started as part of the exercise in Chapter Four. If you are missing any necessary information or it was not included in the term sheet or set forth below, you can make reasonable assumptions regarding the missing information but should bracket any areas where you have made assumptions or require additional information to complete the provision.

The firm and Dutch Elm Company have learned the following information in conjunction with the due diligence investigation of Tree Services, Inc. and you should utilize that information, as needed, in drafting the target's representations and warranties and disclosure schedules:

3.03
No Conflict; Consent • No information was discovered that indicated TSI would have a conflict if it were to enter into this merger transaction.

3.02 (b)
Board approval • The TSI board of directors has approved the merger transaction and recommended it to the common shareholders for approval. The three founders have all indicated they will vote in favor of the merger.

• Erin Mooney used her shares of TSI preferred stock as collateral for a personal loan in the total amount of $45,000 with a current principal balance of $38,000. Union Bank maintains a security interest in her shares.

3.04 (c)
Capitalization • The TSI board of directors declared a dividend of $0.50 per share on its common stock last month with a payment date set for 70 days from today's date.

3.18 Compliance w/ laws + Disclosure Schedule

✗ TSI has been served with a number of county permit violations over the past two years for operating its cherry picker trucks to remove tree branches in violation of county ordinances. The violations are as follows:

✗ County A: Two permit violations; $750 fine for each; paid in full

✗ County C: Five permit violations; $500 fine for each; 3 paid in full; 2 are being contested

✗ County F: Three permit violations; $1,200 fine for each; 2 paid in full; 1 being contested

✗ County G: Two permit violations; $1,100 fine for each; both are being contested

3.18 § b + Disclosure

✗ TSI learned last month that three of its county licenses had expired as a result of an employee transition and had not been renewed. TSI is currently in the process of renewing its licenses in the Counties D, E, and H and believes those licenses will be renewed within the next 45–60 days.

✗ TSI disclosed four litigation-oriented matters (all of which have arisen in the past 12 months) as follows:

3.17 Legal proceed + Disclosure Schedule

✗ Sally Dawson, an employee of TSI, claims she was injured on the job when a limb dropped on her. As she attempted to move out of the limb's way, she fell and broke her arm in several places. She filed a workers' compensation claim.

✗ Sally Dawson has threatened to file a claim against TSI for emotional distress as a result of the previously discussed accident. She has threatened to sue for $500,000 in damages plus attorneys' fees and costs.

✗ ABC Management Company is suing TSI for damage to the roof and HVAC system of one of its apartment buildings that ABC claims was caused when a TSI employee lost control of a limb in windy conditions. ABC has sued for $220,000 plus fees and costs. The lawsuit is in the discovery phase. TSI's insurance carrier has been notified and has indicated it believes the suit is frivolous.

✓ Golf Course Management, Inc. is suing TSI in regard to a tree maintenance contract at one of the golf courses it manages. Golf Course Management claims that TSI did not adequately care for the trees, and as a result 10% of the trees on the course were attacked by the blue spruce beetle and had to be partially cut back or removed entirely. Golf Course Management has sued for $465,000 plus fees and costs. TSI's insurance carrier has been notified. Golf Course Management, Inc. has also threatened to cancel its services contract with TSI, which comprises approximately 2.5% of TSI's gross revenues in the current year.

• TSI indicated the following matters occurred since its most recent year-end financial statements:

✗ TSI recently entered into its largest contract to date with Golf Holdings International. This contract will constitute approximately 5% of TSI's gross revenues over the next 24 months.   *3.08 (h)*

3.11 + Disclos

✗ Approximately one week ago, one of TSI's employees accidentally backed a chipper truck into the side of the building it leases and did substantial damage to the building and the truck. The respective insurance companies and landlord have been notified. An assessment and investigation into the accident are underway.   *~~3.08~~ (~~h~~)*

3. DEC(r)
+
~~Direction~~
Disclosure

- TSI had exceptionally strong results in the most recently ended fiscal quarter and as a result it paid discretionary bonuses to its executive officers, senior staff, and crew leaders in a total amount of $325,000.

3.12(g)
+
Disclosure
Schedule

- TSI holds an active trademark on its name and logo design. The trademark was registered with the U.S. Patent & Trademark Office during May of the first year of the company's operations. The registration number is #445556. TSI recently learned that Thorny Shrubs, Inc., a company operating in northern Colorado and Nebraska, is using a very similar trademark and logo and TSI's legal counsel sent a cease and desist letter approximately three weeks ago and to date has not received an acknowledgement or response.

- TSI has two long term debt arrangements as follows: (i) a term loan with Big Bank of Colorado in the amount of $1,500,000 with interest calculated at the prime rate plus 3.0% on a per annum basis with interest payments due monthly and with the principal due as a lump sum in June 2025, and (ii) a revolving line of credit with Bank of the Rockies of up to $750,000 that TSI uses for day-to-day operations and which is secured by TSI's equipment. The long-term debt arrangements require both banks' prior written consents to any merger and acquisition.

- The three founders pledged their shares of common stock as collateral in conjunction with the Loan Agreement with Big Bank of Colorado.

- Big Bank of Colorado has a lien on TSI's bank accounts with the bank.

- Big Bank of Colorado has a security interest in most of TSI's assets.

- Bank of the Rockies has a lien on TSI's equipment.

Dutch Elm Company provided the following information that you should utilize as needed in drafting DEC's and the merger sub's representations and warranties:

4.02   ✗   DEC and merger sub have no conflicts in regard to this transaction.

4.05   ✗   DEC intends to secure commercial financing to pay any cash consideration.

4.05   •   DEC has adequate authorized common stock to pay any stock consideration.

3.02   ✗   The DEC and merger sub boards of directors each approved the merger transaction.

V. COVENANTS

The covenants in the merger and acquisition agreement address what the parties can and cannot do during the period of time from when the merger and acquisition agreement is executed until the transaction closes, as well as those actions the parties must take in an attempt to ensure that closing takes place. While each party to the agreement will generally agree to specific covenants, the majority are meant to protect the buyer and ensure that the target continues to operate in the normal course of business and takes all actions necessary in order to close the merger transaction. Some covenants are within the entity's direct control, such as how the target conducts its business operations or the target granting access to its books and records. Other covenants are outside the entity's direct control, such as securing third party consents (e.g. landlord's consent to buyer's assumption of the lease) or obtaining the necessary shareholder vote.

VI. DRAFTING COVENANTS

For the purposes of this simulation, you are a junior associate at the law firm of McClelland, Springer & Combelic, PC. Dutch Elm Company has asked the firm to prepare the initial draft of the merger and acquisition agreement based on the information set forth in the term sheet prepared in Chapter Three.

Mr. Combelic has asked you to draft the covenants provision of the merger and acquisition agreement, including the target, buyer, and merger subsidiary's relevant covenants. In addition, you should add any relevant defined terms to the definition section that you started as part of the exercise in Chapter Four. If you are missing any necessary information or it was not included in the term sheet or set forth below, you can make reasonable assumptions regarding the missing information but should bracket any areas where you have made assumptions or require additional information to complete the provision.

DEC has requested that the following additional information be addressed in the covenants provision:

- TSI must operate in the ordinary course of business and may not make any individual or aggregated expenditures (outside the ordinary course of business) that exceed $250,000 without the prior consent of DEC.   *5.01 (J)*

- DEC would like TSI to secure the necessary shareholder consent within 10 days of the execution of the merger and acquisition agreement.   *5.04*

- No public announcements can be made without the other parties' consents   *5.10*

VII. CLOSING CONDITIONS

In those circumstances where the execution of the merger and acquisition agreement and the closing of the merger transaction do not occur simultaneously, which is generally the case, the agreement will contain a closing conditions provision that sets out those obligations the parties must meet in order for the other party to be required to close the transaction. As is true with most provisions of the merger and acquisition agreement, it is the target that will have a greater burden imposed on it by the closing conditions as it will have made the more extensive set of representations and warranties, which form the basis of the main closing conditions. If the specified conditions are not met or waived by the party with the right to waive a condition, then closing of the transaction cannot take place.

VIII. DRAFTING CLOSING CONDITIONS

For the purposes of this simulation, you are a junior associate at the law firm of McClelland, Springer & Combelic, PC. Dutch Elm Company has asked the firm to prepare the initial draft of the merger and acquisition agreement based on the information set forth in the term sheet prepared in Chapter Three.

Mr. Combelic has asked you to draft the closing conditions provision of the merger and acquisition agreement, including the target, buyer, and merger subsidiary's relevant closing conditions. In addition, you should add any relevant defined terms to the definition section that you started as part of the exercise in Chapter Four. If you are missing any necessary information or it was not included in the term sheet or set forth below, you can make reasonable assumptions regarding the missing information but should bracket any areas where you have made assumptions or require additional information to complete the provision.

7.03
- The parties are not aware of any laws or regulations that would prevent this merger transaction from moving forward and being completed.   *7.01*

- Target must provide a representation and warranty bring-down certificate at closing.   *7.03(a)*

- Target must secure all the necessary approvals, consents, or waivers prior to closing.   *7.03(d)*

Target cannot have suffered a material adverse effect. 7.0 7 (a)

Buyer and merger sub must provide a representation and warranty bring-down certificate at closing.

Buyer and merger sub must secure all the necessary approvals, consents, or waivers prior to closing. 7.03

CHAPTER SEVEN

THE MERGER AND ACQUISITION AGREEMENT—PART IV

I. INTRODUCTION

The next step in finalizing the merger and acquisition agreement is to draft those provisions that protect the buyer, merger subsidiary, target, and selling shareholders in the event one of the parties breaches the agreement or cannot meet a condition or obligation, the stockholders' representative's obligations, and lastly, the miscellaneous provisions, which act as a catch-all for important contractual provisions that were not covered elsewhere in the agreement.

II. INDEMNIFICATION

The indemnification provision sets out each party's obligation to indemnify the other parties after the merger transaction has closed and establishes how long various indemnification obligations continue post-closing (e.g. a set number of years, the length of the relevant statute of limitations, or indefinitely). The indemnification provision covers losses that arise (i) due to a party's misrepresentation or breach of a representation and warranty; (ii) due to a party's failure to comply with a covenant; or (iii) as a result of other negotiated terms in the agreement that create potential liability for a specific party. In order to truly understand a party's obligations, the indemnification provision must be read in conjunction with the representations and warranties, as well as the applicable disclosure schedules, and covenants.

While the indemnification provision is mutual in the sense that the selling shareholders indemnify the buyer and merger subsidiary, and the buyer and merger subsidiary indemnify the selling shareholders, the majority of the protection flows from the selling shareholders to the buyer and merger subsidiary. It is the selling shareholders that provide indemnification to the buyer, not the target entity as it becomes owned by the buyer at closing and no longer exists as an entity separate from the buyer. Because the selling shareholders will be the parties on the hook for any potential covered losses, the indemnification provision often results in the creation of an escrow fund so that the buyer can more readily recover the losses it has incurred without having to seek contribution from multiple shareholders.

There are a number of critical factors to be aware of when drafting an indemnification provision including (i) the length of time various representations, warranties, and covenants survive after closing; (ii) the definitions of indemnitees (or indemnified parties) so that a party can ensure that all relevant or affected persons can seek indemnification (e.g. the entity itself, affiliates, and representatives); (iii) whether the selling shareholders are jointly (buyer's preference) or just severally (selling shareholders' preference) liable; (iv) the amount of purchase price consideration the buyer requires to be held in escrow to cover potential losses; (v) any limitations on indemnification such as first dollar or tipping baskets (provides that a party is not liable until losses exceed a certain threshold amount) or caps (limits the amount of total losses for which a party is responsible); (vi) adjustments based on recovery of insurance proceeds; (vii) duty for the party seeking indemnification to mitigate potential losses; or (viii) whether misrepresentations or breaches are determined without taking into account material adverse effect qualifiers.

In addition to covering what triggers indemnification claims, the provision must also address the process a party has to follow in order to seek indemnification for both third-party and direct claims, including notice procedures; which party has the right to control any legal proceedings, including who is responsible for the costs and fees associated with such proceedings; the process for disputing an indemnification claim and which party is responsible for the costs associated with such claim dispute; the process for paying an indemnification claim, including procedures for seeking payment if no escrow agreement exists or the escrow has been used in full; how indemnification payments are treated for tax purposes; and whether indemnification is the exclusive remedy for the parties.

III.   DRAFTING THE INDEMNIFICATION PROVISION

For purposes of this simulation, you are a junior associate at the law firm of McClelland, Springer & Combelic, PC. Dutch Elm Company has asked the firm to prepare the initial draft of the merger and acquisition agreement based on the information set forth in the term sheet prepared in Chapter Three.

Mr. Combelic asked you to draft the indemnification provision of the merger and acquisition agreement. In addition, you should add any relevant defined terms to the definition section that you started as part of the exercise in Chapter Four. If you are missing any necessary information or it was not included in the term sheet or set forth below, you can make reasonable assumptions regarding the missing information but should bracket any areas where you have made assumptions or require additional information to complete the provision.

Dutch Elm Company has provided the firm with the following additional information you should utilize in drafting the indemnification provision:

- *8.04(a)* There is a selling shareholder basket that tips once all claims, in the aggregate, exceed $200,000.

- *8.04 (c)* The selling shareholders' liability is capped at 100% of their pro-rata share of the total purchase price (unless a different percentage was otherwise negotiated in the term sheet).

- *8.04(b)* Indemnification payments are reduced by the amount of any insurance proceeds received.

- *8.5(a)* The indemnifying party has the right to participate in or assume the defense of third party claims, with an exception for those claims that create a potential conflict of interest.

- *8.06(a) ?(b)* All selling shareholders' indemnification payments shall be paid from the indemnification escrow fund until it is depleted and once depleted, paid by the selling shareholders, who are severally, but not jointly, liable.

- There is a buyer basket that tips once all claims, in the aggregate, exceed $500,000.

- The buyer's liability is capped at $1,500,000 (unless a different percentage was otherwise negotiated in the term sheet).

IV.   TERMINATION

The termination provision details those circumstances that permit the parties to terminate the merger and acquisition agreement and thus the merger transaction, whether mutual or unilateral. In addition, it sets out any penalties associated with such termination, as well as the parties' post-termination rights and obligations.

The termination provision will generally provide that the parties can mutually agree to terminate the agreement at any time prior to the closing of the merger transaction. It will also set forth those circumstances that afford a party the unilateral right to terminate the agreement. The most common unilateral termination rights result from (i) a misrepresentation or breach of a representation, warranty, covenant, or other specific term that causes a closing condition to fail, or (ii) the failure to meet a closing condition by a specified date. Other circumstances that generally provide either party with the right to terminate include a law or governmental action that precludes the merger or the failure to close the merger by a specified date.

In some circumstances, the parties may negotiate termination fees. The merger and acquisition agreement may include a break-up fee where the target owes the buyer a payment if the merger transaction does not close as a result of the target company or its selling shareholders' actions. Some common failures that trigger a break-up fee include the target's board of directors changing its decision regarding approval of the merger or the target not obtaining the requisite shareholder approval. The merger and acquisition agreement may also include a reverse break-up fee where the buyer owes the target a payment if the merger transaction does not close as a result of the buyer's actions. Some common failures that trigger a reverse break-up fee include the buyer failing to secure adequate financing to close the merger transaction, failing to secure antitrust approval, or failing to close the merger by a specified date.

V. DRAFTING THE TERMINATION PROVISION

For purposes of this simulation, you are a junior associate at the law firm of McClelland, Springer & Combelic, PC. Dutch Elm Company has asked the firm to prepare the initial draft of the merger and acquisition agreement based on the information set forth in the term sheet prepared in Chapter Three.

Mr. Combelic asked you to draft the termination provision of the merger and acquisition agreement. In addition, you should add any relevant defined terms to the definition section that you started as part of the exercise in Chapter Four. If you are missing any necessary information or it was not included in the term sheet or set forth below, you can make reasonable assumptions regarding the missing information but should bracket any areas where you have made assumptions or require additional information to complete the provision.

Dutch Elm Company has provided the firm with the following additional information you should utilize in drafting the termination provision:

- Any cure period opportunity in the termination provision shall be ten days. 9.01(b)(i)

- Conditions must be met within 120 days of execution of the merger and acquisition 9.01(b)(ii) agreement.

- The merger transaction must close within 180 days of execution of the merger and acquisition agreement.

- Dutch Elm Company has agreed to a reverse break-up fee in amount of $750,000 if it is unable to secure the necessary financing. — ? Covenant or term chin

- Tree Services, Inc. has agreed to a break-up fee in the amount of 1.5% of the total purchase consideration if it is unable to secure the necessary shareholder approval.

VI. STOCKHOLDERS' REPRESENTATIVE

The stockholders' representative provision is generally only found in those merger and acquisition agreements where there are a larger number of shareholders and a representative is appointed to act on behalf of those shareholders in regard to matters that arise after the transaction has closed. By appointing a stockholder representative, the buyer is not placed in a position of having to negotiate with all the selling shareholders on an individual basis in regard to post-closing matters such as purchase price adjustments or indemnification. The stockholder representative may be one of the larger selling shareholders or an independent stockholder representative firm.

The stockholder representative provision should clearly set forth the representative's powers, as well as provide for how the representative may be removed or may resign. This provision should also address how the representative will be indemnified by the selling shareholders and in what circumstances the representative may be held liable. Finally, if the stockholder representative is compensated for this role, the provision should indicate the amount of compensation, as well as which parties, generally the selling shareholders, are responsible for paying the representative.

VII. DRAFTING THE STOCKHOLDERS' REPRESENTATIVE PROVISION

For purposes of this simulation, you are a junior associate at the law firm of McClelland, Springer & Combelic, PC. Dutch Elm Company has asked the firm to prepare the initial draft of the merger and acquisition agreement based on the information set forth in the term sheet prepared in Chapter Three.

Mr. Combelic asked you to draft the stockholders' representative provision of the merger and acquisition agreement. In addition, you should add any relevant defined terms to the definition section that you started as part of the exercise in Chapter Four. If you are missing any necessary information or it was not included in the term sheet or set forth below, you can make reasonable assumptions regarding the missing information but should bracket any areas where you have made assumptions or require additional information to complete the provision.

Dutch Elm Company has provided the firm with the following additional information you should utilize in drafting the stockholders' representative provision:

- Melissa Green will act as the initial stockholder representative.
  10.01(a)(i)-(ix) The selling shareholders are willing to give her broad authority to act in that capacity.

- She will not receive any additional compensation as stockholder representative.

- 10.01(b) She can only be removed by a unanimous vote of both Thomas Shrub and Susan Brown.

- 10.01 (c) Thomas Shrub, Susan Brown, and the other shareholders will indemnify her severally, but not jointly.

VIII. MISCELLANEOUS PROVISIONS

Lastly, the miscellaneous provision sets out pertinent details regarding the agreement, its construction, and interpretation. While the sections in this provision may be referred to as boilerplate, they are anything but that and should be carefully drafted to ensure that no unintended consequences or inconsistencies with other provisions in the agreement are created.

Miscellaneous provisions generally address routine matters such as (i) notice requirements; (ii) expenses; (iii) interpretation and headings; (iv) entire agreement and integration; (v) severability; (vi) amendment and modification; (vii) waiver; (viii) counterparts; (ix) successors and assigns; (x) governing law; (xi) jurisdiction and venue; (xii) waiver of jury trial; (xiii) no third party beneficiaries; and (xiv) force majeure.

IX. DRAFTING THE MISCELLANEOUS PROVISIONS

For purposes of this simulation, you are a junior associate at the law firm of McClelland, Springer & Combelic, PC. Dutch Elm Company has asked the firm to prepare the initial draft of the merger and acquisition agreement based on the information set forth in the term sheet prepared in Chapter Three.

Mr. Combelic asked you to draft the miscellaneous provision of the merger and acquisition agreement. In addition, you should add any relevant defined terms to the definition section that you started as part of the exercise in Chapter Four. If you are missing any necessary information or it was not included in the term sheet or set forth below, you can make reasonable assumptions regarding the missing information but should bracket any areas where you have made assumptions or require additional information to complete the provision.

Dutch Elm Company has provided the firm with the following additional information you should utilize in drafting the miscellaneous provision:

- Each party is responsible for its own expenses unless otherwise indicated in the 10.02 agreement.

- Governing law is Nevada and all matters are subject to jurisdiction within Nevada. 10.11

- The parties have agreed to waive the right to a jury trial. 10.11(b) + (c)

- The agreement cannot be assigned by either party without written consent of the other parties. 10.08

- All parties are entitled to force majeure protection. — ?

CHAPTER EIGHT

APPROVALS

I. INTRODUCTION

In conjunction with any merger transaction, the parties will have to secure various approvals in order to finalize and close the deal. The required approvals will be dependent on the entity, where it is incorporated, and its corporate governance documents, as well as general corporate law principles. Additionally, the structure of the merger transaction will impact whether the parties must seek consents of or assignments by outside third parties as a part of the merger transaction.

II. BOARD OF DIRECTOR APPROVALS

In order to be in a position to close the merger transaction, the buyer, the merger subsidiary (if a triangular merger), and the target will be required to secure the approval of their respective boards of directors. As noted above, the entity's state of incorporation and its corporate governance documents will dictate how it must secure the board of directors approval, as well as the required vote.

In many cases, corporate entities seek board approval through a written consent action process. Most state laws require that board of director consent actions must be unanimous in order to be legally effective. In those circumstances where the entire board is in agreement regarding the potential merger transaction, the consent action process is far less cumbersome and time consuming than calling and holding a meeting of the board of directors. However, if the entire board is not in agreement regarding the potential merger transaction, the entity will have to comply with its corporate governance documents and state law requirements regarding the calling and holding of a special meeting of the board of directors to secure the required approval of the transaction.

While the board of director resolutions, whether secured through a duly held meeting or written consent action, are unique to each specific deal and the relevant party, there are some common resolutions. The board of directors will need to approve the transaction itself and the proposed structure, all of the necessary documents to effect the transaction, any forms or filings that are required pursuant to state law, any additional actions required to effect the transaction, as well as traditional catch-all resolutions such as granting the entity's "authorized persons" the authority to do what is required to finalize the merger and acquisition and ratifying any prior actions related to the transaction.

III. PREPARING BOARD OF DIRECTOR CONSENT ACTIONS

For purposes of this simulation you are a junior associate at the law firm of Williams & Rader, LLC. Tree Services, Inc. has asked the firm to prepare the board of directors' unanimous written consent action to approve the merger transaction with Dutch Elm Company based on the draft merger and acquisition agreement that was prepared in conjunction with Chapters Four–Seven.

Ms. Williams asked you to prepare a standard board of directors unanimous written consent action for a merger transaction of this type. If you are missing any necessary information, you can make reasonable assumptions regarding the missing information but should bracket any areas where you have made assumptions or require additional information to complete the consent action. Tree Services, Inc. and its board of directors has indicated that Melissa Green and Thomas Shrub will be the authorized persons for the company in regard to the merger transaction.

IV. SHAREHOLDER APPROVALS

In addition to the required board of directors approval of the merger and acquisition by each of the entities, a party to the merger may also have to secure the requisite approval of its shareholders. As previously noted, the structure of the merger and the entity's state of incorporation and its corporate governance documents will dictate whether it must secure shareholder approval and how it must secure that approval.

A. TARGET SHAREHOLDER APPROVAL

No matter the structure of the merger, the target shareholders will have to approve the proposed transaction and its terms. In the event that there are a limited number of common shareholders and the majority, if not all, are in favor of the merger transaction or if a majority of the stock holdings are concentrated in a small group of common shareholders, the target may seek such approval through a written consent action process (dependent upon state law requirements and limitations). In those circumstances where there are a large number of common shareholders and the holdings are widely disbursed, the target will generally call a special meeting of the shareholders to secure the necessary approval.

While the matters that the shareholders will approve are unique to each deal and the relevant party, there are some commonalities. The target's common shareholders will need to approve the transaction itself; the proposed structure; the merger and acquisition agreement, and in particular those terms that directly impact the shareholders; the purchase price, including any related escrow or holdback amounts; the appointment of a stockholder representative, if there is one; all of the necessary documents to effect the transaction; and any additional actions required to effect the transaction, as well as traditional catch-all resolutions such as granting the entity's "authorized persons" the authority to do what is required to finalize the merger transaction.

B. MERGER SUBSIDIARY SHAREHOLDER APPROVAL

In those circumstances where the transaction is structured as a forward or reverse triangular merger, the merger subsidiary's shareholders will have to approve the proposed transaction and its terms. Since the merger subsidiary is wholly-owned by the buyer, these approvals are generally just formalities and occur through a written consent action process.

The merger subsidiary's common shareholder will need to approve the transaction itself; the proposed structure; the merger and acquisition agreement; and any additional actions required to effect the transaction, as well as traditional catch-all resolutions such as granting the entity's "authorized persons" the authority to do what is required to finalize the merger transaction.

C. BUYER SHAREHOLDER APPROVAL

In those circumstances where the transaction is structured as a forward merger, meaning the target merges with and into the buyer and ceases to exist as a stand-alone entity, the buyer shareholders will have to approve the proposed transaction and its terms except in those limited circumstances where the forward merger does not impact the buyer's corporate governance documents or there are no changes to the shares of the buyer's stock as a result of the merger.

V. PREPARING SHAREHOLDER CONSENT ACTIONS

For purposes of this simulation you are a junior associate at the law firm of Williams & Rader, LLC. Tree Services, Inc. has asked the firm to prepare the shareholders' written consent action to approve the merger transaction with Dutch Elm Company based on the draft merger and acquisition agreement that was prepared in conjunction with Chapters Four–Seven.

Ms. Williams asked you to prepare a standard shareholders' written consent action for a merger transaction of this type. If you are missing any necessary information, you can make reasonable assumptions regarding the missing information but should bracket any areas where you have made assumptions or require additional information to complete the consent action.

Tree Services, Inc. has provided the firm with the following additional information you should utilize in drafting the shareholders' consent action:

- The TSI board of directors has determined that the merger transaction and merger and acquisition agreement are fair and in the best interests of the company and has entered into a unanimous written consent action approving the merger transaction.

- The three founders and other shareholders are in favor of the merger transaction and are comfortable with the terms of the draft merger and acquisition agreement, the draft escrow agreement, and the other ancillary documents.

- The three founders and other shareholders are in favor of appointing Melissa Green as the initial stockholder representative.

- The three founders and other shareholders are willing to waive their appraisal rights.

VI.   THIRD PARTY CONSENTS, ASSIGNMENTS, AND ASSUMPTIONS

In some merger transactions, the consent of third parties may be necessary in order to close the transaction or before a contract can be assigned and assumed by the buyer. The issue of third party consents is unlikely to arise when the merger is structured as a straight stock purchase, meaning the buyer simply acquires all the stock of the target and the target continues to operate as it always has, or when the merger is structured as a reverse triangular merger, meaning the merger subsidiary merges with and into the target and the target is the surviving entity. However, if a target contract contains a change of control provision the buyer will need to secure the requisite approval or waiver. A change of control provision provides the other party to the contract with certain rights in the event of a change in ownership of the other party or a sale of substantially all of the other party's assets. These rights often include the right to consent to the continuation of the contract in the event of a change of control or a right to terminate the contract.

On the other hand, when the merger is structured as a forward merger or forward triangular merger, meaning the target ceases to exist once the merger transaction closes, third party consents will likely be required for contracts of the target that contain anti-assignment provisions. An anti-assignment provision limits either one or both of the parties to the contract from assigning the contract to a third party without first obtaining the prior written consent of the non-assigning party. However, in some cases there may be exceptions to anti-assignment clauses such as in the case of an assignment to an affiliate or a successor-in-interest. In these merger structure situations, it is critical that the buyer closely examine the target's contracts as part of the due diligence process to adequately assess those contracts that will require the target to secure the assignment and assumption of the contract by the buyer at the closing of the merger transaction so that those required assignments and assumptions can be included as part of the target's closing conditions.

The other circumstance that may give rise to a third party consent is when a contract of the target contains a negative covenant that prevents the target from engaging in a merger and acquisition or causing a change of control without first obtaining the prior written consent of the other party or parties. Some of the most common types of agreements that contain these types of negative covenants are commercial loan agreements, promissory notes, or indentures (i.e. the contract governing a corporate bond issuance). In this situation, the buyer will either require the target to secure the necessary consent as part of the target's closing conditions or require that these creditors be paid in full out of the purchase consideration at the closing of the merger transaction.

VII. PREPARING A THIRD PARTY CONSENT, ASSIGNMENT, AND ASSUMPTION

For purposes of this simulation you are a junior associate at the law firm of Williams & Rader, LLC. Tree Services, Inc. has asked the firm to prepare the requisite documents to seek the consent of TSI's landlord, Giant Real Estate Company, to the merger and acquisition transaction with Dutch Elm Company based on the terms of the Industrial Lease Agreement by and between Giant Real Estate Company and Tree Services, Inc. dated April 1, 2014 that is included as one of the due diligence contracts in Appendix C.

Ms. Williams asked you to prepare a cover letter to TSI's landlord, Giant Real Estate Company, explaining the situation and include the third party consent due to the change of control provision in the lease for execution by Giant Real Estate.

Tree Services, Inc. has provided the firm with the following additional information you should utilize in drafting the third party consent:

- Dutch Elm Company desires to continue to lease this building.

- Tree Services, Inc. must secure the landlord's consent to the change of control of TSI prior to closing of the merger transaction.

CHAPTER NINE

FILINGS AND NOTICES

I. INTRODUCTION

In addition the various board of director, shareholder, and third party approvals that the parties to a merger transaction must secure, there are filings and notices that must be made or provided. The characteristics of the entities (e.g. size, financial condition, and industry), as well as how the target will be operated post-closing will dictate the additional filings and notices that must be made. These filings and notices could include a Hart-Scott-Rodino filing to meet antitrust regulations, a WARN Act notice if there will be a plant closing or mass layoff, and other required federal or state regulatory approvals.

II. HART-SCOTT-RODINO FILING

In many mergers and acquisitions, the parties may have to make a Hart-Scott-Rodino ("HSR") filing with the Federal Trade Commission and Department of Justice—Antitrust Division and observe the required waiting period before closing the merger transaction. The HSR pre-merger notification and filing requirements are triggered when the merger transaction exceeds a certain size (or value) or if the parties exceed a certain size. The Federal Trade Commission maintains the current thresholds on its website. As the HSR process can hold up a merger transaction, the parties should assess whether or not they are required to make the HSR filing as early as possible, as well as if there is an exemption if they fall into one of the required categories. In the event the parties fail to make a required HSR filing, they may face monetary penalties.

If the HSR pre-merger notification and filing requirements are triggered, generally each party is required to file the HSR form with the supporting documentation. The waiting period commences once both parties have filed the HSR form and the buyer has paid the applicable filing fee. There is a mandatory 30-day waiting period and once the waiting period has expired or the parties have received an early termination notice (assuming there has been no request for additional information or documents) the merger transaction can be closed.

The purpose of the HSR filing and waiting period is to put the antitrust agencies on notice of the potential merger transaction. This allows the agencies time to determine whether the transaction should be reviewed or blocked under current antitrust laws. While in many circumstances the antitrust agencies will simply allow the initial 30-day waiting period to pass and lapse or provide notice of early termination of the waiting period, in some cases the agencies will ask for additional information and documentation. A request for additional information generally results in a delayed closing of the merger transaction until such information is provided, reviewed by the agencies, and the parties are permitted to proceed with the transaction.

III. PREPARING THE HART-SCOTT-RODINO FILING

For purposes of this simulation, you are a junior associate at the law firm of McClelland, Springer & Combelic, PC. Dutch Elm Company has asked the firm to assess whether the merger transaction with Tree Services, Inc. triggers the HSR filing requirement.

Mr. Combelic has asked you to review the current HSR pre-merger notification requirements to assess whether DEC and TSI must make the requisite filings and prepare a memo summarizing your analysis and findings. Additionally, Mr. Combelic has indicated that if the HSR pre-merger notification is triggered, you should prepare DEC's initial HSR filing and attach it to the memo.

IV. WORKERS' ADJUSTMENT AND RETRAINING NOTIFICATION ACT NOTICE

The Workers' Adjustment and Retraining Notification Act ("WARN Act") requires an employer to provide its employees with advance notice in the event of a "plant closing" or "mass layoff." This WARN Act notice is only triggered in certain circumstances and is dependent upon the number of employees and the parties' intentions in regard to the target company's employees, whether known prior or subsequent to the closing of the merger transaction. Depending on the circumstances, it may be the target or buyer that is responsible for complying with the WARN Act and its notice requirements.

V. PREPARING THE WARN ACT NOTICE

For purposes of this simulation, you are a junior associate at the law firm of McClelland, Springer & Combelic, PC. Dutch Elm Company has asked the firm to assess whether the merger transaction with Tree Services, Inc. triggers any concerns under the WARN Act.

Mr. Combelic has asked you to review the current WARN Act requirements to assess whether DEC will face any concerns in regard to the merger with TSI and prepare a memo summarizing your analysis and findings. Additionally, Mr. Combelic has indicated that if a WARN Act notice is triggered, you should prepare the WARN Act notice and attach it to the memo.

Dutch Elm Company has provided the firm with the following additional information you should utilize in assessing the WARN Act notice provisions:

- DEC plans to maintain TSI's current location and offices in Commerce City, Colorado.

- DEC hopes to retain TSI's arborists and office staff, but will require them to apply and interview with DEC in order to determine if they should be retained.

- DEC plans to lay off approximately 10% of TSI's current year-round crew workers.

CHAPTER TEN

ANCILLARY DOCUMENTS

I. INTRODUCTION

While the merger and acquisition agreement is the critical document that sets forth the overarching terms of the merger transaction, there are also a number of ancillary agreements that are required to finalize the transaction. As every merger transaction is unique, each will require its own set of ancillary documents that are pertinent to the terms of that particular merger. Generally, the ancillary agreements are negotiated and the parties reach a final agreed upon form of the ancillary agreement prior to the closing of the merger transaction, with the ancillary agreements being executed and effective as of the closing date (or executed prior to closing but not effective until the closing date). It is also often the case that the finalization of an ancillary agreement is one of the listed closing conditions in the merger and acquisition agreement.

While the ancillary documents will be distinct for each deal, there are a number of agreements that are often part of many merger transactions. These common agreements include the escrow agreement, non-competition and non-solicitation agreement, executive (or key employee) employment agreement, and consulting agreement.

II. ESCROW AGREEMENT

When the merger and acquisition agreement requires that funds (or other property) be held in escrow for disbursement at some point in the future, whether funds (or property) of the target, selling shareholders, or buyer, an escrow agreement will be required to govern that situation and relationship. The agreement will appoint an escrow agent, who is typically a third party, to manage the escrow in compliance with the terms and provisions of the escrow agreement. In some merger transactions, there may be multiple escrow funds that are established and governed by one over-arching escrow agreement or by separate escrow agreements. While there are any number of scenarios that might require an escrow agreement in a merger transaction, the most typical reasons are to cover post-closing indemnification obligations, to cover post-closing purchase price adjustments, or for holding source code.

The next sections discuss the most critical components of the escrow agreement in conjunction with an escrow agreement for holding funds to meet a future monetary obligation.

A. ESTABLISHMENT OF ESCROW ACCOUNT; INVESTMENT OF ESCROW FUNDS

These provisions address the amount of funds to be deposited into the escrow account or accounts, when such funds must be deposited, how the funds may be invested, and which party is entitled to any earnings that result from the investments. The agreement should be clear on whether all escrowed funds will be held in one general escrow account or parsed into separate escrow accounts to deal with the potential matters that may give rise to a claim (e.g. a separate escrow account for selling shareholder indemnification obligations and a separate escrow account for the potential earn-out payment). Generally, the parties will dictate that the escrow agent only invest escrow funds in conservative and short-term investment vehicles to ensure that the money deposited is not lost or diminished as a result of the manner in which it is invested and is readily available. Lastly, the parties should indicate who receives any interest or earnings on invested funds. Typically, the interest or earnings will remain in the escrow account and be reinvested until the escrow account is terminated and any remaining funds are released. In most circumstances, any interest or earnings are distributed equally to the parties or fully to the party entitled to receive any funds that remained in the escrow account.

B. RELEASE OF ESCROW FUNDS

The escrow agreement should contain very detailed terms regarding when and how the escrow funds can be released. It should clearly set forth the procedures for how one or both parties make a claim for escrowed funds so that the escrow agent has a firm set of instructions to follow in that regard. Additionally, the agreement should set forth the procedures the escrow agent must follow in regard to any disputed claims for escrow funds. Lastly, the agreement should set forth how and when (e.g. periodically or only upon termination of the escrow) remaining escrow funds are to be disbursed to the party entitled to such funds.

C. PROVISIONS RELATING TO THE ESCROW AGENT

The escrow agreement should clearly delineate the rights and duties of the escrow agent; the limitations on an escrow agent's liability, including provisions regarding indemnification of the escrow agent; how the escrow agent can resign, be replaced, or be removed; and how the escrow agent will be compensated and reimbursed for expenses.

D. TERMINATION

The escrow agreement termination provision should set forth when and how the escrow agreement terminates, meaning after all escrowed funds have been disbursed or a date certain. Additionally, it should indicate how open claims are managed and how any remaining funds are disbursed upon termination if the escrow terminates as of a certain date.

III. PREPARING THE ESCROW AGREEMENT

For purposes of this simulation, you are a junior associate at the law firm of McClelland, Springer & Combelic, PC. Dutch Elm Company has asked the firm to prepare the initial draft of the escrow agreement based on the draft merger and acquisition agreement that was prepared in conjunction with Chapters Four–Seven.

Mr. Combelic asked you to prepare a standard escrow agreement. If you are missing any necessary information, you can make reasonable assumptions regarding the missing information but should bracket any areas where you have made assumptions or require additional information to complete the escrow agreement.

Dutch Elm Company has provided the firm with the following additional information you should utilize in drafting the escrow agreement:

- The parties have agreed to use Nevada State Bank as the escrow agent.

- The parties have agreed that the escrow funds can only be invested in traditional types of conservative investment vehicles.

- The parties have agreed that whoever is entitled to the disbursement of any remaining funds when the escrow terminates is entitled to any interest or earnings on those funds at that time of final disbursement.

- The parties have agreed to share the costs and expenses of the escrow agent 50/50.

- The parties have agreed that the escrow agent can only be removed or replaced upon the consent of all the parties.

IV. NON-COMPETITION AND NON-SOLICITATION AGREEMENT

A non-competition and non-solicitation agreement is often an ancillary contract in a merger transaction, whether as a separate document or as provisions tied in with an employment or consulting agreement. The purpose of this agreement is to establish the pertinent restrictions on a party's ability to compete with or solicit employees and customers from the target company post-closing of the merger transaction. Generally in those circumstances where the target's founders or executive officers will not remain employed after the merger closes, they will be required to execute a stand-alone non-compete and non-solicitation agreement to prevent them from competing with the target or poaching employees or customers from the target after the merger has closed. In this scenario, the non-competition and non-solicitation agreement is generally a closing condition. In those circumstances where the target's founders or executive officers will remain employed with or act as consultants for the target after the merger closes, the non-compete and non-solicitation provisions will typically be wrapped into their respective employment or consulting agreement.

The next sections discuss the most critical components of the non-competition and non-solicitation agreement as a stand-alone agreement.

A. NON-COMPETE PROVISION

The non-competition provision prevents the party from competing with the target's business (post-closing) by placing limitations on the types of businesses and business activities in which the party can be involved for a specified amount of time and limited to a certain geographic region. This is critical when the party will no longer work for the target after the merger closes (or terminates their relationship at some future date) and so the buyer wants to prevent the party from entering into a directly competitive business and diminishing the value of the acquired entity as a result of that party's inside knowledge and information. The types of prohibited business activities, geographic scope, and length of time should be clearly set out in this provision.

B. NON-SOLICITATION PROVISION

The non-solicitation provision prevents the party from soliciting both employees and customers of the target (post-closing) for a specified amount of time. This is essential when the party will no longer work for the target after the merger closes (or terminates their relationship at some future date). It enables the buyer to protect and retain the employees and customers of the acquired entity and prevent a diminishment in the acquired entity's value. The length of time for non-solicitation of employees and customers should be clearly set out in this provision.

C. OTHER COVENANTS

The agreement may also contain non-disparagement and non-interference provisions. The non-disparagement provision prevents the party from making negative comments about the other party (the target or buyer) whether in spoken or written form. The non-interference provision prevents the party from interfering with the business and related aspects of the other party (the target or buyer) such as interfering with customers or suppliers. Both of these provisions protect the buyer by preventing the former founder or employee from harming the target's business (post-closing).

D. SAVINGS CLAUSE AND REMEDIES

Due to the fact that non-competition provisions are often contested at some point by the party that has agreed to the non-compete, and state laws can be strict on the term and geographic scope, the agreement should contain a savings clause that allows for the contract to be reformed by the court so that it remains enforceable.

Because the non-competition and non-solicitation agreement is personal in nature, in addition to monetary remedies, the agreement should include the right to seek an injunction and to require specific performance.

V.   PREPARING THE NON-COMPETITION AND NON-SOLICITATION AGREEMENT

For purposes of this simulation, you are a junior associate at the law firm of McClelland, Springer & Combelic, PC. Dutch Elm Company has asked the firm to prepare the initial draft of the non-competition and non-solicitation agreement for Timothy Han (Tree Services Inc.'s Senior Vice President & Secretary) as he plans to terminate his employment relationship with TSI as of the closing date and will not be involved in any capacity after the merger closes.

Mr. Combelic asked you to prepare a standard non-competition and non-solicitation agreement. If you are missing any necessary information, you can make reasonable assumptions regarding the missing information but should bracket any areas where you have made assumptions or require additional information to complete the non-competition and non-solicitation agreement.

Dutch Elm Company has provided the firm with the following additional information you should utilize in drafting the non-competition and non-solicitation agreement:

- Han's employee relationship will terminate upon the closing of the merger transaction.
- Han has agreed to a two-year non-compete, but it must be strictly tailored as to the types of prohibited activities with a limited geographic restriction.
- Han has agreed to a one-year non-solicitation of TSI employees with standard exceptions.
- Han has agreed to a three-year non-solicitation of TSI customers with standard exceptions.
- Han has agreed to a non-disparagement provision.
- Han has agreed to a standard confidentiality and trade secrets protection provision.

VI.   EMPLOYMENT AGREEMENT

In conjunction with a merger transaction, the purchaser often desires to retain some of the founders, executive officers, or key employees of the target company as employees of the surviving entity after the merger closes. This helps to ensure a smooth transition, as well as maintain continuity with the target's customers and can be especially important when the target is a closely held entity and the founders are intimately involved in the day-to-day management and operations of the company. In some circumstances, finalizing employment agreements with key employees will be included as part of the target's closing conditions.

Employment agreements, while not required to create an employer-employee relationship, establish the terms and obligations of the employee in a formal and contractual manner. An employment agreement is most often used for executives and key employees. The employment agreement should set out the specific terms of the relationship including the term and termination, employee's duties and responsibilities, employee's compensation and benefits, and restrictions on the employee during and following termination or non-renewal.

The next sections discuss the most critical components of the employment agreement (not including non-competition and non-solicitation which are discussed in Section IV above).

A. TERM AND TERMINATION

The term provision should set forth the initial term of the employment agreement and timing requirements in regard to how the agreement and employment relationship may be renewed going forward, whether automatically or only upon consent of both parties.

The termination provision should explicitly set forth the circumstances that permit the employer to terminate the agreement and employment relationship, which is generally permitted "for cause" and "without cause," and the circumstances that permit the employee to terminate the agreement and employment relationship, which is generally permitted for "good reason" or "without good reason." In conjunction with these concepts, the phrases "for cause" and "good reason" should be clearly defined. Additionally, the termination provision should make it clear what amounts and benefits the employee is entitled to in the various termination scenarios.

B. DUTIES AND RESPONSIBILITIES

This provision should set forth the employee's title (e.g. Chief Financial Officer or Vice President of Marketing) and position with the company. Additionally, the provision should detail the employee's duties and responsibilities in the specified position, including who or which group the employee reports to in this role (e.g. Chief Executive Officer or Board of Directors). This provision will generally stipulate that the employee must devote full attention to this position and may also indicate the location from where the employee must work.

C. COMPENSATION AND BENEFITS

The compensation provision should cover all the details of the employee's compensation package. In particular it should set forth the employee's base salary, including when and how it is subject to adjustment, as well as information regarding any signing bonus, annual bonuses, including when and how they are determined, and equity awards.

The benefits provisions should cover all the details regarding the employee's benefits. In particular it should set out all the various types of benefits to which the employee is entitled, such as health, retirement plans, vacation or paid time off, relocation expenses, and business expense reimbursement.

VII. PREPARING THE EMPLOYMENT AGREEMENT

For purposes of this simulation, you are a junior associate at the law firm of McClelland, Springer & Combelic, PC. Dutch Elm Company has asked the firm to prepare the initial draft of the employment agreement for Melissa Green (Tree Services Inc.'s current Chief Executive Officer) as DEC wants to retain Green after the merger transaction closes.

Mr. Combelic asked you to prepare a standard employment agreement. If you are missing any necessary information, you can make reasonable assumptions regarding the missing information but should bracket any areas where you have made assumptions or require additional information to complete the employment agreement.

Dutch Elm Company has provided the firm with the following additional information you should utilize in drafting Green's employment agreement:

- Green has agreed to be President of the surviving entity for an initial term of 18 months that automatically renews for consecutive 12 month terms unless otherwise terminated.

- Green will report to the Chief Executive Officer of DEC.

- Green has agreed to a base salary of $400,000 to be reviewed and adjusted on the same basis as other officers of DEC and the surviving entity.

- Green has agreed to a potential annual bonus of up to 10% of her base salary calculated on the same basis as other officers of DEC and the surviving entity.

- Green is willing to accept DEC's standard benefits package in regard to health, dental, long-term disability, and 401k.

- Green has agreed to four weeks paid time off during each calendar year.

- In the event of termination without cause or for good reason (including as a result of a change in control), Green is entitled to 2X her current salary plus the target bonus (or bonus she would have earned) for that year and any benefits due.

- Green has agreed to a two-year non-compete and non-solicitation after her employment ends, whether voluntary or involuntary.

- Green is fine with DEC's standard confidentiality terms.

- Green is not receiving a signing bonus or any equity award.

VIII.   CONSULTING AGREEMENT

In conjunction with a merger transaction, the buyer often desires to utilize the knowledge and skill set of some of the founders, executive officers, or key employees of the target company after the merger closes, but only for a shorter period of time and not as full time employees. In those circumstances, the buyer may enter into consulting (or independent contractor) agreements with those key individuals to help ensure a smooth transition of the acquired entity and its business operations after the closing. In some circumstances, finalizing consulting agreements with key employees will be included as part of the target's closing conditions.

The consulting agreement creates a contractual relationship between the buyer and the former employee of the target to provide the agreed upon services as a consultant. Consulting agreements do not create an employer-employee relationship, but instead create an independent contractor relationship between the parties. These types of agreements provide greater flexibility for the parties, such as the ability to create a relationship that requires a limited time commitment from the consultant, is of a shorter duration, or is non-exclusive.

The consulting agreement will establish the terms of the relationship. It should specifically address the consultant's duties and obligations, the expected time commitment, the compensation arrangement, termination rights, and restrictions on or other obligations of the consultant during and after termination of the relationship.

The next sections discuss the most critical components of the consulting agreement (not including non-competition and non-solicitation which are discussed in Section IV above).

A.   TERM AND TERMINATION

The term provision should set forth the initial term of the consulting agreement and should generally be of a finite duration to ensure that it is an independent contractor relationship and not deemed to be an employee relationship. The term may be for a set amount of time or upon completion of the specific project or services to be provided. This provision should also indicate how the term may be renewed or extended, if at all.

The termination provision should explicitly set forth the circumstances that permit the consultant or the company to terminate the agreement and independent contractor relationship. Generally termination may happen upon mutual agreement, without cause after so many days' notice, and upon a material breach of the agreement. The termination provision should make it clear what amounts are due the consultant and what things must be delivered by the consultant to the company upon termination.

B. DUTIES AND RESPONSIBILITIES

This provision should set forth that the individual is an independent contractor and detail the services the individual is expected to provide in that capacity. In addition, it should indicate where the consultant may work from (e.g. on site or from a home office), the amount of time the consultant is expected to work (e.g. so many hours per week or month), who the consultant will report to (e.g. Chief Marketing Officer), that the consultant is not entitled to any of the benefits that employees receive, and that the consultant is responsible for their own taxes.

C. COMPENSATION

The compensation provision should cover all the details of the consultant's compensation arrangement. Generally consultants are paid an hourly rate or a per project fixed rate. In particular this provision should set forth the consultant's rate, if hourly, or total payment, if project based; whether the consultant will be reimbursed for travel or other expenses, and if so the types of travel and other expenses eligible for reimbursement; and how the consultant will invoice the company and be paid its fees.

D. RESTRICTIONS AND OTHER OBLIGATIONS

As the buyer is retaining a former founder, executive officer, or key employee in the role of a consultant, the buyer will want to protect itself by requiring the consultant to entire into non-compete and non-solicitation provisions during the term of the relationship and for a specified period of time after it ends. Additionally, there should be restrictions that require the consultant to maintain the confidentiality of information to which it is privy. Lastly, there should be provisions that indicate that any work produced by the consultant is a "work made for hire" and that the company retains all intellectual property rights to that work.

IX. PREPARING THE CONSULTING AGREEMENT

For purposes of this simulation, you are a junior associate at the law firm of McClelland, Springer & Combelic, PC. Dutch Elm Company has asked the firm to prepare the initial draft of the consulting agreement for Susan Brown (Tree Services Inc.'s current Senior Vice President—Marketing) as DEC wants to retain Brown as a consultant after the merger transaction closes.

Mr. Combelic asked you to prepare a standard consulting agreement. If you are missing any necessary information, you can make reasonable assumptions regarding the missing information but should bracket any areas where you have made assumptions or require additional information to complete the consulting agreement.

Dutch Elm Company has provided the firm with the following additional information you should utilize in drafting Brown's consulting agreement:

- Brown is being retained as a consultant to ensure a smooth transition and to assist with the retention of the target's customers and suppliers, as well as any other pertinent matters that arise as a result of the merger.

- Brown shall be accessible to the executive officers, board of directors, and legal counsel of DEC in her consulting role, but ultimately reports to the Chief Executive Officer of DEC.

- The initial term is six months, with an option for the parties to agree to mutually extend the term.

- Brown shall provide up to a maximum of 20 hours per week.

- Brown shall be paid $125/hour.

- Brown is entitled to reimbursement of any pre-approved travel or reasonable expenses related to her consulting duties.

- Brown is fine with DEC's standard confidentiality terms.

CHAPTER ELEVEN

THE CLOSING PROCESS

I. INTRODUCTION

Once the merger and acquisition agreement, as well as the ancillary documents have been finalized, it is time for the parties to start planning for the closing of the merger transaction. Closing the merger involves more than simply executing all the documents, paying the purchase price consideration, and taking ownership of the target entity. Closing is a very detailed process and one that requires great organization as it must ensure that the parties have fulfilled all of their closing conditions (or the condition has been waived), including those obligations that are completed at closing, and that the parties are prepared for the closing.

II. THE CLOSING CHECKLIST

A critical component of ensuring that the merger closes as smoothly as possible, is the closing checklist. The checklist should set forth all of the documents that must be drafted and delivered at closing, the party responsible for each document, any other closing items or actions that must take place in order to finalize the merger transaction, and those matters that must occur or documents that must be filed post-closing. The checklist is not a static document, but should be updated as the parties move through the merger transaction so that it is an accurate reflection of the status of each item on the list. The ultimate goal of the checklist is to help facilitate the closing of the merger transaction and make certain that all necessary items are completed prior to or at the closing.

III. PREPARING THE CLOSING CHECKLIST

For purposes of this simulation, you are a junior associate at the law firm of McClelland, Springer & Combelic, PC. Dutch Elm Company has asked the firm to prepare the initial draft of the closing checklist for the merger transaction with Tree Services, Inc.

Mr. Combelic indicated that if you are missing any necessary information, you can make reasonable assumptions regarding the missing information but should bracket any areas where you have made assumptions or require additional information to complete the closing checklist.

Dutch Elm Company has provided the firm with the following additional information you should utilize in preparing the closing checklist:

The following documents have been finalized and executed or the filings have been made:

- Confidentiality Agreement
- Term Sheet
- Merger and Acquisition Agreement
- Hart-Scott-Rodino filing (if necessary)
- Boards of Directors' Consent Actions (completed)

The following documents and filings are in process or will be completed by closing:

- Escrow Agreement (final form)
- Green Employment Agreement (in final stage negotiations)

- Shrub Employment Agreement (in final stage negotiations)
- Brown Consulting Agreement (in early stage negotiations)
- Han's Non-Competition and Non-Solicitation Agreement (in mid stage negotiations)
- Formation of Merger Sub (in process)
- Third Party Consents (in process)
- Payoff Letters (requested)
- Merger Certificates (prepared)
- Officers' and Secretaries' Certificates
- Shareholders' Consent Actions (in process)
- Legal Opinion from Target's outside counsel
- Letters of Transmittal
- Officer and Director Resignations
- Certified Corporate Governance Documents
- Wire Transfer Instructions

IV. CERTIFICATE, ARTICLES, OR STATEMENT OF MERGER

In conjunction with a merger transaction, state corporation laws will require the entities involved in the merger to file either a Certificate, Articles, or Statement of Merger with the applicable state authority (generally, the Secretary of State) in their state of incorporation. Once the forms have been filed with the appropriate state authorities, the merger transaction has legal effect, meaning it can be recognized as a completed and legally effective merger transaction. The merger transaction will be deemed effective on the same date the Certificate, Articles, or Statement of Merger is filed or on a later date specified in that particular filing. The various state filings should be made simultaneously or should state the same effective date and time in order to avoid any potential issues due to inconsistent timing.

Each state has its own statutes that specify the process for legally effecting a merger transaction and the required information that must be filed with the particular state. In order to determine the specific requirements for the filing, the state statutes for the entity's state of incorporation must be examined and complied with.

V. PREPARING THE CERTIFICATE, ARTICLES, OR STATEMENT OF MERGER

A. PREPARING DUTCH ELM COMPANY'S ARTICLES OF MERGER

For purposes of this simulation, you are a junior associate at the law firm of McClelland, Springer & Combelic, PC. Dutch Elm Company has asked the firm to prepare the required Articles of Merger to legally effect the merger transaction in Nevada.

Mr. Combelic has asked you to review the relevant Nevada Revised Statutes and prepare a brief memo explaining the requirements under Nevada law. Additionally, Mr. Combelic has indicated that you should prepare the Articles of Merger and attach them to the memo.

B. PREPARING TREE SERVICES, INC.'S STATEMENT OF MERGER

For purposes of this simulation you are a junior associate at the law firm of Williams & Rader, LLC. Tree Services, Inc. has asked the firm to prepare the required Statement of Merger to legally effect the merger transaction in Colorado.

Ms. Williams has asked you to review the relevant Colorado Revised Statutes and prepare a brief memo explaining the requirements under Colorado law. Additionally, Ms. Williams has indicated that you should prepare the Statement of Merger and attach it to the memo.

VI. OFFICER'S CERTIFICATE: ACCURACY OF REPRESENTATIONS AND WARRANTIES

When there is a gap period between the execution of the merger and acquisition agreement and the closing of the merger transaction, an important closing condition for all parties is the officer's certificate. The officer's certificate is delivered at closing and certifies that all of the representations and warranties that the particular party made in the merger and acquisition agreement remain true and correct as of the closing date, which certification is often referred to as a "bring down" certificate, and that the party has satisfied all of its obligations pursuant to the agreement. The party preparing the officer's certificate should ensure that the language conforms to the requirements set forth in the merger and acquisition agreement.

In the event that a new matter arose between execution of the agreement and closing of the transaction (e.g. a new lawsuit was filed), the party should ensure that the disclosure schedule for that particular representation and warranty is updated to reflect the new information in order to ensure that the disclosure schedule is accurate and thus the representations and warranties are still true and correct. The officer's certificate should detail any updates to the disclosure schedules so that the other parties are aware of the changes as such changes may allow them to exercise other rights (i.e. termination) pursuant to the merger and acquisition agreement.

VII. PREPARING THE OFFICER'S CERTIFICATE

For purposes of this simulation you are a junior associate at the law firm of Williams & Rader, LLC. Tree Services, Inc. has asked the firm to prepare the officer's certificate based on the draft merger and acquisition agreement that was prepared in conjunction with Chapters Four–Seven.

Ms. Williams asked you to prepare a standard officer's certificate for a merger transaction of this type. If you are missing any necessary information, you can make reasonable assumptions regarding the missing information but should bracket any areas where you have made assumptions or require additional information to complete the officer's certificate.

Tree Services, Inc. has provided the firm with the following additional information you should utilize in drafting the officer's certificate:

- The merger and acquisition agreement was executed six weeks ago and closing is scheduled to take place in one week.

- TSI has operated its business consistent with past practices and in the ordinary course since executing the merger and acquisition agreement.

- Unless otherwise noted here, TSI has met all of its obligations under the merger and acquisition agreement.

- The following matters have arisen since execution of the merger and acquisition agreement:

- Three large TSI customers opted not to renew their annual contracts as they secured a better deal with another provider. In the aggregate, these three customers comprise less than 1% of TSI's most recent year end revenues.

- TSI settled the pending lawsuit with ABC Management Company for $175,000 plus related attorneys' fees and costs of $22,500. TSI's insurance provider agreed to the terms of the settlement.

- The pending lawsuit with Golf Course Management, Inc. is proceeding, but to date Golf Course Management has not cancelled its services contract with TSI.

- TSI's revolving line of credit has a current outstanding balance of $313,000 as TSI engaged in some ordinary purchases to replace aging trucks and equipment.

VIII.   SECRETARY'S CERTIFICATE

The secretary's certificate is a document prepared and delivered at the closing of the merger. The purpose of this document is to certify the authenticity of corporation's organizational documents, the board of director and shareholder resolutions or consent actions authorizing the merger transaction, and those officers who have authority to execute the merger and acquisition agreement and ancillary documents.

IX.   PREPARING THE SECRETARY'S CERTIFICATE

For purposes of this simulation you are a junior associate at the law firm of Williams & Rader, LLC. Tree Services, Inc. has asked the firm to prepare the secretary's certificate based on the draft merger and acquisition agreement that was prepared in conjunction with Chapters Four–Seven.

Ms. Williams asked you to prepare a standard secretary's certificate for a merger transaction of this type. If you are missing any necessary information, you can make reasonable assumptions regarding the missing information but should bracket any areas where you have made assumptions or require additional information to complete the secretary's certificate.

Tree Services, Inc. has provided the firm with the following additional information you should utilize in drafting the secretary's certificate:

- TSI will provide copies of all its corporate governance documents for you to attach to the certificate.

- TSI has requested the certified certificate of good standing from the state of Colorado and will provide it once received.

- TSI will provide the executed board of director and shareholder consent actions for you to attach to the certificate.

- Melissa Green and Thomas Shrub are authorized to execute any necessary agreements to effect the merger transaction.

X.   LEGAL OPINION

A third party legal opinion is a professional opinion generally issued, in the form of a letter, by the client's law firm to a third party upon the request of the client. The opinion expresses legal conclusions as to certain matters related to the transaction that the specified third party may rely upon. In the context of a merger transaction, the third party legal opinion that the target's law firm issues is relatively standard and is generally one of the target's closing conditions. In essence, the opinion is meant to provide the purchaser with added protection or comfort in proceeding with the transaction. While a legal opinion does not act as a guarantee, the law firm issuing the opinion should undertake sufficient due diligence in order to be in a position to render the requested opinion. As a result of recent concerns regarding legal opinions, they have become less commonplace in merger transactions.

The next sections discuss the most critical components of a third party legal opinion in the context of a merger transaction.

A. DESCRIPTION OF DOCUMENTS REVIEWED

The opinion letter should set forth a list of documents that were reviewed in conjunction with the rendering of the opinion, as well as the type of due diligence that was undertaken. These documents are usually those that pertain to the merger transaction and the target's corporate governance documents and approvals. Additionally, each document should be briefly described and reference any relevant dates (e.g. the date of the Good Standing Certificate).

B. FACTUAL ASSUMPTIONS

The opinion letter should set forth any assumptions that the law firm made in conjunction with the rendering of the opinion. In order to render the opinion, the law firm will have to assume that certain facts are true and should set forth those specific assumptions. Common factual assumptions include that the signatures on documents are genuine, documents are authentic or copies conform to the authentic document, the truthfulness and completeness of the documents reviewed, that the other parties have the requisite power and authority to enter into the transaction and that all the transaction documents are binding upon and enforceable against the other parties, and the accuracy of other opinions relied upon, if any.

C. LEGAL OPINIONS

The opinion letter should set forth the legal opinions that the law firm is rendering in conjunction with the review of the described documents and based upon the various factual assumptions. The most common opinions include (i) target's corporate status; (ii) target's power and authority to enter into the transaction and deliver all the transaction documents; (iii) that target's entering into this transaction will not result in other violations; (iv) that the transaction documents will be valid and binding upon target; (v) that target does not have to seek any additional approvals, consents, or opinions to enter into the transaction; and (vi) target's capitalization. Lastly, the letter should indicate the applicable laws, which are generally federal laws and the laws of the state where the law firm is situated or where the attorney is admitted to practice.

D. EXCEPTIONS

The opinion letter should set forth any exceptions to or limitations on the scope of the opinion. Generally, the letter will list those matters to which the law firm is not granting an opinion (e.g. bankruptcy, insolvency, equity principles, or good faith). The letter should provide any applicable limitations, such as date limitations, meaning the opinion speaks only as of a certain date (e.g. date of the Good Standing Certificate) or certificate limitations, meaning the opinion relies on information provided in an officer's certificate. Other common exceptions or limitations include no opinions regarding a particular jurisdiction, choice of law, indemnification, or a severability provision in a transaction document.

E. RELIANCE

The opinion letter should indicate the date of the opinions and those parties that may rely upon the rendered opinions. It should also indicate that it is limited to the matters specifically set forth and that the law firm has no obligation to update the opinions or advise the third party of any changes that arise after the date of the opinion letter. Lastly, it should specify that the opinion letter may not be shared with or relied upon by any other party without the law firm's prior written consent.

XI. PREPARING THE LEGAL OPINION

For purposes of this simulation you are a junior associate at the law firm of Williams & Rader, LLC. Tree Services, Inc. has asked the firm to prepare the legal opinion requested by Dutch Elm Company in conjunction with the merger transaction.

Ms. Williams asked you to prepare an initial draft of the opinion letter that is standard for a merger transaction of this type and based upon federal and Colorado state laws. If you are missing any necessary information, you can make reasonable assumptions regarding the missing information but should bracket any areas where you have made assumptions or require additional information to complete the legal opinion.

Tree Services, Inc. has provided the firm with the following additional information you should utilize in drafting the opinion letter:

- TSI is validly existing and in good standing and has provided authentic copies of all its corporate governance documents and a Good Standing Certificate dated within the past three business days.

- TSI has secured all the necessary approvals to undertake the merger transaction and has provided authentic copies of all that documentation.

- TSI has indicated there are no other approvals necessary in order for it to enter into this merger transaction.

- TSI has provided the firm with copies of the officer's and secretary's certificates certifying any necessary information or matters so that the firm can render the opinion.

CHAPTER TWELVE

MISCELLANEOUS MATTERS

I. INTRODUCTION

The previous eleven chapters walked through a traditional merger transaction between two private companies from the inception of the client relationship to negotiating the terms of the merger transaction to drafting the merger and acquisition agreement and ancillary documents to finalizing all the necessary approvals and filings in order to close the transaction. This final chapter discusses two concepts that occur throughout the merger transaction process, marking up opposing counsel's drafted documents and communicating with the client via email. Additionally, the final section in this chapter introduces the concept of drafting a press release once the transaction is complete.

II. REDLINES OR MARK-UPS

An important skill set for every transactional lawyer is the ability to review a draft of a document and respond to that document with comments and concerns in the form of a mark-up of the document. Marking up a draft agreement is part of, and plays a role in, the overall negotiation process of the terms of the proposed merger transaction.

In order to provide comments and prepare a mark-up, the lawyer must clearly understand the client's goals and objectives. This will enable the lawyer to best address the client's concerns in the comments and mark-up and to suggest revisions that place the client in a better position. The lawyer and client must work together to determine how far to push with comments and mark-ups without jeopardizing the transaction.

III. PREPARING A REDLINE OR MARK-UP

For purposes of this simulation you are a junior associate at the law firm of Williams & Rader, LLC. Tree Services, Inc. has asked the firm to prepare a redline of the indemnification provision of the draft merger and acquisition. The indemnification provision is included in Appendix D.

Ms. Williams asked you to review the indemnification provision and prepare an initial mark-up of the provision based on your knowledge of the merger transaction and taking into account the information provided below. Ms. Williams indicated that you should use your best judgment as to when to make an actual change to the provision versus providing a comment for further discussion.

Tree Services, Inc. has provided the firm with the following additional information you should utilize in preparing the mark-up of the indemnification provision:

- The selling shareholders want to limit their indemnification obligations as much as is reasonably possible.

- The selling shareholders do not want to be jointly liable.

- The selling shareholders do not want to escrow funds in excess of 10–15% of the total purchase consideration.

- The selling shareholders do not want the escrow funds to be held for longer than 18–24 months post-closing.

- The selling shareholders would like a tiered release of the escrow funds over the course of the escrow period.

- The selling shareholders would like the option to assume the defense of third party litigation when there is no conflict.

IV.   EMAIL COMMUNICATION WITH THE CLIENT

Lawyers communicate with clients in many ways over the course of a large transaction, such as a merger. Some of these methods of communication include in person meetings, telephone or conference calls, virtual meetings, and email correspondence. It has become commonplace for lawyers and clients to frequently communicate by email. Email is often a quick and easy way for the parties to communicate about day-to-day matters, as well as about larger issues or the status of various documents in conjunction with a transaction.

While email messages may be viewed as an informal type of communication, lawyers should treat this type of correspondence with a client as a professional interaction. Email deserves the same attention to professionalism and detail as any other type of written correspondence or communication with a client. Additionally, as with every type of client communication, both parties must be acutely aware of protecting the attorney-client privilege, as well as protecting the confidentiality of electronically exchanged information.

A good client email should be structured similar to a traditional letter. An email should (i) contain information in the "subject line" that makes it clear the topic and importance of the email; (ii) lead off with a salutation; (iii) keep the content as succinct as possible with the most important information at the beginning of the email; (iv) indicate if there are attachments and what is attached; (v) include a wrap-up statement that indicates next steps in regard to the email; (vi) include a signature block; and (vii) include a confidentiality notice.

V.   PREPARING A CLIENT EMAIL

For purposes of this simulation you are a junior associate at the law firm of Williams & Rader, LLC. Ms. Williams has asked you to prepare a draft of a client cover email to be sent in conjunction with the mark-up of the indemnification provision you prepared in the prior assignment in Section III.

Ms. Williams indicated that the email should inform the client about the firm's concerns with the indemnification provision and provide TSI with any relevant and necessary information so that they can review the mark-up and be prepared to discuss it on the next client conference call in a few days.

VI.   PRESS RELEASE

In the context of a merger transaction between two private entities, there is generally no statutory obligation to issue a press release, make an announcement to the public, or submit a securities law filing regarding the acquisition. However, the buyer and target may want to publicly announce the transaction so that those parties who might be interested are alerted to the fact that it has been completed. In particular, the buyer and target may want shareholders, customers, suppliers, and other entities operating within the same industry to know about the merger transaction.

One of the primary reasons to publish a press release is to inform the general public and stakeholders of the companies about the news, as well as to prevent the circulation of false or inaccurate information regarding the transaction. The press release should convey the pertinent details of the transaction in a clear and succinct manner. It should be written in a professional business voice, omitting legalese, and should convey how the transaction will impact the future of both companies.

VII. PREPARING A PRESS RELEASE

For purposes of this simulation, you are a junior associate at the law firm of McClelland, Springer & Combelic, PC. Dutch Elm Company has asked the firm to prepare the initial draft of the press release announcing the merger with Tree Services, Inc.

Mr. Combelic asked you to prepare the initial draft of the press release. If you are missing any necessary information, you can make reasonable assumptions regarding the missing information but should bracket any areas where you have made assumptions or require additional information to complete the press release.

Dutch Elm Company has provided the firm with the following additional information you can utilize in drafting the press release:

- The tentative issuance of the press release is one week from today.

- DEC's marketing department will issue the press release and Mason Star, Vice President of Marketing Communications, is the contact person.

- The company's taglines are as follows:

  - DEC is one of the leading providers of premier landscape maintenance services in the continental United States. DEC has over 24,500 customers nationwide. Its website is www.dec.com.

  - TSI is the preeminent provider of commercial landscaping services in the state of Colorado and the Midwest. TSI has over 1,750 customers. It's new website is www.dec.com/tsi.

- DEC provided the following DEC representative quotes:

  - The merger of TSI into DEC's newly formed subsidiary and the securing of TSI's customers enables DEC to establish a strong presence in the state of Colorado and neighboring states. As a result, DEC will grow its market share and presence in Colorado and the neighboring states immediately and be positioned for greater success in the Midwest region. (Michelle Smith, Senior Vice President of Sales & Marketing at DEC)

  - TSI's well-established business and customer relationships afford DEC immediate entry into the local marketplace. We can hit the ground running and further establish DEC as the premier provider of landscaping services in the Midwest region. (Bernard Thompson, Chief Operating Officer of DEC)

  - We are thrilled about the TSI merger and the hiring of Melissa Green and Thomas Shrub as part of the DEC team. Melissa and Thomas bring a wealth of experience and expertise to the business operations and long-standing relationships that TSI has in the Colorado community and neighboring states. They will help ensure a smooth transition. (Fred Wilcox, Chief Executive Officer of DEC)

- DEC provided the following TSI representative quotes:

  - By merging TSI into DEC's subsidiary and joining the DEC management team, we can more effectively serve our customer base. Not only will all of our customers continue to receive the quality service they have come to expect, but they will now have the opportunity to consider additional services as a result of this merger. (Melissa Green, former Chief Executive Officer of TSI)

  - TSI's merger with DEC was a wise decision. Melissa and I will remain an integral part of the consolidated operations and TSI's customers will continue to receive the quality service they have come to expect. It is a win-win situation for both companies as well as the customers of TSI. (Thomas Shrub, former Chief Financial Officer of TSI)

Appendix A

Information Regarding Tree Services, Inc.

I. Corporate Governance Information

Tree Services, Inc. ("TSI") was incorporated in the state of Colorado in 2009 and has been in continuous operation since that time. TSI is a Colorado C corporation and it authorized two classes of stock upon incorporation:

(i) 10,000,000 shares of Common Stock, $0.01 par value ("TSI CS"), and

(ii) 1,000,000 shares of Preferred Stock, $0.10 par value ("TSI PS").

TSI has not increased the authorized shares for either class of stock since its inception. Pursuant to TSI's bylaws, all matters that TSI common shareholders are entitled to vote on require a simple majority vote. The TSI preferred shareholders have no voting rights.

Upon its incorporation, TSI issued 5,000,000 shares of TSI CS to the three founders as set forth in the table below:

Founder's Name	Number of CS Shares Issued	CS %	Price Paid
Melissa Green	2,000,000	40%	$200,000
Thomas Shrub	2,000,000	40%	$200,000
Susan Brown	1,000,000	20%	$100,000

Each of the founders signed a simple common stock purchase agreement with TSI when the TSI CS shares were issued.

In 2013, TSI created an employee stock option plan and funded the plan with 1,000,000 shares of TSI CS. To date, TSI has granted options to five of its senior level employees, who are all still employees of TSI. The options vested immediately upon their grant date and can be exercised at any time provided the employee remains an employee of TSI. The details of the option grants are set forth in the table below:

	# of Options Granted	Option Exercise Price	# of Options Exercised	# of Options Unexercised
Employee #1	50,000	$1.10	40,000	10,000
Employee #2	25,000	$1.15	20,000	5,000
Employee #3	25,000	$1.15	20,000	5,000
Employee #4	10,000	$1.20	10,000	0
Employee #5	10,000	$1.20	10,000	0

The following table sets forth the current common stock ownership structure of TSI:

Founder's Name	Number of CS Shares Owned	CS %
Melissa Green	2,000,000	39.22%
Thomas Shrub	2,000,000	39.22%
Susan Brown	1,000,000	19.61%
Exercised Options (by non-Founders)	100,000	1.95%

While TSI is currently in good financial standing, about two years after it was incorporated, the founders made a decision to grow the business and its operations and in order to do that, TSI raised the needed capital through sales of its TSI PS. TSI issued 50,000 shares of TSI PS to three investors as set forth in the table below:

Investor's Name	Number of PS Shares Issued	PS %	Price Paid
Erin Mooney	25,000	50%	$125,000
Joe Rosen	12,500	25%	$62,500
Stanley Danger	12,500	25%	$62,500

The TSI PS has an annual guaranteed cumulative dividend payment of $0.50 per share that is required to be paid in December of each year provided TSI is legally able to pay such dividend. To date, TSI has met each dividend payment and no dividend payments are in arrears or have accumulated. The TSI PS also has a guaranteed liquidation preference upon the dissolution or sale of TSI ("PS Preference"). The PS Preference guarantees the TSI PS shareholders the return of his or her initial investment. Each of the TSI PS investors signed a TSI PS purchase agreement that sets forth these rights.

TSI has four executive officers, three of which are also the original founders of the company. Their pertinent information is set forth in the table below:

Name	Position	Base Salary	Potential Annual Bonus
Melissa Green	Chief Executive Officer	$375,000	$75,000
Thomas Shrub	Chief Financial Officer	$315,000	$60,000
Susan Brown	Senior Vice President—Marketing	$275,000	$35,000
Timothy Han	Senior Vice President & Secretary	$250,000	$25,000

TSI maintains a five-person board of directors. A simple majority vote is required to implement any action requiring a vote. Members of the board of directors do not receive compensation for sitting on TSI's board. However, independent directors are reimbursed for any travel, lodging, and food expenses related to attending in-person board meetings. The information regarding the directors is as follows:

Director's Name	Director's Age	Date Directorship Commenced	Independent
Melissa Green, Chairperson of the Board	48	Upon incorporation	No
Thomas Shrub	49	Upon incorporation	No
Jonathon Nixon	44	Upon incorporation	Yes
Erin Mooney	47	On January 2, 2012	Yes
Rolland Brown	63	On January 2, 2012	Yes

II. Business Information

TSI is a large Colorado-based company in the landscaping services industry. The company provides landscape care and maintenance services for both residential and commercial customers. TSI primarily operates in the state of Colorado with some customers in neighboring states. The commercial customers account for approximately 50% of TSI's revenues and the residential customers account for approximately 40%. TSI's remaining 10% of revenues come from its winter month service offerings. The company has a total customer base of approximately 1,750 regular commercial and residential customers, and provides services to many one-time customers as well. TSI has a number of large commercial contracts with both private and public parks, golf courses, apartment and condominium complexes, and office parks. Its residential customers range from townhomes and small single-family homes to large single-family and mountain homes.

TSI's primary focus is on the care and maintenance of trees and shrubs, but it also offers other related landscaping services. TSI offers the following tree services: tree pruning, tree removal, emergency tree care, branch removal around utility lines, and other related services such as fertilization, cabling and bracing, and insect and disease control. TSI also provides landscape maintenance services such as spring and fall clean up and cut back, leaf clearing, lawn mowing and care, basic irrigation systems, and pest control. During the winter months, TSI offers snow removal and holiday light hanging services.

TSI maintains an average fleet of 20–25 trucks and trailers, including tree trucks with chippers and grapples, tree trucks with aerial lifters, site trucks, trucks with snow removal plows, and spray, fertilizer, and injection trucks. In addition to its trucks and trailers, TSI also maintains a number of hydraulic truck cranes, stump and limb grinders, stump removers, brush chippers, chain saws, clippers, snow blowers, and other related tools.

TSI employs 120 crew workers, two arborists, and five office staff in addition to the four executive officers. Of the 120 crew workers, approximately 40–55 are seasonal employees who work for TSI only during the months of March–November, which are typically TSI's busiest months. The remaining 55–70 crew workers are employed by TSI year-round. Of the year-round crew workers, 15 are crew leaders and supervisors.

III. Financial Information

TSI's fiscal year end is December 31 and the company prepares its audited financial statements in accordance with generally accepted accounting principles. TSI has provided its projected balance sheet and income statement for the current fiscal year and its actual balance sheets and income statements for the prior two fiscal years.

Tree Services, Inc.
Balance Sheets

	Current FY Ending December 31 (Projected)	FY Ended December 31 (One Year Prior)	FY Ending December 31 (Two Years Prior)
Assets			
Current assets:			
Cash	$ 3,145,000	$ 2,985,000	$ 3,224,000
Accounts receivable, net	5,623,000	5,198,000	6,546,000
Other current assets	1,672,000	1,278,000	1,887,000
Total current assets	10,440,000	9,461,000	11,657,000
Property, plant, and equipment	3,856,000	3,552,000	4,232,000
Less: accumulated depreciation	(2,236,000)	(1,953,000)	(2,358,000)
Net property, plant, and equipment	1,620,000	1,599,000	1,874,000
Other long-term assets	1,741,000	1,604,000	1,911,000
Total Assets	$ 13,801,000	$ 12,664,000	$ 15,442,000
Liabilities and Stockholders' Equity			
Current liabilities:			
Accounts payable	1,743,000	1,856,000	2,143,000
Accrued expenses	1,176,000	1,211,000	1,482,000
Other current liabilities	1,932,000	2,157,000	2,561,000
Total current liabilities	4,851,000	5,224,000	6,186,000
Long-term debt	1,862,000	1,572,000	1,982,000
Other long-term liabilities	1,544,875	818,875	1,685,875
Total liabilities	8,257,875	7,614,875	9,853,875
Stockholders' equity:			
Common stock	5,010	5,010	5,010
Preferred stock	5,000	5,000	5,000
Additional paid-in-capital	741,115	741,115	741,115
Retained earnings	4,792,000	4,298,000	4,837,000
Total stockholders' equity	5,543,125	5,049,125	5,588,125
Total liabilities and stockholders' equity	$ 13,801,000	$ 12,664,000	$ 15,442,000

Tree Services, Inc.
Income Statements

	Current FY Ending December 31 (Projected)	FY Ended December 31 (One Year Prior)	FY Ending December 31 (Two Years Prior)
Revenues	$ 29,713,000	$ 27,622,000	$ 33,247,000
Less: Costs and expenses:			
Operating	17,124,000	15,849,000	18,615,000
Selling, general, and administrative	6,833,000	6,353,000	7,646,000
Depreciation	2,971,000	2,731,000	3,362,000
Total costs and expense	26,928,000	24,933,000	29,623,000
Income from operations	2,785,000	2,689,000	3,624,000
Other income (expense):			
Interest income (expense), net	(297,030)	(276,432)	(323,746)
Other income (expense), net	(224,970)	(378,568)	(641,254)
Income before income taxes	2,263,000	2,034,000	2,659,000
Less: Income taxes	481,000	432,000	565,000
Net income	$ 1,782,000	$ 1,602,000	$ 2,094,000

APPENDIX B

INFORMATION REGARDING DUTCH ELM COMPANY

I. Corporate Governance Information

Dutch Elm Company ("DEC") was incorporated in the state of Nevada in 2002 and has been in continuous operation since incorporation. DEC is a C Corporation and it authorized one class of stock:

   (i)   50,000,000 shares of Common Stock, $0.01 par value ("DEC CS").

DEC has not increased the authorized shares of DEC CS since its inception. Pursuant to DEC's bylaws, all matters that DEC common shareholders are entitled to vote on require a simple majority vote.

Upon its incorporation, DEC issued 10,000,000 shares of DEC CS to the three founders as set forth in the table below:

Founder's Name	Number of CS Shares Issued	CS %	Price Paid
Fred Wilcox	4,500,000	45%	$450,000
Bernard Thompson	3,000,000	30%	$300,000
Margaret Fine	2,500,000	25%	$250,000

Each of the founders signed a simple common stock purchase agreement with DEC when the DEC CS shares were issued.

In 2004, DEC created an employee stock option plan and funded the plan with 5,000,000 shares of DEC CS. To date, DEC has granted 1,350,000 stock options to various employees of DEC. Of those 1,350,000 options, to date 1,000,000 have been exercised. The options vest over four years at the rate of 25% year. DEC has also granted 150,000 options to its founders. Of those 150,000 options, to date 75,000 have been exercised. Any unexercised options are forfeited upon an employee's termination with DEC.

The following table sets forth the current ownership structure of DEC:

Founder's Name	Number of CS Shares Owned	CS %
Fred Wilcox	4,525,000	40.86%
Bernard Thompson	3,025,000	27.31%
Margaret Fine	2,525,000	22.80%
Exercised Options (by non-Founders)	1,000,000	9.03%

DEC has five executive officers, three of which are also the original founders of the company. Their pertinent information is set forth in the table below:

Name	Position	Base Salary	Potential Annual Bonus
Fred Wilcox	Chief Executive Officer & President	$550,000	$120,000
Bernard Thompson	Chief Operating Officer	$525,000	$60,000
Margaret Fine	Chief Financial Officer	$525,000	$60,000
Michelle Smith	Senior Vice President of Sales & Marketing	$475,000	$40,000
Robert Lawson	Senior Vice President & Secretary	$415,000	$30,000

DEC maintains a five-person board of directors. A simple majority vote is required to implement any action requiring a vote. Members of the board of directors do not receive compensation for sitting on DEC's board. However, independent directors are reimbursed for any travel, lodging, and food expenses related to attending in-person board meetings. The information regarding the directors is as follows:

Director's Name	Director's Age	Date Directorship Commenced	Independent
Fred Wilcox, Chairperson of the Board	55	Upon incorporation	No
Bernard Thompson	58	Upon incorporation	No
Margaret Fine	46	Upon incorporation	No
William Carlton	62	On January 2, 2006	Yes
Lisa Montgomery	37	On January 2, 2006	Yes

II. Business Information

DEC is a national company in the landscaping services industry. DEC provides tree care, landscape care, and on-going maintenance services for both residential and commercial customers throughout the continental United States. The commercial customers account for approximately 60% of DEC's revenues and the residential customers account for approximately 35%. DEC's remaining 5% of revenues come from its winter month service offerings. The company has a total customer base of over 24,500 regular customers, as well as thousands of one-time customers. DEC has many local and large national commercial contracts with private and public parks, private and public golf courses, apartment and condominium complexes, planned communities, small and large office parks, and small ski resorts. Its residential customers range from townhomes and small single-family homes to large single-family and vacation homes.

DEC provides all types of horticultural services including a broad array of tree-related and landscaping services. It also works with a number of utility companies to clear tree growth from power lines. DEC's tree-related service offerings include: pruning, removal, emergency tree care, surgery, spraying, clearing around utility lines, cabling and bracing, watering, and fertilization. Additionally, DEC provides a wide array of landscaping services including construction and design, leaf clearing, lawn mowing and care, small and large irrigation systems, and disease and pest control. During the winter months, DEC provides snow removal to all of its customers, as well as winter landscape maintenance services. In addition, in severe storm conditions, DEC may assist small towns and cities with snow removal.

In order to meet the needs of its commercial and residential customers, DEC maintains a large fleet of trucks and trailers, including tree trucks with chippers and grapples, tree trucks with aerial lifters, site trucks, trucks with snow removal plows, and spray, fertilizer and injection trucks. In addition to its trucks and trailers, DEC also maintains a number of hydraulic truck cranes, stump and limb grinders, stump removers, brush chippers, chain saws, clippers, snow blowers, and other related tools.

DEC employs more than 700 crew workers and one to two arborists for each geographic region it serves. Approximately 30% of its crew workers are seasonal employees who work for DEC only during the months of March-November. DEC's corporate headquarters are located in Las Vegas, Nevada where it employs a staff of 60 full-time employees to oversee and run its national operations.

III. Financial Information

DEC's fiscal year end is December 31 and the company prepares audited financial statements annually. DEC has provided its projected balance sheet and income statement for the current fiscal year and its actual balance sheets and income statements for the prior two fiscal years.

Dutch Elm Company
Balance Sheets

	Current FY Ending December 31 (Projected)	FY Ended December 31 (One Year Prior)	FY Ending December 31 (Two Years Prior)
Assets			
Current assets:			
Cash	$ 64,578,000	$ 53,121,000	$ 43,006,000
Accounts receivable, net	141,920,000	128,671,000	112,134,000
Other current assets	31,592,000	27,333,000	23,633,000
Total current assets	238,090,000	209,125,000	178,773,000
Property, plant, and equipment	637,104,000	616,036,000	588,650,000
Less: accumulated depreciation	(435,504,000)	(422,853,000)	(409,214,000)
Net property, plant, and equipment	201,600,000	193,183,000	179,436,000
Other long-term assets	28,131,000	29,156,000	31,354,000
Goodwill, net	41,671,000	41,671,000	34,376,000
Total Assets	$ 509,492,000	$ 473,135,000	$ 423,939,000
Liabilities and Stockholders' Equity			
Current liabilities:			
Accounts payable	49,050,000	45,093,000	41,283,000
Current portion of long-term debt	15,926,000	16,315,000	16,701,000

Accrued expenses	48,891,000	42,816,000	37,659,000
Other current liabilities	25,622,000	24,433,000	23,262,000
Total current liabilities	139,489,000	128,657,000	118,905,000
Long-term debt, net of current portion	122,254,000	105,469,000	72,194,000
Other long-term liabilities	76,048,000	77,619,000	80,661,000
Total liabilities	337,791,000	311,745,000	271,760,000
Stockholders' equity:			
Common stock	101,750	101,750	101,750
Additional paid-in-capital	1,425,750	1,425,750	1,425,750
Retained earnings	170,173,500	159,862,500	150,651,500
Total stockholders' equity	171,701,000	161,390,000	152,179,000
Total liabilities and stockholders' equity	$ 509,492,000	$ 473,135,000	$ 423,939,000

Dutch Elm Company
Income Statements

	Current FY Ending December 31 (Projected)	FY Ended December 31 (One Year Prior)	FY Ending December 31 (Two Years Prior)
Revenues	$ 841,354,000	$ 819,605,000	$ 801,831,000
Less: Costs and expenses:			
Operating	549,822,000	541,486,000	533,899,000
Selling, general, and administrative	223,657,000	213,895,000	204,032,000
Depreciation and amortization	45,914,000	44,926,000	44,865,000
Total costs and expense	819,393,000	800,307,000	782,796,000
Income from operations	21,961,000	19,298,000	19,035,000
Other income (expense):			
Interest income (expense), net	(4,707,000)	(4,138,000)	(3,106,000)
Other income (expense), net	(3,890,000)	(2,989,000)	(5,744,000)
Income before income taxes	13,364,000	12,171,000	10,185,000
Less: Income taxes	3,053,000	2,960,000	1,833,000
Net income	$ 10,311,000	$ 9,211,000	$ 8,352,000

APPENDIX C

DUE DILIGENCE CONTRACTS

1.   Industrial Lease Agreement

**INDUSTRIAL LEASE AGREEMENT
BY AND BETWEEN**

**GIANT REAL ESTATE COMPANY
("LANDLORD")**

**AND
TREE SERVICES, INC.
("TENANT")**

DATED: APRIL 1, 2014

INDUSTRIAL LEASE SUMMARY

LANDLORD: Giant Real Estate Company
                                55555 Tower Road
                                Brighton, CO 80602

TENANT: Tree Services, Inc.
                                6789 120th Street
                                Commerce City, CO 80022

PREMISES: Commerce City Industrial Complex
                                6789 120th Street
                                Units A–C
                                Commerce City, CO 80022

LEASED SQUARE FEET: 16,000 square feet

PERMITTED USE: Commercial landscape business operations and related office
                                use

TERM: 60 months

COMMENCEMENT DATE: April 1, 2014

EXPIRATION DATE: March 31, 2019

RENT PER SQUARE FOOT: Months 1–24 at $5.50 psf

Months 25–48 at $6.25 psf

Months 49–60 at $7.00 psf

RENT PER MONTH: Months 1–24 at $7,333.33

Months 25–48 at $8,333.33

Months 49–60 at $9,333.33

SECURITY DEPOSIT: $43,999.98 (six months rent)

OPERATING EXPENSES: $1.10 psf, estimated

BASE YEAR: 2012

OPTIONS: Option 1: Three years at $7.45 psf

Option 2: Three years at $7.90 psf

Option 3: Three years at $8.35 psf

INDUSTRIAL LEASE AGREEMENT

This Industrial Lease Agreement (the "Lease") is made this 1st day of April 2014 by and between Giant Real Estate Company, a Colorado limited liability company ("Landlord") and Tree Services, Inc., a Colorado C Corporation (the "Tenant"), who mutually covenant and agree as follows:

I.   Leased Premises; Term; and Use

1.1. *The Leased Premises.* Landlord, for and in consideration of the rents herein reserved and of the covenants and agreements herein contained on the part of the Tenant to be kept, observed, and performed, demises and leases to the Tenant that part of the building, located at 6789 120th Street, Units A–C, Commerce City, Colorado in the Commerce City Industrial Complex, as shown on the floor plan attached to this Lease as Exhibit A, and containing approximately 16,000 square feet of leasable space (the "Leased Premises"). The leasing of the Leased Premises to Tenant includes, with no additional rent or other charge payable therefore, the right of Tenant (a) to use related driveways, walkways, drainage facilities, and other site improvements, (b) to enjoy all easements, rights, licenses, privileges, and other appurtenances in any way pertaining to or beneficial to the Leased Premises, (c) to use, on a non-exclusive basis, 12 parking spaces in the parking lot, and (d) to install, at Tenant's sole cost and subject to any required municipal approvals, signage at the Leased Premises in accordance with the terms of this Lease.

1.2. *Preparation of Leased Premises.* On or before April 1, 2014, the Tenant will have possession of the Leased Premises in "as-is, where-is" condition. The Landlord will not be liable to Tenant for damages nor will the Tenant be relieved from any obligations under this Lease if the Tenant is unable to occupy the space on April 1, 2014 because of holding over or retention of possession of the Leased Premises by a prior tenant or occupant or any other cause beyond the reasonable control of the Landlord. In such event, however, the rent under this Lease shall abate on a per diem basis until the Leased Premises are available.

1.3. *Term.* The initial lease term of the Leased Premises shall be 60 months (the "Term") commencing on April 1, 2014 (the "Commencement Date"), and ending sixty months from the Commencement Date, unless sooner terminated or extended as provided in this Lease.

1.4. *Use.* The Leased Premises shall be occupied and used by the Tenant for its commercial landscape business operations and related office use and for no other purpose whatsoever without Landlord's prior written consent, which may be withheld in Landlord's sole discretion. Tenant shall obtain any permits, approvals, or certificates of occupancy related to Tenant's proposed use of the Leased Premises prior to the Commencement Date.

Tenant shall not permit the Leased Premises to be used in any manner that would render the insurance thereon void. Tenant shall not use or occupy the Leased Premises, or permit the Leased Premises to be used or occupied, contrary to any statute, rule, order, ordinance, requirement, or regulation applicable thereto; or in any manner which would violate any certificate of occupancy affecting the same, or which would cause structural injury to the improvements or cause the value or usefulness of the Leased Premises or any part thereof to diminish, or which would constitute a public or private nuisance or waste.

II.   Rent and Security Deposit

2.1. *Rent.* Beginning with the Commencement Date, Tenant shall pay to Landlord, until otherwise notified in writing by Landlord, as rent for the Leased Premises, at such place or places as Landlord may designate in writing from time-to-time, annual "Base Rent" as follows: during the first twenty-four months of the Term, the annual Base Rent will be $88,000.00 payable monthly in advance in installments of $7,333.33; during months twenty-five through forty-eight of the Term, the annual Base Rent will be increased to $100,000.00 payable monthly in advance in installments of $8,444.44; and during months forty-nine through sixty, the annual Base Rent of the Term will be $112,000.00 payable monthly in advance in installments of $9,333.33. All payments of Base Rent shall be made without deduction, set off, discount, or abatement in lawful money of the United States.

2.2. *Interest on Late Payments.* Each and every installment of Base Rent, and each and every payment of other charges due under this Lease, which shall not be paid when due, shall bear interest at a rate equal to 18% per annum from the date due until paid.

2.3. *Security Deposit.* Intentionally Omitted

III.   Additional Rent for Operating Expenses

3.1. *Monthly Operating Expense Payment.* In addition to the Base Rent set forth in Section 2.1, on the first day of each month, Tenant shall pay to the Landlord an amount equal to the Tenant's proportionate share of Operating Expenses (as defined in Section 3.3 below) for that calendar year divided by twelve (this amount is referred to as "Additional Rent"). For the calendar year 2014, the estimated Operating Expenses are $1.10 per square foot. The Tenant's proportionate share of the Operating Expenses shall be an amount equal to the total building Operating Expenses divided by the leasable square feet in the building, which Landlord represents to be 34,500 square feet (as of the date of this Lease), times the number of square feet leased by the Tenant as set forth in Section 1.1. On or before December 15 of each year during the Term, the Landlord shall estimate the Operating Expenses for the next calendar year and shall notify the Tenant in writing of the Tenant's proportionate share of the estimated Operating Expenses. Then, in addition to the Base Rent set forth in Section 2.1, on January 1 and on the first day of each month during the next calendar year, with the Base Rent the Tenant shall pay to the Landlord the Tenant's Additional Rent (Base Rent and Additional Rent collectively referred to as, "Rent").

3.2. *Annual Operating Expenses Adjustments.* On or before May 15 of each year and after the first calendar year of the Term, whether the first year is full or partial, the Landlord shall determine the actual Operating Expenses for the total building and the land on which the building is located, including on-site parking related to the building, for the preceding calendar year. Therefore, on or before May 15 of each calendar year through the year following the termination of the Term, with any options and extensions, the total amount of the Tenant's estimated Operating Expenses paid during the preceding calendar year shall be corrected or reflect the actual Operating Expenses for such preceding calendar year, and the Landlord shall submit a statement reflecting the correction to the Tenant. On or before June 1 of each such year, the Tenant shall pay to the Landlord, an amount equal to the difference between the Tenant's proportionate share of the actual Operating Expenses for the preceding calendar year less the Tenant's proportionate share of the estimated Operating Expenses, which were paid by the Tenant during such preceding calendar year.

3.3. *Audit Right.* Landlord shall maintain books and records of account that shall be open to Tenant and its representatives. Tenant shall have the right, at Tenant's sole cost and expense, to examine Landlord's books and records relating to the Leased Premises and the building so that Tenant can (i) determine that any Operating Expenses or other expenses have been paid or incurred; (ii) confirm that certain Operating Expenses charged by Landlord include costs that are properly within the term "Operating Expenses," and (iii) confirm Landlord's calculation of Operating Expenses; provided that if Tenant fails to exercise such right for more than four months following its receipt of Landlord's final written determination of Operating Expenses for a particular calendar year, Tenant shall be deemed to have waived its right to audit and contest Landlord's determination of such Operating Expenses for that calendar year, and, in such event, Landlord's determination for the applicable calendar year shall become final and binding on Landlord and Tenant for all purposes under this Lease. Tenant shall exercise such audit right by providing Landlord with a written notice of Tenant's exercise of such audit right within forty-five days following Tenant's receipt of Landlord's final written determination of Operating Expenses for a particular calendar year (the "Audit Notice"). If Tenant provides a timely Audit Notice, Landlord's books and records relating to Operating Expenses shall be open for copying and inspection at Landlord's corporate business office upon reasonable notice and at reasonable times by Tenant and its duly authorized representatives, who shall have reasonable access to the same and the right to require Landlord, its agents, and employees, to provide such information or explanation with respect to the same as may reasonably be necessary for a proper examination.

In the event that it is determined as a result of any audit by Tenant that the actual Operating Expenses for any calendar year are less than the amount paid by Tenant for such calendar year, then the amount of the excess shall be taken by Tenant as a credit against the next following installments of Additional Rent payable by Tenant to Landlord until Tenant has deducted an amount equal to the amount of such credit or, if the Term has expired, the credit amount shall be paid by Landlord to Tenant within ninety days after the date the amount Landlord owes Tenant has been determined. If Tenant's audit reveals Tenant has overpaid Operating Expenses for any calendar year by more than twenty-five percent of the total actual Operating Expenses for such calendar year, Landlord shall, within ninety days after the date Landlord receives from Tenant an invoice, pay to Tenant the actual cost of such audit less any expenses that Landlord determines are unreasonable in the circumstances. If Tenant's audit reveals that Tenant has underpaid Operating Expenses for any calendar year, then Tenant shall pay to Landlord the amount of underpayment within ten business days after the date the amount Tenant owes has been determined.

3.4. *Operating Expenses Defined.* The term "Operating Expenses" means and includes the total reasonable operating expenses related to the total building and building site (collectively, the "Real Estate") which are incurred by the Landlord, and shall include without limitation, taxes and assessments levied, assessed, or imposed at any time by any municipal, county, state, or federal government or any governmental authority, upon or against the Real Estate ("Real Estate Taxes"); fees contingent on tax savings realized from an appeal; any tax or assessment levied, assessed, or imposed at any time by any governmental authority in connection with the receipt of any income or rents from the building to the extent that any such tax or assessment is in lieu of all or a portion of any of the Real Estate Taxes, personal property, and ad valorem taxes; costs of water and sewage; management expenses (management expense not to exceed fifteen percent of the Base Rent for the Leased Premises), labor, including all wages, salaries, Social Security taxes which may be levied upon such wages and salaries according to generally accepted accounting practices; and supplies, repairs, maintenance, painting, general exterior cleaning, insurance, landscaping, snow removal, and other items properly constituting direct operating costs according to standard accounting practices. The term "Operating Expenses" does not mean or include depreciation of the building or equipment; interest expense on borrowed money of any form or nature; costs of maintaining the Landlord's corporate or business existence; franchise taxes; federal or state income taxes; expenditures required to be capitalized for federal income tax purposes; office expenses or salaries of Landlord's executive officers; commissions and fees paid for the rental of the building, or any parts thereof; tenant improvements; wage taxes or Social Security payments of Landlord or its property manager; or Landlord's transfer, recording, inheritance, estate, succession, franchise, excise, business privilege, personal property, income, gross receipts, or profit tax. Costs incurred for capital improvements shall be included in Operating Expenses for the calendar year in which the costs are incurred and for subsequent calendar years depreciated on a straight line basis over the ordinary, useful life of the improvement (as determined by the Internal Revenue Code of 1986, as amended, and the regulations thereto).

3.5. *Annual Notice.* The Landlord shall notify the Tenant in writing by May 15 of each year of the actual Operating Expenses during the preceding calendar year, together with the computation of the additional payments for Operating Expenses due from the Tenant by June 1 of such year pursuant to sections 3.1, 3.2, and 3.3 above.

3.6. *Real Estate Tax Abatement.* To the extent that a program for the abatement of Real Estate Taxes (the "Tax Abatement") has been approved for the building by the City of Commerce City, Colorado, such Tax Abatement during the Term shall be solely for the benefit of the Landlord and shall not reduce Tenant's Additional Rent payment.

3.7. *Alternative Taxes.* If, at any time during the Term, the method of taxation prevailing at the commencement of the Term shall be altered so that any new tax, assessment, levy, imposition, or charge, or any part thereof, shall be measured by or be based in whole or in part upon the Lease, Leased Premises, building, or the Real Estate, or the Base Rent, Additional Rent, or other income therefrom and shall be imposed upon Landlord, then all such taxes, assessments, levies, impositions, or charges, or the part thereof, to the extent that they are so measured or based, shall be deemed to be included within the term impositions for the purposes hereof, to the extent that such impositions would be payable if the Leased Premises were the only property of Landlord subject to such impositions as so defined. There shall be excluded from impositions all municipal, county, state, or federal income taxes, federal excess profit taxes, franchise, capital stock, and federal or state estate or inheritance taxes of Landlord.

IV. Insurance

4.1. *Tenant's Insurance.* In addition to the Base Rent and Additional Rent for the Leased Premises, Tenant shall procure and maintain policies of insurance, at its own cost and expense, insuring:

(a) Landlord and Tenant from all claims, demands, or actions made by or on behalf of any person or persons, firm or corporation, arising from, related to, or connected with, the Leased Premises or any act or omission of Tenant, for injury to or death of any person in an amount of not less than $3,000,000, for injury to or death of more than one person in any one occurrence in an amount of not less than $5,000,000, for damage to property in an amount of not less than

$7,500,000, plus excess liability coverage with a combined limit of $10,000,000. Said insurance shall provide comprehensive full coverage of the indemnity set forth in Section 11.1 hereof;

(b) Tenant from all workers' compensation claims; and

(c) Tenant's personal property located in the Leased Premises in amounts reasonably deemed adequate by Landlord to fully insure such personal property pursuant to Fire and Extended Coverage Insurance.

4.2. *Form of Insurance.* The aforesaid insurance shall be in companies and in form, substance, and amount (where not stated above) satisfactory to Landlord in its sole and absolute discretion and any mortgagee of Landlord. The insurance shall not be subject to cancellation except after at least one hundred twenty days' prior written notice to Landlord and any mortgagee of Landlord. The original insurance policies (or certificates thereof satisfactory to Landlord) together with satisfactory evidence of payment of the premiums, shall be deposited with Landlord at the Commencement Date, and renewals thereof not less than sixty days prior to the end of the term of each such coverage.

4.3. *Building Insurance Premium.* Tenant shall pay all of the costs of procuring and maintaining a policy or policies insuring the improvements at any time situated upon the Leased Premises against loss or damage by fire, lightning, wind storm, hail storm, aircraft, vehicles, smoke, explosion, riot, or civil commotion as provided by the Standard Fire and Extended Coverage Policy and all other risks of direct physical loss as insured against under Special Extended Coverage Endorsement, and flood insurance whenever such protection is necessary and is available. The insurance coverage shall be in amounts not less than the full replacement cost of such improvements, which shall be determined by Landlord in its sole and absolute discretion. Tenant shall also pay the premium for insurance against loss of Rents during the period while the Leased Premises are untenantable due to fire or other casualty (for a period of at least eighteen months). The policy or policies shall name Landlord as the insured, with all proceeds payable to Landlord, and, if required by any mortgagee of Landlord, shall contain a standard mortgage clause satisfactory to Landlord's mortgagee.

4.4. *Mutual Waiver of Subrogation Rights.* Whenever (a) any loss, cost, damage, or expense resulting from fires, explosion, or any other casualty or occurrence is incurred by either of the parties to this Lease, or anyone claiming by, through, or under it in connection with the Leased Premises, and (b) such party is then covered in whole or in part by insurance with respect to such loss, cost, damage, or expense or required under this Lease to be so insured, then the party so insured (or so required) releases the other party from any liability the other party may have on account of such loss, cost, damage, or expense to the extent of any amount recovered by reason of such insurance (or which could have been recovered had such insurance been carried as so required) and waives any right of subrogation which might otherwise exist in or accrue to any person on account thereof, provided that such release of liability and waiver of the right of subrogation shall not be operative in any case where the effect is to invalidate such insurance coverage or increase the cost thereof (provided that in the case of increased cost, the other party shall have the right, within ten days following written notice, to pay such increased cost, thereupon keeping such release and waiver in full force and effect).

V. Damage or Destruction

5.1. *Landlord's Obligation to Rebuild.* In the event the Leased Premises are damaged by fire, explosion, or other casualty, Landlord shall commence the repair, restoration, or rebuilding thereof within two hundred seventy days of such damage, and shall complete such restoration, repair, or rebuilding within one hundred eighty days after the commencement thereof, provided that if construction is delayed because of changes, deletions, or additions in construction requested by Tenant, strikes, lockouts, casualties, acts of God, war, material or labor shortages, governmental regulation, or control of other causes beyond the control of Landlord, the period for restoration, repair, or rebuilding shall be extended for the amount of time Landlord is so delayed. If the proceeds of insurance are insufficient to pay the cost of such repair, restoration, or rebuilding, Tenant shall reimburse Landlord for any deficiency required to be expended by Landlord for such work, as such deficiency is paid to contractors for such work. If the casualty or the repair, restoration, or rebuilding caused thereby shall render the Leased Premises untenantable, in whole or in part, Rent shall abate to the extent and during the period of untenantability, and Tenant shall have no liability therefor; provided, however, that Tenant shall, on a monthly basis, advance to Landlord a sum equal to the monthly payment of Rent and other charges otherwise due hereunder, and such advances shall be repaid to Tenant solely from the proceeds, if any, of rental insurance on the Leased Premises collected and retained by Landlord for the period of such untenantability. If such a fire, explosion, or other casualty damages the building or the Leased Premises to the extent of twenty-five percent or more, Landlord may, in lieu of repairing, restoring, or rebuilding the same, terminate this Lease within thirty days after occurrence of the event causing the damage. In such event, the obligation of Tenant to pay Rent and other charges hereunder shall end as of the date of such notice from Landlord.

VI. Condemnation

6.1. *Taking of Whole.* If the whole of the Leased Premises shall be taken or condemned for a public or quasi-public use or purpose by a competent authority, or if such a portion of the Leased Premises shall be so taken that as a result thereof the balance cannot be used for the same purpose as expressed in Article I, then in either of such events, the Lease shall terminate upon delivery of possession to the condemning authority, and any award, compensation, or damages shall be paid to and be the sole property of Landlord, but nothing herein shall preclude Tenant from proving (to the extent allowable by law) its damages with respect to moving expenses and loss of personal property, and receiving an award therefor. Tenant shall continue to pay Rent until the Lease is terminated, and any impositions prepaid by Tenant shall be adjusted between the parties.

6.2. *Partial Taking.* If only a part of the Leased Premises shall be so taken or condemned, and, as a result thereof, the balance of the Leased Premises can be used for the same purpose as expressed in Article I, this Lease shall not terminate, and Landlord shall repair and restore the Leased Premises and all improvements thereon. Rent shall be equitably abated following such taking as determined by Landlord in its sole and absolute discretion. Any portion of the award which has not been expended by Landlord for such repair or restoration shall be retained by Landlord as Landlord's sole property. If twenty-five percent or more of the building or the Leased Premises shall be so taken or condemned, the Landlord may terminate this Lease by giving written notice thereof to Tenant within thirty days after such taking. In such event, the award shall be paid to and be the sole property of Landlord, but nothing herein shall preclude Tenant from proving (to the extent allowable by law) its damages with respect to moving expenses and loss of personal property, and receiving an award therefor. Tenant shall continue to pay Rent until the Lease is terminated, and any excess impositions prepaid by Tenant shall be adjusted between the parties, retroactive to the date of taking.

VII. Maintenance and Alterations

7.1. *Maintenance.* Tenant shall keep and maintain the entire interior of the Leased Premises (including, without limitation, interior walls, electrical, heating, and other mechanical equipment, lighting fixtures, interior plumbing fixtures, and interior pipes and conduits below the floor of the Leased Premises) in good condition and repair including, without limitation, any necessary replacements, necessary interior painting, window replacement of equal quality, and maintaining and repairing doors. Tenant shall, to the extent possible, keep the Leased Premises from falling temporarily out of repair or deteriorating. Tenant shall fully comply with all health and police regulations in force, and shall conform with the rules and regulations of fire underwriters or their fire protection engineers. Tenant shall promptly remove any debris left in the parking area or other exterior areas of the Leased Premises by Tenant, its employees, agents, contractors, or invitees.

7.2. *Alterations.* Tenant shall not create any openings in the roof or exterior walls, nor shall Tenant make any alterations or additions to the Leased Premises without the prior written consent of Landlord, which consent can be withheld or conditioned in Landlord's sole discretion. In the event of an improvement or alteration, Landlord shall have the right to determine whether it shall be left or removed at the expiration or termination of the Lease, except as required by any governmental authority. Tenant shall be responsible to make all additions, improvements, alterations, and repairs on the Leased Premises and on and to the appurtenances and equipment thereof, required by any governmental authority or which may be made necessary by the act or neglect of any person, firm, or corporation, claiming by, through, or under Tenant. Any improvement or alteration shall be done in a good and workmanlike manner and in compliance with all applicable permits and authorizations and building and zoning laws, and with all other laws, ordinances, rules, regulations, and requirements of all Federal, State, and Municipal governments, departments, commissions, boards, and officers, and in accordance with the orders, rules and regulations of the National Board of Fire Underwriters or any other body exercising similar functions. Upon completion of any work by or on behalf of Tenant, such Tenant shall provide Landlord with documents as Landlord may require (including, without limitation, sworn contractors' statements and supporting lien waivers) evidencing payment in full for such work.

VIII.   Assignment and Subletting

8.1. *Consent Required.* Tenant shall not, without Landlord's prior written consent, (a) assign, convey, or mortgage this Lease or any interest under it; (b) allow any transfer thereof or any lien upon Tenant's interest by operation of law; (c) sublet the Leased Premises or any part thereof; or (d) permit the use or occupancy of the Leased Premises or any part thereof by anyone other than Tenant. Landlord agrees that it will not unreasonably withhold its consent to any assignment or sublease, provided that if Tenant requests Landlord's consent to an assignment of the Lease or to a sublease of all or a substantial portion of the Leased Premises, Landlord may, in lieu of granting such consent or reasonably withholding the same, terminate this Lease, effective on the effective date of said assignment or on the commencement date specified in the sublease, as the case may be, to which Landlord's consent is requested. No permitted assignment or subletting shall relieve Tenant of Tenant's covenants and agreements hereunder, and Tenant shall continue to be liable as a principal and not as a guarantor or surety, to the same extent as though no assignment or subletting had been made.

8.2. *Merger, Consolidation, or Intra-Corporate Transfer.* Tenant may not in any circumstance, without Landlord's prior written consent, assign this Lease to any corporation resulting from a merger or consolidation of Tenant. In the event that Landlord consents to such assignment, the successors shall execute an instrument in writing fully assuming all of the obligations and liabilities imposed upon Tenant hereunder and deliver the same to Landlord. Upon receipt by Landlord of such assumption, Tenant shall be discharged from any further liability hereunder.

8.3. *Other Transfer of Lease.* Tenant shall not allow or permit any transfer of this Lease or any interest hereunder by operation of law, or convey, mortgage, pledge, or encumber this Lease or any interest herein.

8.4. *Landlord Assignment.* The Landlord may transfer and assign, in whole or in part, all of its rights and obligations under this Lease and in the Real Estate. After such transfer or assignment the Landlord will have no further liability to the Tenant under this Lease for the obligations assumed by the assignee or transferee from and after the date of such assumption.

IX. Liens and Encumbrances

9.1. *Encumbering Title.* Tenant shall not do any act which shall in any way encumber the title of Landlord in and to the building or the Leased Premises, nor shall the interest or estate of Landlord in the building or the Leased Premises be in any way subject to any claim by way of lien or encumbrance, whether by operation of law or by virtue of any express or implied contract by Tenant. Any claim to, or lien upon, the building or the Leased Premises arising from any act or omission of Tenant shall accrue only against the leasehold estate of Tenant and shall be subject and subordinate to the paramount title and rights of Landlord in and to the building and the Leased Premises.

9.2. *Liens and Right to Contest.* Tenant shall not permit the building or the Leased Premises to become subject to any mechanics', laborers', or materialmen's lien on account of labor or material furnished to Tenant or claimed to have been furnished to Tenant in connection with work of any character performed or claimed to have been performed on the building or the Leased Premises by, or at the direction or sufferance of, Tenant; provided, however, that Tenant shall have the right to contest in good faith and with reasonable diligence the validity of any such lien or claimed lien, if Tenant shall give to Landlord such security as may be deemed satisfactory to Landlord in its sole discretion to insure payment thereof and to prevent any sale, foreclosure, or forfeiture of the building or the Leased Premises by reason of non-payment thereof; provided further, however, that on final determination of the lien or claim for lien, Tenant shall immediately pay any judgment rendered, with all proper costs and charges, and shall have the lien released and any judgment satisfied.

X. Utilities and Security

10.1. *Utilities.* Tenant shall purchase all utility services, including but not limited to fuel, water, sewer, and electricity from the utility or municipality providing such service, and shall pay for such services when such payments are due.

10.2. *Security System.* Landlord may install, in Landlord's sole discretion, a security system to monitor the building and the Leased Premises. If Landlord elects to install such system, Landlord shall bill Tenant for its proportionate share of the costs of such installation, which shall be paid within fifteen days of Tenant's receipt of the bill. Additionally, Landlord shall bill Tenant a monthly fee, as determined in Landlord's sole discretion, for utilizing such system, which Tenant shall pay in conjunction with its Base Rent and Additional Rent on the first day of each month of the Term.

XI. Indemnity and Waiver

11.1. *Indemnity.* Tenant will protect, indemnify, and save harmless Landlord from and against any and all liabilities, obligations, claims, damages, penalties, causes of action, costs, and expenses (including without limitation, attorneys' fees and expenses) imposed upon or incurred by or asserted against Landlord by reason of (a) any accident, injury to, or death of persons, or loss of or damage to property occurring on or about the Leased Premises or resulting from any act or omission of Tenant or anyone claiming by, through, or under Tenant; (b) any failure on the part of Tenant to perform or comply with any of the terms of this Lease; or (c) performance of any labor or services or the furnishings of any materials or other property in respect of the Leased Premises or any part thereof. In case any action, suit, or proceeding is brought against Landlord by reason of any such occurrence, Tenant will, at Tenant's expense, resist and defend such action, suit, or proceeding, or cause the same to be resisted and defended by counsel approved by Landlord. In either case, all at Tenant's sole cost and expense.

11.2. *Waiver of Certain Claims.* Tenant waives all claims it may have against Landlord for damage or injury to person or property sustained by Tenant or any persons claiming through Tenant or by any occupant of the building or the Leased Premises, or by any other person, resulting from any part of the building or the Leased Premises or any of its improvements, equipment, or appurtenances becoming out of repair, or resulting directly or indirectly from any act or neglect of any tenant or occupant of any part of the building or the Leased Premises or of any other person, including Landlord to the extent permitted by law. This Section 11.2 shall include, without limitation, damage caused by water, snow, frost, steam, excessive heat or cold, sewage, gas, odors, or noise, or caused by bursting or leaking of pipes or plumbing fixtures, and shall apply equally whether any such damage results from the act or neglect of Tenant or of other tenants, or occupants of any part of the building or the Leased Premises or of any other person, including Landlord (and its representatives) to the extent permitted by law, and whether such damage is caused by or results from anything or circumstance above mentioned or referred to, or to any other thing or circumstance whether of a like nature or of a wholly different nature. All personal property belonging to Tenant or any occupant of the building or the Leased Premises that is in or on any part of the building or the Leased Premises shall be there at the risk of Tenant or of such other person only, and Landlord shall not be liable for any damage thereto or for the theft or misappropriation thereof.

XII. Rights Reserved to Landlord

12.1. *Rights Reserved to Landlord.* Without limiting any other rights reserved or available to Landlord under this Lease, at law or in equity, Landlord, on behalf of itself and its agents reserves the following rights to be exercised at Landlord's election:

(a) To enter the Leased Premises with reasonable frequency during business hours (at any time during an emergency) for the purpose of inspecting the same, and making necessary repairs as per the terms of this Lease.

(b) To show the Leased Premises to prospective purchasers, mortgagees, or other persons having a legitimate interest in viewing the same, and, at any time during the final two years of the Term, to persons wishing to lease the Leased Premises.

(c) During the final two years of the Term, to place and maintain "For Rent" or "For Sale" signs in or on the Leased Premises.

Landlord may enter upon the Leased Premises for any and all of said purposes and may exercise any and all of the foregoing rights hereby reserved without being deemed guilty of any eviction or disturbance of Tenant's use or possession of the Leased Premises, and without being liable in any manner to Tenant.

XIII. Quiet Enjoyment

13.1. *Quiet Enjoyment.* As long as Tenant is not in default under the covenants and agreements of this Lease, Tenant's quiet and peaceable enjoyment of the Leased Premises shall not be disturbed or interfered with by Landlord or by any person claiming by, through, or under Landlord.

XIV. Subordination or Superiority

14.1. *Subordination or Superiority.* The rights and interest of Tenant under this Lease shall be subject and subordinate to any first mortgage or first trust deed that hereafter may be placed upon the building or the Leased Premises by Landlord and to any and all advances to be made thereunder, and to the interest thereof, if the mortgagee or trustee named in said mortgage or trust deed shall elect to subject and subordinate the rights and interest of Tenant under this Lease to the lien of its mortgage or deed of trust and shall agree to recognize the Lease of Tenant in the event of foreclosure if Tenant is not in default (which agreement may, at such mortgagee's option, require attornment by Tenant). Any such mortgagee or trustee may elect to give the rights and interest of Tenant under this Lease priority over the lien of its mortgage or trust deed. In the event of each such election and upon notification by such mortgagee or trustee to Tenant to that effect, the rights and interest of Tenant under this Lease shall be deemed to be subordinate to, or have priority over, as the case may be, the lien of said mortgage or trust deed, whether this Lease is dated prior to or subsequent to the date of said mortgage or trust deed. Tenant shall execute and deliver whatever instruments may be required for such purposes, and in the event Tenant fails to do so within ten days after demand in writing, Tenant does hereby make, constitute, and irrevocably appoint Landlord as its attorney in fact and in its name, place, and stead to do so.

XV.   Surrender

15.1. *Surrender.* Upon the termination of this Lease, whether by forfeiture, lapse of time, or otherwise, or upon the termination of Tenant's right to possession of the Leased Premises, Tenant will at once surrender and deliver up the Leased Premises, together with all improvements thereon, to Landlord in good condition and repair, reasonable wear and tear and loss by fire or other casualty excepted. Said improvements shall include all plumbing, lighting, electrical, heating, cooling and ventilating fixtures and equipment, and other articles of personal property used in the operation of the Leased Premises (as distinguished from operations incident to the business of Tenant; articles of personal property incident to Tenant's business are hereinafter referred to as Trade Fixtures). All additions, hardware, non-Trade Fixtures, and all improvements, temporary or permanent, in or upon the Leased Premises placed there by Tenant shall become Landlord's property and shall remain upon the Leased Premises upon such termination of this Lease by lapse of time or otherwise, without compensation or allowance or credit to Tenant, unless Landlord requests their removal in writing at or before the time of such termination of this Lease. If Landlord so requests removal of said additions, hardware, non-Trade Fixtures, and improvements, and Tenant does not make such removal at said termination of this Lease, or within fifteen days after such request, whichever is later, Landlord may remove and deliver the same to any other place of business of Tenant or warehouse the same, and Tenant shall pay the actual cost of such removal, delivery, and warehousing to Landlord plus an additional ten percent fee on demand.

15.2. *Removal of Tenant's Property.* Upon the termination of this Lease by lapse of time, Tenant may remove Tenant's Trade Fixtures; provided, however, that Tenant shall repair any injury or damage to the Leased Premises which may result from removals. If Tenant does not remove Tenant's Trade Fixtures from the Leased Premises prior to the end of the Term, however ended, Landlord may, at its option, remove the same and deliver the same to any other place of business of Tenant or warehouse the same, and Tenant shall pay the actual cost of such removal (including the repair of any injury or damage to the Leased Premises resulting from such removal), delivery, and warehousing to Landlord plus a ten percent fee on demand, or Landlord may treat such Trade Fixtures as having been conveyed to Landlord with this Lease as a Bill of Sale, without further payment or credit by Landlord or Tenant.

15.3. *Holding Over.* If Tenant retains possession of the Leased Premises, or any part thereof, after the termination of this Lease by lapse of time or otherwise, the Tenant shall pay to the Landlord rent at two and one-half times the Base Rent then in effect pursuant to this Lease for the time that Tenant remains in possession. If the Tenant remains in possession of the Leased Premises, or any part thereof, after the termination of the Term by lapse of time or otherwise, the Landlord may terminate the tenancy immediately and without notice. The provisions of this Section 15.3 do not waive the Landlord's right of re-entry or any other right under this Agreement.

XVI.   Remedies

16.1. *Defaults.* Tenant agrees that any one or more of the following events shall be considered events of default as said term is used herein:

(a) Tenant shall be adjudged an involuntary bankrupt, or a decree or order approving, as properly filed, a petition or answer filed against Tenant asking reorganization of Tenant under the Federal bankruptcy laws as now or hereafter amended, or under the laws of any state, shall be entered, and any such decree or judgment or order shall not have been vacated or set aside within fifteen days from the date of the entry or granting thereof; or

(b) Tenant shall file or admit the jurisdiction of the court and the material allegations contained in any petition in bankruptcy or any petition pursuant or purporting to be pursuant to the Federal bankruptcy laws as now or hereafter amended, or Tenant shall institute any proceedings or shall give its consent to the institution of any proceedings for any relief of Tenant under any bankruptcy or insolvency laws or any laws relating to the relief of debtors, readjustment of indebtedness, reorganization, arrangements, composition, or extension; or

(c) Tenant shall make any assignment for the benefit of creditors or shall apply for or consent to the appointment of a receiver for Tenant or any of the property of Tenant; or

(d) The Leased Premises are levied upon by any revenue officer or similar officer; or

(e) A decree or order appointing a receiver of the property of Tenant shall be made, and such decree or order shall not have been vacated or set aside within fifteen days from the date of entry or granting thereof; or

(f) Tenant shall abandon the Leased Premises or vacate the same during the term hereof; or

(g) Tenant shall default in any payment of Rent or in any other payment required to be made by Tenant hereunder when due as herein provided, and such default shall continue for three days after notice in writing to Tenant; or

(h) Tenant shall fail to contest the validity of any lien or claimed lien and give security to Landlord to insure payment thereof, or having commenced to contest the same and having given such security, shall fail to prosecute such contest with diligence, or shall fail to have the same released and satisfy any judgment rendered thereon, and such default continues for three days after notice in writing to Tenant; or

(i) Tenant shall default in keeping, observing, or performing any of the other covenants or agreements herein contained to be kept, observed, and performed by Tenant, and such default shall continue for five days after notice thereof in writing to Tenant; or

(j) Tenant shall repeatedly be late in the payment of Rent or other charges required to be paid hereunder or shall repeatedly default in the keeping, observing, or performing of any other covenants or agreements herein contained to be kept, observed, or performed by Tenant (provided notice of such payment or other defaults shall have been given to Tenant, but whether or not Tenant shall have timely cured any such payment or other defaults of which notice was given).

Upon the occurrence of any one or more of such events of default, Landlord may, at its election, terminate this Lease, or terminate Tenant's right to possession only, without terminating the Lease. Upon termination of the Lease, or upon any termination of Tenant's right to possession without termination of the Lease, Tenant shall surrender possession and vacate the Leased Premises immediately, and deliver possession to Landlord, and grant to Landlord the full and free right, without demand or notice of any kind to Tenant (except as expressly provided for in this Lease), to enter into and upon the Leased Premises in such event, with or without process of law, and to repossess the Leased Premises as Landlord's former estate, and to expel or remove Tenant and any others who may be occupying or within the Leased Premises, without being deemed in any manner guilty of trespass, eviction, or forcible entry or detainer, without incurring any liability for any damage resulting therefrom, and without relinquishing Landlord's rights to Rent or any other right given to Landlord hereunder or by operation of law. Upon termination of the Lease, Landlord shall be entitled to recover, as damages, all Rent and other sums due and payable by Tenant on the date of termination, plus (1) an amount equal to the value of the Rent and other sums provided herein to be paid by Tenant for the residue of the stated Term, less the fair rental value of the Leased Premises for the residue of the stated Term (taking into account the time and expenses necessary to obtain a replacement tenant or tenants, including expenses hereinafter described relating to recovery of the Leased Premises, preparation for reletting, and for reletting itself), and (2) the cost of performing any other covenants to be performed by Tenant. If Landlord elects to terminate Tenant's right to possession only, without terminating the Lease, the Landlord may, at Landlord's option, enter into the Leased Premises, remove Tenant's signs and other evidences of tenancy, and take and hold possession thereof as hereinabove provided, without such entry and possession terminating the Lease or releasing Tenant, in whole or in part, from Tenant's obligations to pay the Rent hereunder for the full term or from any other of its obligations under this Lease. Landlord may, but shall be under no obligation to, relet all or any part of the Leased Premises for such rent and upon such terms as shall be satisfactory to Landlord (including the right to relet the Leased Premises for a term greater or lesser than that remaining under the Lease, the right to relet the Leased Premises as a part of a larger area, and the right to change the character or use made of the Leased Premises). For the purpose of such reletting, Landlord may decorate or make any repairs, changes, alterations, or additions in or to the Leased Premises that may be necessary or convenient and charge Tenant for such costs. If Landlord does not relet the Leased Premises, Tenant shall pay to Landlord on demand damages equal to the amount of the Rent and other sums provided herein to be paid by Tenant for the remainder of the Term. If the Leased Premises are relet and a sufficient sum shall not be realized from such reletting after paying all of the expenses of such decorations, repairs, changes, alterations, additions, the expenses of such reletting, and the collection of the rent accruing therefrom (including, but not by way of limitation, attorneys' fees and brokers' commissions), to satisfy the Rent and other charges provided to be paid for the remainder of the Term, Tenant shall pay to Landlord on demand any deficiency, and Tenant agrees that Landlord may file suit to recover any sums falling due under the terms of this Section 16.1 from time-to-time. If Tenant shall default under subsection (i) hereof, and if such default cannot with due diligence be cured within a period of five days, and if notice thereof in writing shall have been given to Tenant, and if Tenant promptly commences to eliminate the causes of such default, then Landlord shall not have the right to declare said Term ended by reason of such default or to repossess without terminating the Lease as long as Tenant is proceeding diligently and with reasonable dispatch to take all steps and do all work required to cure such default, and does so cure such default, provided, however, that the curing of any default in such manner shall not be construed to limit or restrict the right of Landlord to declare the said Term ended or to repossess without terminating the Lease, and to enforce all of its rights and remedies hereunder for any other default not so cured.

16.2. *Remedies Cumulative.* No remedy herein or otherwise conferred upon or reserved to Landlord shall be considered to exclude or suspend any other remedy, but the same shall be cumulative and shall be in addition to every other remedy given hereunder, or now or hereafter existing at law or in equity or by statute, and every power and remedy given by this Lease to Landlord may be exercised from time-to-time and so often as occasion may arise or as may be deemed expedient.

16.3. *No Waiver.* No delay or omission of Landlord to exercise any right or power arising from any default shall impair any such right or power or be construed to be a waiver of any such default or any acquiescence therein. No waiver of any breach of any of the covenants of this Lease shall be construed, taken, or held to be a waiver of any other breach, or as a waiver, acquiescence in, or consent to any further or succeeding breach of the same covenant. The acceptance by Landlord of any payment of Rent or other charges hereunder after the termination by Landlord of this Lease or of Tenant's right to possession hereunder shall not, in the absence of agreement in writing to the contrary by Landlord, be deemed to restore this Lease or Tenant's right to possession hereunder, as the case may be, but shall be construed as a payment on account, and not in satisfaction of damages due from Tenant to Landlord.

XVII. Environmental

17.1. *Compliance with Laws.* As a principle element of the consideration for the lease of the Leased Premises to the Tenant by the Landlord, the Tenant acknowledges and agrees that it is familiar and shall comply with all applicable federal, state, and local statutes, laws, rules, regulations, and ordinances (the "Laws") relating to the use, handling, and disposal of hazardous and toxic substances and wastes ("Hazardous Substances"), including all air, water, soil, solid waste, and other environmental requirements, as an operating business on the Leased Premises under this Lease. The Tenant agrees to comply with all of the Laws to obtain all applicable permits, and to file all required notices and reports during the Term and the Tenant's possession of the Leased Premises.

17.2. *Environmental Indemnification.* The Tenant shall indemnify, release, discharge, defend, and hold the Landlord harmless from and against, and shall assume, any and all liability including, without limitation, all liability for reporting, assessment, investigation, removal, and remediation, and all costs and expenses, arising out of, as a result of, or in connection with any failure of the Tenant or its employees, agents, or assigns, to comply with any of the Laws and any and all contamination or the results thereof in the air, soil, and ground water at the Leased Premises and the Real Estate, or at a disposal site to which waste materials generated by the Tenant at the Leased Premises or the Real Estate or elsewhere, were disposed, as well as any and all release of contamination from the Leased Premises or the Real Estate caused by or contributed to by the Tenant during the Term and the Tenant's possession of the Leased Premises. However, Tenant's indemnification and other obligations to Landlord in the immediately preceding sentence due to release of contamination from the Leased Premises contributed by Tenant shall be limited to the proportion that the contamination of the Leased Premises contributed by Tenant bears to the total amount of contamination of the Leased Premises. The Tenant's obligations under this paragraph shall arise on the discovery of any violation of or non-compliance with any Law by the Tenant, or the contamination of the Leased Premises or the Real Estate, whether or not any Federal, state, or local agency has taken or threatened any action. The foregoing indemnification of Landlord by Tenant shall be limited to any liability directly associated with the change of condition of the building, the Leased Premises, or the Real Estate after the Commencement Date.

XVIII. Miscellaneous

18.1. *Estoppel Certificates.* Tenant shall at any time and from time-to-time upon not less than five days prior written request from Landlord execute, acknowledge, and deliver to Landlord, in form reasonably satisfactory to Landlord and/or Landlord's mortgagee, a written statement certifying (if true) that Tenant has accepted the Leased Premises, that this Lease is unmodified and in full force and effect (or if there have been modifications, that the same is in full force and effect as modified and stating the modifications), that the Landlord is not in default hereunder, the date to which the rental and other charges have been paid in advance, if any, and such other accurate certification as may reasonably be required by Landlord or Landlord's mortgagee, and agreeing to give copies to any mortgagee of Landlord of all notices by Tenant to Landlord. It is intended that any such statement delivered pursuant to this subsection may be relied upon by any prospective purchaser or mortgagee of the building or the Leased Premises and their respective successors and assigns. Tenant understands that its failure to meet its obligations under this section will cause financial damages to Landlord and Tenant agrees to indemnify and hold Landlord harmless from such damages.

18.2. *Landlord's Right to Cure.* Landlord may, but shall not be obligated to, cure any default by Tenant (specifically including, but not by way of limitation, Tenant's failure to obtain insurance, make repairs, or satisfy lien claims); and whenever Landlord so elects, all costs and expenses paid by Landlord in curing such default, including, without limitation, reasonable attorneys' fees, shall be due on the next Rent date after such payment, together with interest (except in the case of said attorneys' fees) at a rate equal to eighteen percent per annum, from the date of the advance to the date of repayment by Tenant to Landlord.

18.3. *Amendments Must Be in Writing.* None of the covenants, terms, or conditions of this Lease, to be kept and performed by either party, shall in any manner be altered, waived, modified, changed, or abandoned except by a written instrument, duly signed and delivered by the other party.

18.4. *Notices.* All notices to or demands upon Landlord or Tenant, desired or required to be given under any of the provisions of this Lease, shall be in writing. Any notices or demands from Landlord to Tenant shall be deemed to have been duly and sufficiently given if a copy thereof has been mailed by United States registered or certified mail in an envelope properly stamped and addressed to Tenant as follows: 6789 120th Street, Commerce City, CO 80022, or at such address as Tenant may have furnished by written notice to Landlord, and any notices or demands from Tenant to Landlord shall be deemed to have been duly and sufficiently given if mailed in an envelope properly stamped and addressed to Landlord as follows: 55555 Tower Road, Brighton, CO 80602, or at such other address as Landlord may have furnished by written notice to Tenant, with a copy to any first mortgagee of the Leased Premises, the identity and address of which Tenant shall have received written notice. The effective date of such notice shall be one day after delivery of the same to the United States Postal Service.

18.5. *Short Form Lease.* This Lease shall not be recorded, but the parties agree, at the request of either of them, to execute a Short Form Lease for recording, containing the names of the parties, the legal description, and the Term of the Lease.

18.6. *Time of Essence.* Time is of the essence of this Lease, and all provisions herein relating thereto shall be strictly construed.

18.7. *Relationship of Parties.* Nothing contained herein shall be deemed or construed by the parties to this Lease, nor by any third party, as creating the relationship of principal and agent or of partnership, or of joint venture by the parties hereto, it being understood and agreed that no provision contained in this Lease, nor any acts of the parties, shall be deemed to create any relationship other than the relationship of Landlord and Tenant.

18.8. *Captions.* The captions of this Lease are for convenience only and are not to be construed as part of this Lease and shall not be construed as defining or limiting in any way the scope or intent of the provisions hereof.

18.9. *Severability.* If any term or provision of this Lease shall to any extent be held invalid or unenforceable, the remaining terms and provisions of this Lease shall not be affected thereby, but each term and provision of this Lease shall be valid and be enforced to the fullest extent permitted by law.

18.10. *Law Applicable.* This Lease shall be construed and enforced in accordance with the laws of the State of Delaware.

18.11. *Covenants Binding on Successors.* All of the covenants, agreements, conditions, and undertakings contained in this Lease shall extend and inure to and be binding upon the heirs, executors, administrators, successors, and assigns of the respective parties hereto, the same as if they were in every case specifically named, and wherever in this Lease reference is made to either of the parties hereto, it shall be held to include and apply to, wherever applicable, the heirs, executors, administrators, successors, and assigns of such party. Nothing herein contained shall be construed to grant or confer upon any person or persons, firm, corporation, or governmental authority, other than the parties hereto, their heirs, executors, administrators, successors, and assigns, any right, claim, or privilege by virtue of any covenant, agreement, condition, or understanding in this Lease contained.

18.12. *Landlord Means Owner*. The term *Landlord* as used in this Lease, so far as covenants or obligations on the part of Landlord are concerned, shall be limited to mean and include only the owner or owners at the time in question of the fee of the building and the Leased Premises, and in the event of any transfer or transfers of the title to such fee, Landlord herein named (and in case of any subsequent transfer or conveyances, the then grantor) shall be automatically freed and relieved, from and after the date of such transfer or conveyance, of all liability as respects the performance of any covenants or obligations on the part of Landlord contained in this Lease thereafter to be performed; provided that any funds in the hands of such Landlord or the then grantor at the time of such transfer, in which Tenant has an interest, shall be turned over to the grantee, and any amount then due and payable to Tenant by Landlord or the then grantor under any provisions of this Lease, shall be paid to Tenant.

18.13. *Lender's Requirements*. If any mortgagee or committed financier of Landlord should require, as a condition precedent to the closing of any loan or the disbursal of any money under any loan, that this Lease be amended or supplemented in any manner (other than in the description of the Leased Premises, the Term, the purpose, or the Rent or other charges hereunder) Landlord shall give written notice thereof to Tenant, which notice shall be accompanied by a Lease Supplement Agreement embodying such amendments and supplements. Tenant shall, within five days after the effective date of Landlord's notice, either consent to such amendments and supplements (which consent shall not be unreasonably withheld) and execute the tendered Lease Supplement Agreement, or deliver to Landlord a written statement of its reason or reasons for refusing to so consent and execute. Failure of Tenant to respond within the five-day period shall be a default under this Lease without further notice. If Landlord and Tenant are then unable to agree on a Lease Supplement Agreement satisfactory to each of them and to the lender within five days after delivery of Tenant's written statement, Landlord shall have the right to terminate this Lease immediately after the end of the five days.

18.14. *Signs*. Tenant shall install no exterior sign without Landlord's prior written approval, which shall not be unreasonably withheld. Upon the expiration or termination of this Lease, Tenant shall remove the exterior sign and return the Leased Premises to its original condition.

18.15. *Financial Statements*. From time to time and upon written request, Tenant shall provide Landlord audited financial statements reflecting the Tenant's current financial condition.

18.16. *Arbitration*. Any controversy or claim arising out of or relating to equitable Rent abatement in Section 6.2 shall be settled by arbitration in accordance with the rules of the American Arbitration Association. Rent shall continue to be paid during arbitration in the amount determined by Landlord to be due, but the amount in controversy shall be paid into an escrow to be invested in United States obligations with interest to be paid in the shares ultimately determined to be payable to the parties hereto. The arbitration decision will be final and binding upon the parties.

18.17. *Self-Help*. In the event that Landlord shall default in the performance of any of its obligations under this Lease, and such default continues for more than one hundred eighty days after written notice from Tenant to Landlord, the Tenant shall have the right, after the giving of a second written notice to Landlord, to cause such default to be cured, and Landlord shall reimburse Tenant for the reasonable cost to Tenant in curing such default after Tenant bills Landlord therefor. Tenant's bill shall be accompanied by detailed evidence of such cost to Tenant. If Landlord fails to make such payment within sixty days after receipt of such bill and detailed itemization of cost, Tenant shall have the right to deduct the cost of such cure from Rent thereafter payable under the Lease. Anything herein to the contrary notwithstanding, if Landlord's default cannot with due diligence be cured within a period of one hundred eighty days, and if Landlord promptly commences to eliminate the cause of such default within one hundred eighty days after Tenant's original notice of such default, then Tenant shall not have the right to pursue its remedies under this Section 18.17 as long as Landlord is proceeding diligently and with reasonable dispatch to take all steps and do all the work required to cure such default and does so cure such default.

18.18. *Rules and Regulations.* The Landlord reserves the right to make, amend, or change rules and regulations for the building and the Leased Premises and the Real Estate at any time. The Tenant shall immediately abide by all rules and regulations adopted by the Landlord pertaining to the operation and management of the building, the Leased Premises, and the Real Estate. If any rules or regulations adopted by the Landlord are contrary to the provisions of this Lease, the terms of this Lease shall govern.

XIX.   Option to Extend

19.1.   *Option to Extend.* Provided no default has occurred and is continuing, and provided Tenant (and not a sublessee or assignee) shall then be in occupancy of the Leased Premises, at the expiration of the initial Term, Tenant shall have the option of extending the Term for one additional three year term (the "First Option Term) at a rental rate of $7.45 psf. Tenant may exercise this option by giving Landlord written notice of its intention on or before the date that is one year before the expiration of the then current Term. At the expiration of the First Option Term, provided no default has occurred and is continuing, and provided Tenant (and not a sublessee or assignee) shall then be in occupancy of the Leased Premises, Tenant shall have the option of extending the Term for one additional three year term (the "Second Option Term") at a rental rate of $7.90 psf. Tenant may exercise this option by giving Landlord written notice of its intention on or before the date that is one year before the expiration of the First Option. At the expiration of the Second Option Term, provided no default has occurred and is continuing, and provided Tenant (and not a sublessee or assignee) shall then be in occupancy of the Leased Premises, Tenant shall have the option of extending the Term for one additional three year term (the "Third Option Term") at a rental rate of $8.35 psf. Tenant may exercise this option by giving Landlord written notice of its intention on or before the date that is one year before the expiration of the Second Option Term.

IN WITNESS WHEREOF, Landlord and Tenant have executed this Lease the day and year first above written.

GIANT REAL ESTATE COMPANY

By: /s/Jackson Money   Date: May 10, 2014

     Jackson Money, President

TREE SERVICES, INC.

By: /s/ Melissa Green   Date: April 1, 2014

     Melissa Green, CEO

Exhibit A

Intentionally Omitted

(you can assume there are no issues with his exhibit)

2. Loan Agreement

LOAN AGREEMENT

This Loan Agreement ("Agreement"), made June 15, 2018, between Tree Services, Inc., a corporation organized under the laws of Colorado, having its principal office at 6789 120th Street, Commerce City, CO 80022 ("Borrower") and Big Bank of Colorado, a Bank organized under the laws of the Colorado, having its principal office at 100 19th Street, Denver, CO 80202 ("Bank").

RECITALS

A.   Borrower has requested Bank to lend it $1,500,000 on a term loan basis (the "Loan").

B.   Bank is willing to lend Borrower $1,500,000 on a term loan basis pursuant to the terms and the conditions set forth below.

In consideration of the matters described above, and of the mutual benefits and obligations set forth in this Agreement, the parties agree as follows:

SECTION ONE.
DEFINITIONS

As used in this Agreement, the following terms have the following definitions:

A.   "accounts," "chattel paper," "contracts," "contract rights," "documents," "equipment," "fixtures," "general intangibles," "goods," "instruments," and "inventory" shall have the same respective meaning as are given to those terms in the Uniform Commercial Code as enacted in Colorado.

B.   "Collateral Documents" means all those documents specified in Section Three, subparagraphs A(2) through A(4), of this Agreement.

C.   "Consolidated Cash Flow" means, as to Borrower, the aggregate of (1) net income after taxes; (2) amortization of intangible assets; (3) depreciation and depletion; and (4) deferred taxes and expenses, all as shown by the consolidated income statement of Borrower, calculated in accordance with generally accepted accounting principles.

D.   "Consolidated Current Assets" and "Consolidated Current Liabilities" mean, at any time, all assets or liabilities, respectively, that, in accordance with generally accepted accounting principles consistently applied, should be classified as current assets or current liabilities, respectively, on a consolidated balance sheet of Borrower.

E.   "Consolidated Fixed Assets" means, at any time, all assets (other than Consolidated Current Assets) that, in accordance with generally accepted accounting principles consistently applied, should be classified as fixed assets on a consolidated balance sheet of Borrower.

F.   "Consolidated Liabilities" means all Indebtedness that, in accordance with generally accepted accounting principles consistently applied, should be classified as liabilities on a consolidated balance sheet of Borrower.

G.   "Consolidated Long-Term Liabilities" means Consolidated Liabilities less the portion that constitutes Consolidated Current Liabilities.

H.   "Consolidated Net Working Capital" means, at any time, the amount by which Consolidated Current Assets exceed Consolidated Current Liabilities.

I.   "Consolidated Tangible Net Worth" means, at any time, stockholders' equity, less the sum of:

    1.   any surplus resulting from any write-up of assets subsequent to June 15, 2018;

2.   goodwill, including any amounts, however designated on a consolidated balance sheet of Borrower, representing the excess of the purchase price paid for assets or stock acquired over the value assigned to them on the books of Borrower;

3.   patents, trademarks, trade names, and copyrights;

4.   any amount at which shares of capital stock of Borrower appear as an asset on Borrower's balance sheet;

5.   loans and advances to stockholders, directors, officers, or employees; and

6.   deferred expenses.

J.   "Financial Statements" means the consolidated balance sheets of Borrower as of March 31, 2018, December 31, 2017, September 30, 2017, and June 30, 2017, and consolidated statements of income of Borrower for the years or months ended on those dates.

K.   "Indebtedness" means, as to Borrower or any Subsidiary, all items of indebtedness, obligation, or liability, whether matured or unmatured, liquidated or unliquidated, direct or contingent, joint or several, including, but not limited to:

1.   all indebtedness guaranteed, directly or indirectly, in any manner, or endorsed (other than for collection or deposit in the ordinary course of business) or discounted with recourse;

2.   all indebtedness in effect guaranteed, directly or indirectly, through agreements, contingent or otherwise:

a.   to purchase such indebtedness;

b.   to purchase, sell, or lease (as lessee or lessor) property, products, materials, or supplies, or to purchase or sell services, primarily for the purpose of enabling Borrower to make payment of such indebtedness or to assure the owner of the indebtedness against loss; or

c.   to supply funds to or in any other manner invest in the debtor;

3.   all indebtedness secured by (or for which the holder of the indebtedness has a right, contingent or otherwise, to be secured by) any mortgage, deed of trust, pledge, lien, security interest, or other charge or encumbrance on property owned or acquired subject to the same, whether or not the liabilities secured by the same have been assumed; and

4.   all indebtedness incurred as the lessee of goods or services under leases that, in accordance with generally accepted accounting principles, should not be reflected on the lessee's balance sheet.

L.   "Laws" means all ordinances, statutes, rules, regulations, orders, injunctions, writs, or decrees of any government or political subdivision or agency, or any court or similar entity.

M.   "Obligations" means the obligation of Borrower:

1.   to pay the principal of any interest on the Note in accordance with its terms and to satisfy all of its other liabilities to Bank, whether under this Agreement or otherwise, whether now existing or later incurred, matured or unmatured, direct or contingent, joint or several, including any extensions, modifications, renewals, and substitutions;

2.   to repay to Bank all amounts advanced by Bank under this Agreement or otherwise on behalf of Borrower, including, but not limited to, advances for principal or interest payments to prior secured parties, mortgagees, or lienors, or for taxes, levies, insurance, rent, repairs to or maintenance or storage of any of the Collateral (as defined in Section Four); and

3.   to reimburse Bank, on demand, for all of Bank's expenses and costs, including all fees and expenses of its counsel, in connection with the preparation, administration, amendment, modification, or enforcement of this Agreement and the documents required under this Agreement,

including, but not limited to, any proceeding brought or threatened to enforce payment of any of the obligations referred to in subparagraphs 1 and 2 of this paragraph M.

N.   "Permitted Liens" means:

1.   liens for taxes, assessments, or similar charges, incurred in the ordinary course of business, that are not yet due and payable;

2.   pledges or deposits made in the ordinary course of business to secure payment of workers' compensation, or to participate in any fund in connection with workers' compensation, unemployment insurance, old-age pensions, or other social security programs;

3.   liens of mechanics, materialmen, warehousemen, carriers, or other like liens, securing Obligations incurred in the ordinary course of business, that are not yet due and payable;

4.   good faith pledges or deposits made in the ordinary course of business to secure performance of bids, tenders, contracts (other than for the repayment of borrowed money), or leases, not in excess of 5% of the aggregate amount due under the same, or to secure statutory Obligations, or surety, appeal, indemnity, performance, or other similar bonds required in the ordinary course of business;

5.   encumbrances consisting of zoning restrictions, easements, or other restrictions on the use of real property, none of which materially impairs the use of such property by Borrower or any Subsidiary in the operation of its business, and none of which is violated in any material respect by existing or proposed structures or land use;

6.   liens in favor of Bank;

7.   existing liens set forth or described on Exhibit B, attached to and by this reference made a part of this Agreement;

8.   purchase money security interests granted to secure not more than 5% of the purchase price of assets, the purchase of which is permitted by SECTION SIX, subparagraph B(9);

9.   the following, if the validity or amount is being contested in good faith by appropriate and lawful proceedings, so long as levy and execution on them have been stayed and continue to be stayed and they do not, in the aggregate, materially detract from the value of the property of Borrower or in any Subsidiary, or materially impair its use in the operation of the business:

a.   claims or liens for taxes, assessments, or charges due and payable and subject to interest or penalty;

b.   claims, liens, and encumbrances on, and defects of title to, real or personal property, including any attachment of personal or real property or other legal process prior to adjudication of a dispute on the merits;

c.   claims or liens of mechanics, materialmen, warehousemen, carriers, or other like liens; and

d.   adverse judgments on appeal.

O.   "Person" means any individual, corporation, limited liability company, partnership, association, joint-stock company, trust, unincorporated organization, joint venture, court, or government or political subdivision or agency.

P.   "Records" means correspondence, memoranda, tapes, disks, papers, books, and other documents, or transcribed information of any type, whether expressed in ordinary or machine-readable language.

Q. "Shareholders' Equity" means, at any time, the aggregate of Shareholders' Equity plus the sum of the following accounts set forth in a consolidated balance sheet of the Borrower, prepared in accordance with generally accepted accounting principles consistently applied:

1. the par or stated value of all outstanding capital stock;

2. capital surplus (or additional paid-in-capital); and

3. retained earnings.

R. "Subordinated Indebtedness" means all Indebtedness incurred at any time by Borrower or any Subsidiary, repayment of which is subordinated to the Obligations in form and manner satisfactory to Bank. All existing Subordinated Indebtedness is so specified in Exhibit C.

S. "Subsidiary" means any corporation of which more than 20% of the outstanding voting securities, at the time of determination, shall be owned directly or indirectly through one or more intermediaries by Borrower.

SECTION TWO.
THE LOAN

A. <u>Disbursement of the Loan</u>. The Bank will credit the proceeds of the Loan to Borrower's deposit account with Bank.

B. <u>General Terms</u>. Subject to the terms of this Agreement, Bank will lend Borrower the principal sum of $1,500,000 on a term basis.

C. <u>The Note</u>. At the time of the making of the Loan, Borrower will execute and deliver a note to Bank, in the form of Exhibit A (the "Note").

D. <u>Payments of Principal</u>. The principal of the Loan will be repaid in whole in the form of one lump sum payment on June 14, 2025 or the next business day.

E. <u>Prepayment</u>. Borrower may prepay the principal of the Loan in whole or, from time to time, in part, any partial payment to be made in the sum of $10,000 or an integral multiple of such sum. All such partial prepayments shall be applied against the installments of principal required by paragraph D of this Section in the inverse order of maturity. Each such partial payment shall be charged an early payment penalty fee of the lesser of (i) 10% of the amount of the pre-payment, or (ii) $1,500. A prepayment of the whole shall be charged an early prepayment penalty fee of the lesser of (i) 5% of the prepayment amount, or (ii) $37,500.

F. <u>Interest Rate and Payments of Interest</u>.

1. Interest shall be paid as follows:

a. Subject to the provisions of subparagraph 3 of this paragraph F, interest on the principal balance of the Loan, from time to time outstanding, will be payable at the rate of three percent above the prime rate in effect from time to time prior to maturity or six percent above the prime rate in effect from time to time after maturity (the "Rate"), whether maturity is brought about by acceleration in the event of default or otherwise. For these purposes, "prime rate" shall mean the prime commercial rate announced by the Bank from time to time as its prime rate.

b. Each time the prime rate shall change, the Rate shall change contemporaneously with such change. Interest shall be calculated on the basis of a 360-day year, counting the actual number of days elapsed, and shall be payable on the last day of each month, commencing on June 30, 2018. After maturity, whether by acceleration or otherwise, accrued interest shall be payable on demand.

2.   The Rate is predicated on the condition that Borrower will maintain aggregate demand deposit balances with Bank in which (1) the average free balances will equal fifty percent of the unpaid principal amount of the term Loan; and (2) in addition, in which the average free balances will equal twenty-five percent of the undisbursed portion of any revolving Loan commitment, if one exits now or in the future. If, during any quarterly period, Borrower shall fail to maintain the aggregate demand deposit balances required, Borrower shall pay Bank a deficient balances fee calculated by multiplying the dollar amount of the deficiency in demand deposit balances by Bank's average per annum interest rate charged on domestic commercial loans during the quarterly period plus 2%. For these purposes, "free balances" shall mean gross balances minus the aggregate amount of deposits required to cover activity in the Borrower's deposit accounts, based on Bank's standard analysis.

3.   It is the intention of the parties to conform strictly to applicable usury Laws in effect from time to time during the term of the Loan. Accordingly, if any transaction or transactions contemplated would be usurious under applicable Law—including the Laws of the United States of America or of any other jurisdiction whose Law may be applicable—then, in that event, notwithstanding anything to the contrary in this Agreement, or any other agreement entered into in connection with this Agreement, it is agreed as follows:

    a.   the provisions of this subparagraph 3 shall govern and control;

    b.   the aggregate of all interest under applicable Law that is contracted for, charged, or received under this Agreement, or under any of the other above-mentioned agreements or otherwise in connection with this Agreement, shall under no circumstances exceed the maximum amount of interest allowed by applicable Law, and any excess shall be promptly credited to Borrower by Bank (or, if the consideration shall have been paid in full, the excess shall be promptly refunded to Borrower by Bank);

    c.   neither the Borrower nor any Person or entity now or later liable in connection with this Agreement shall be obligated to pay the amount of such interest to the extent that it is in excess of the maximum interest permitted by the applicable usury Laws; and

    d.   the effective rate of interest shall be ipso facto reduced to the highest lawful rate defined below.

4.   All sums paid, or agreed to be paid, to Bank for the use, forbearance, and detention of the Indebtedness of Borrower to Bank, to the extent permitted by applicable Law, shall be amortized, prorated, allocated, and spread throughout the full term of the Note until payment is made in full so that the actual rate of interest does not exceed the highest lawful rate in effect in any particular time during the full term. The maximum lawful interest rate, if any, referred to in subparagraph 3 of this paragraph F, that may accrue pursuant to this Agreement is referred to as the "highest lawful rate." If at any time the Rate exceeds the highest lawful rate, the rate of interest to accrue pursuant to this Agreement shall be limited, notwithstanding anything to the contrary in this Agreement, to the highest lawful rate, but any subsequent reductions in the prime rate shall not reduce the interest to accrue pursuant to this Agreement below the highest lawful rate until the total amount of interest accrued pursuant to this Agreement equals the amount of interest that would have accrued if a varying rate per annum equal to the Rate had at all times been in effect. If the total amount of interest paid or accrued pursuant to this Agreement under the preceding provisions is less than the total amount of interest that would have accrued if a varying rate per annum equal to the Rate had at all times been in effect, then Borrower agrees to pay to Bank an amount equal to the difference between (a) the lesser of (i) the amount of interest that would have accrued if the highest lawful rate had at all times been in effect; or (ii) the amount of interest that would have accrued if a varying rate per annum equal to the Rate had at all times been in effect; and (b) the amount of interest accrued in accordance with the other provisions of this Agreement.

G. <u>Payment to Bank</u>. All sums payable to Bank shall be paid directly to Bank in immediately available funds. Bank shall send Borrower statements of all amounts due, which statements shall be considered correct and conclusively binding on Borrower unless Borrower notifies Bank to the contrary within one day of its receipt of any statement that it deems to be incorrect. Alternatively, at its sole discretion, Bank may charge against any deposit account of Borrower all or any part of any amount due.

SECTION THREE.
CONDITIONS PRECEDENT

The obligation of Bank to make the Loan is subject to the following conditions precedent:

A. <u>Documents Required for Closing</u>. Borrower shall have delivered to Bank, prior to the disbursement of the Loan (the "Closing"), the following:

> 1. the Note;

> 2. a pledge agreement in the form attached as Exhibit D, including Schedules D1, D2, and D3, executed by Melissa Green, Thomas Shrub, and Susan Brown, respectively, together with certificates representing the shares of common stock of Borrower pledged, endorsed in blank;

> 3. a duly executed guaranty agreement dated June 15, 2018, in the form attached as Exhibit E;

> 4. the financing statements and lessors' and mortgagees' waivers required by SECTION FOUR;

> 5. a certified (as of the date of the Closing) copy of resolutions of Borrower's board of directors authorizing the execution, delivery, and performance of this Agreement, the Note, the Collateral Documents, and each other document to be delivered pursuant to this Agreement;

> 6. a certified (as of the date of the Closing) copy of Borrower's bylaws;

> 7. a certificate (as of the date of the Closing) of Borrower's corporate secretary as to the incumbency and signatures of the officers of Borrower signing this Agreement, the Note, the Collateral Documents, and each other document to be delivered pursuant to this Agreement;

> 8. a copy, certified as of the most recent date practicable, by the Secretary of State of Colorado, of Borrower's articles of incorporation, together with a certificate (as of the date of the Closing) of Borrower's corporate secretary to the effect that the articles of incorporation have not been amended since the date of the certification;

> 9. certificates, as of the most recent dates practicable, of the Secretary of State of Colorado, from each state in which the Borrower is qualified as a foreign corporation, and the department of revenue or taxation of each such state, as to the good standing of Borrower;

> 10. a written opinion of Williams & Rader, LLC, the Borrower's counsel, as of the date of the Closing and addressed to the Bank, in form satisfactory to the Bank in its sole and absolute discretion, to the effect that:

> > a. Borrower is a corporation organized, existing, and in good standing under the Laws of its respective state of incorporation (naming such state) and is qualified to transact business and is in good standing in those states where the nature of business or property owned by it requires qualification, as set forth in Exhibit F, attached to and by this reference made a part of this Agreement, and, to the knowledge of such counsel, is not required to be qualified as a foreign corporation in any other jurisdiction;

b.   Borrower has the power to execute and deliver this Agreement, to borrow money under this Agreement, to grant the Collateral required under it, to execute and deliver the Note and the Collateral Documents, and to perform such obligations;

c.   all corporate action by Borrower and all consents and approvals of any Persons necessary to the validity of this Agreement, the Note, the Collateral Documents, and each other document to be delivered, has been obtained, and this Agreement, the Note, the Collateral Documents, and such other documents do not conflict with any provision of the charter or bylaws of Borrower, or of any applicable Laws, or any other agreement binding Borrower or its property of which such counsel has knowledge;

d.   this Agreement, the Note, the Collateral Documents, and all other agreements and documents to be delivered have been executed by, and each is a valid and binding obligation of, Borrower, enforceable in accordance with its terms;

e.   the pledged stock constitutes 98.05% all of the issued and outstanding capital stock of the Borrower, and all pledged stock is fully paid and nonassessable; and

f.   such counsel is without any knowledge of any matters contrary to the representations and warranties contained in SECTION FIVE, paragraph A;

11.   A certificate, as of the date of the Closing, signed by the president or a vice president of Borrower, to the effect that:

a.   the representations and warranties set forth within SECTION FIVE, paragraph A, are true as of the date of the Closing; and

b.   no event of default, and no event that with the giving of notice or passage of time, or both, would become such an event of default, has occurred as of such date;

12.   Copies of all documents evidencing the terms and conditions of any debt specified as "Subordinated Indebtedness" on Exhibit C; and

13.   A Federal Reserve Form U-1, completed and executed by Borrower.

B.   Certain Events. At the time of the Closing:

1.   No event of default shall have occurred and be continuing, and no event shall have occurred and be continuing that, with the giving of notice or passage of time, or both, would be an event of default;

2.   No material adverse change shall have occurred in the financial condition of Borrower or any Subsidiary since the date of this Agreement or the Closing, as applicable; and

3.   All of the Collateral Documents shall have remained in full force and effect.

C.   Legal Matters. At the time of the Closing, all incidental legal matters shall be satisfactory to Chang, Connolly & Weil, LLC, counsel to Bank.

SECTION FOUR.
COLLATERAL SECURITY

A.   Composition of the Collateral. The property in which a security interest is granted pursuant to the provisions of paragraphs B and C of this SECTION FOUR is collectively called the "Collateral."

The Collateral, together with all of Borrower's other property of any kind held by Bank, shall stand as one general, continuing, collateral security for all Obligations and may be retained by Bank until all Obligations have been satisfied in full.

B.   Rights in Property Held by Bank. As security for the prompt satisfaction of all Obligations, Borrower assigns, transfers, and sets over to Bank all of its right, title, and interest in and to, and grants Bank a lien on and a security interest in, all amounts that may be owing from time to time by Bank to Borrower in any capacity, including, but not limited to, any balance or share belonging to Borrower, or any deposit or other account with Bank, which lien and security interest shall be independent of any right of setoff that Bank may have.

C.   <u>Rights in Property Held by Borrower</u>. As further security for the prompt satisfaction of all Obligations arising under this Agreement, Borrower assigns to Bank all of its right, title, and interest in and to, and grants Bank the lien on and a security interest in, all of the following, wherever located, whether now owned or later acquired, together with all replacements and proceeds (including, but not limited to, insurance proceeds):

1.   accounts;

2.   chattel paper;

3.   contracts;

4.   contract rights;

5.   documents;

6.   equipment;

7.   fixtures;

8.   general intangibles;

9.   instruments;

10. inventory;

11. the pledged stock;

12. rights as seller of goods and rights to return or repossessed goods; and

13. all records pertaining to any other collateral.

D.   <u>Priority of Liens</u>. The above-stated liens shall be first and prior liens except for Permitted Liens.

E.   <u>Financing Statements</u>.

1.   Borrower will:

     a.   join with the Bank in executing such financing statements (including amendments and continuation statements) in form satisfactory to Bank, as Bank may from time to time specify;

     b.   pay to or reimburse Bank for all costs and taxes of filing or recording the statements in such public offices as Bank may designate; and

     c.   take such other steps as Bank may direct, including the noting of Bank's lien on the Collateral and on any certificates of title, to perfect Bank's interest in the Collateral.

2.   In addition to the foregoing, and not in limitation:

     a.   a carbon, photographic, or other reproduction of this Agreement shall be sufficient as a financing statement and may be filed in any appropriate office in lieu of a financing statement; and

     b.   to the extent lawful, Borrower appoints Bank as its attorney-in-fact (without requiring Bank to act as such) to execute any financing statement in the name of Borrower, and to perform all other acts that Bank deems appropriate to preserve and continue its security interest in, and to protect and preserve, the Collateral.

F. <u>Mortgagees' and Lessors' Waivers</u>. Borrower will cause each mortgagee of all real estate owned by Borrower and each lessor of premises leased by Borrower to execute and deliver to Bank instruments, in form and substance satisfactory to Bank, by which such mortgagee or lessor waives its rights, if any, to all goods composing a part of the Collateral.

SECTION FIVE.
REPRESENTATIONS AND WARRANTIES

A. <u>Borrower Representations and Warranties</u>. To induce Bank to enter into this Agreement, Borrower represents and warrants to Bank as follows:

1.   Borrower is a corporation organized, validly existing, and in good standing under the Laws of Colorado; Borrower has the lawful power to own its properties and to engage in the business it conducts, and is qualified and in good standing as a foreign corporation in the jurisdictions in which the nature of the business transacted by it or property owned by it makes such qualification necessary; the states in which Borrower is qualified to do business are set forth in Exhibit F; the addresses of all places of business of Borrower are as set forth in Exhibit F; and Borrower has not changed its name, been the surviving corporation in a merger, acquired any business, or changed its principal executive office within five years prior to the effective date of this Agreement, except as set forth in Exhibit G;

2.   Borrower is not in default with respect to any of its existing Indebtedness, and the making and performance of this Agreement, the Note, and the Collateral Documents will not immediately or with the passage of time, or the giving of notice, or both:

   a.   violate the charter or bylaw provisions of Borrower, or violate any Laws or result in a default under any contract, agreement, or agreement to which Borrower or any Subsidiary is a party or by which Borrower or any Subsidiary or its property is bound; or

   b.   result in the creation or imposition of any security interest in, or lien or encumbrance on, any of the assets of Borrower or any Subsidiary, except in favor of Bank;

3.   Borrower has the power and authority to enter into and perform this Agreement, the Note, and the Collateral Documents, and to incur such Obligations, and has taken all corporate action necessary to authorize the execution, delivery, and performance of this Agreement, the Note, and the Collateral Documents;

4.   This Agreement and the Collateral Documents are, and the Note when delivered will be, valid, binding, and enforceable in accordance with their respective terms;

5.   Except as disclosed in Exhibit H, there is no pending order, notice, claim, litigation, proceeding, or investigation against or affecting Borrower or any Subsidiary, whether or not covered by insurance, that would involve the payment of $1,500 or more or materially and adversely affect the business or prospects of Borrower or any Subsidiary if adversely determined;

6.   Borrower has good and marketable title to all of its assets, which are not subject to any security interest, encumbrance, lien, or claim of any third Person, except for Permitted Liens;

7.   The Financial Statements, including any schedules and notes pertaining to the statements, have been prepared in accordance with generally accepted accounting principles consistently applied, and fully and fairly present the financial condition of Borrower at the dates of the Financial Statements and the results of operations for the periods covered by the same, and there has been no material adverse changes in the consolidated financial condition or business of Borrower from June 16, 2017 to the date of this Agreement;

8.   As of January 1, 2018 Borrower had no material Indebtedness of any nature, including, but not limited to, liabilities for taxes and any interest or penalties relating to the same, except to

the extent reflected (in a footnote or otherwise) and reserved against in the March 31, 2018 Financial Statements, or any material Indebtedness of any nature not fully reflected and reserved against in the March 31, 2018 Financial Statements;

9.　Except as otherwise permitted in this Agreement, Borrower has filed all federal, state, and local tax returns and other reports required by Law to be filed prior to the effective date of this Agreement and that are material to the conduct of its business; has paid or caused to be paid all taxes, assessments, and other governmental charges that are due and payable prior to the effective date of the same; and has made adequate provision for the payment of such taxes, assessments, or other charges accruing but not yet payable; and Borrower has no knowledge of any deficiency or additional assessment in a materially important amount in connection with any taxes, assessments, or charges, not provided for on its books;

10.　Except as otherwise disclosed in Exhibit I, or except to the extent that the failure to comply would not materially interfere with the conduct of the business of Borrower or any Subsidiary, Borrower has complied with all applicable Laws with respect to:

　　a.　any restrictions, specifications, or other requirements pertaining to products that Borrower or any Subsidiary manufactures or sells or to the services each performs;

　　b.　the conduct of their respective businesses; and

　　c.　the use, maintenance, and operation of the real and personal properties owned or leased by them in the conduct of their respective businesses.

11.　No representation or warranty by Borrower contained in this Agreement or in any certificate or other document furnished by Borrower pursuant to this Agreement contains any untrue statement of material fact or omits to state a material fact necessary to make such representation or warranty not misleading in light of the circumstances under which it was made;

12.　Each consent, approval, or authorization of, or filing, registration, or qualification with, any Person required to be obtained or effected by Borrower in connection with the execution and delivery of this Agreement, the Note, and the Collateral Documents, or the undertaking or performance of such Obligations, has been obtained or effected;

13.　all existing Indebtedness of Borrower:

　　a.　for money borrowed; or

　　b.　under any security agreement, mortgage, or agreement covering the lease by Borrower as lessee or real or personal property, is described in Exhibit J;

14.　Except as described in Exhibit K, Borrower has no material lease, contract, or commitment of any kind (such as employment agreements; collective bargaining agreements; powers of attorney; distribution arrangements; patent license agreements; contracts for future purchase or delivery of goods or rendering of services; bonus, pension, and retirement plans; or accrued vacation pay, insurance, and welfare agreements); all parties to all such material leases, contracts, and other commitments to which Borrower is a party have complied with provisions of such leases, contracts, and other commitments; no party is in default under any such leases, contracts, and other commitments, and no event has occurred that, but for the giving of notice or the passage of time, or both, would constitute a default;

15.　Borrower has not made any agreement or taken any action that may cause anyone to become entitled to a commission or finder's fee as a result of the making of the Loan;

16.　Borrower's consolidated federal tax return for the year ended 2017 has been audited and accepted as filed by the United States Internal Revenue Service; and

17. All defined benefit pension plans, as defined in the Employee Retirement Income Security Act of 1974 ("ERISA"), as amended, of Borrower meet, as of this date, the minimum funding standards of Section 302 of ERISA, and, with respect to all employee benefit plans, as defined in ERISA, of Borrower and each Subsidiary, no reportable event or prohibited transaction, as defined in ERISA, has occurred.

B. Survival. All of the representations and warranties set forth in paragraph A of this SECTION FIVE shall survive until all Obligations are satisfied in full.

SECTION SIX.
BORROWER'S COVENANTS

Borrower agrees with Bank that, so long as any of its Obligations arising under this Agreement remain unsatisfied, Borrower will comply with the following covenants:

A. Affirmative Covenants.

1. Borrower will use the proceeds of the Loan only for the purposes set forth in Exhibit L, and will furnish Bank such evidence as it may reasonably require with respect to such use.

2. Borrower will furnish Bank:

a. within thirty days after the close of each quarterly accounting period in each fiscal year (i) a consolidated statement of shareholders' equity and a consolidated statement of changes in financial position of Borrower for the quarterly period; (ii) consolidated income statements of Borrower for the quarterly period; and (iii) consolidated balance sheets of Borrower as of the end of the quarterly period—all in reasonable detail, subject to year-end audit adjustments, and certified by Borrower's president or principal financial officer to have been prepared in accordance with generally accepted accounting principles consistently applied;

b. within forty-five days after the close of each fiscal year (i) a consolidated statement of shareholders' equity and a consolidated statement of changes in financial position of Borrower for the fiscal year; (ii) consolidated income statements of Borrower for the fiscal year; and (iii) consolidated balance sheets of Borrower as of the end of the fiscal year—all in reasonable detail, including all supporting schedules and comments—the consolidated statement and balance sheet to be audited by Grant Thornton LLP or another independent certified public accountant selected by Borrower and acceptable to Bank in its sole discretion, and certified by the accountants to have been prepared in accordance with generally accepted accounting principles consistently applied by Borrower, except for any inconsistencies explained in the certification. In addition, Borrower will obtain from the independent certified public accountants and deliver to Bank, within forty-five days after the close of each fiscal year, the accountants' written statement that, in making the examination necessary to their certification, they have obtained no knowledge of any event of default by Borrower, or disclosing all events of default of which they have obtained knowledge; provided, however, that in making their examination the accountants shall not be required to go beyond the bounds of generally accepted auditing procedures for the purpose of certifying Financial Statements; Bank shall have the right, from time to time, to discuss Borrower's affairs directly with Borrower's independent certified public accountants after written notice to Borrower and opportunity of Borrower to be present at any such discussion;

c. contemporaneously with each quarterly and year-end financial report required by subparagraphs A(2)(a) and A(2)(b) above, a certificate of the president or principal financial officer of Borrower stating that he or she has individually reviewed the provisions of this Agreement and that a review of the activities of Borrower during such year or quarterly period, as the case may be, has been made by or under the supervision of the signer of the certificate with a view to determine whether Borrower has kept, observed, performed, and fulfilled all its Obligations under this Agreement, and that, to the best of his or her knowledge, Borrower has observed and performed every undertaking contained in this Agreement and is not at the time in default in the observance or performance of any of its terms and conditions or, if Borrower shall be so in default, specifying all such defaults and events of which he or she may have knowledge; and

d.   promptly after the sending or making available or filing of the same, copies of all reports, proxy statements, and Financial Statements that Borrower sends or makes available to its shareholders and all registration statements and reports that Borrower files with the Securities and Exchange Commission or any successor (if any).

3.   Borrower will maintain its inventory, equipment, real estate, and other properties in good condition and repair (normal wear and tear excepted); will pay and discharge or will cause to be paid and discharged when due the cost of repairs to or maintenance of the same; and will pay or cause to be paid all rental or mortgage payments due on the real estate. Borrower agrees that if it fails to pay or cause to be paid any such payment, Bank may do so and on demand be reimbursed by Borrower.

4.   Borrower will maintain, or cause to be maintained, public liability insurance and fire and extended coverage insurance on all assets owned by it, all in such form and amounts as are consistent with industry practices and with such insurers as may be satisfactory to Bank. The policies shall contain a provision by which they cannot be canceled except after one hundred twenty days' written notice to the Bank. Borrower will furnish to Bank such evidence of insurance as Bank may require. Borrower agrees that if it fails to pay or cause to be paid the premium on any such insurance, Bank may do so and on demand be reimbursed by Borrower. Borrower assigns to Bank any returned or unearned premiums that may be due Borrower on cancellation of any such policies for any reason whatsoever and directs the insurers to pay Bank any amounts so due. Bank is appointed Borrower's attorney-in-fact (without requiring Bank to act as such) to endorse any check that may be payable to Borrower to collect such returned or unearned premiums or the proceeds of the insurance, and any amount so collected may be applied by Bank toward the satisfaction of any of the Obligations.

5.   Borrower will pay or cause to be paid when due all taxes, assessments, and charges or levies imposed on it or on any of its property or that it is required to withhold and pay over, except when contested in good faith by appropriate proceedings, with adequate reserves for the same having been set aside on their books. But Borrower shall pay or cause to be paid all such taxes, assessments, charges, or levies promptly when foreclosure on any lien that has attached (or security for the same) appears imminent.

6.   Borrower will maintain:

a.   Consolidated Net Working Capital in the following minimum amounts:

i.   Months 1–12: $3,800,000

Months 12–24: $4,050,000

Months 25–36: $4,450,000

Months 37–48: $5,100,000

Months 49–60: $5,450,000

b.   Consolidated Tangible Net Worth in the following minimum amounts:

i.   Months 1–12: $4,500,000

Months 12–24:	$4,750,000
Months 25–36:	$5,000,000
Months 37–48:	$5,250,000
Months 49–60:	$5,500,000

    c.   a ratio of Consolidated Liabilities to Consolidated Tangible Net Worth of not more than:

i.	Months 1–12:	2.7 to 1.0
	Months 12–24:	2.6 to 1.0
	Months 25–36:	2.4 to 1.0
	Months 37–48:	2.3 to 1.0
	Months 49–60:	2.1 to 1.0; and

    d.   a ratio of Consolidated Current Assets to Consolidated Current Liabilities of not less than:

i.	Months 1–12:	1.50 to 1.0
	Months 12–24:	1.55 to 1.0
	Months 25–36:	1.65 to 1.0
	Months 37–48:	1.75 to 1.0
	Months 49–60:	1.80 to 1.0.

7.   Borrower, within a reasonable time after written request, will make available for inspection by authorized representatives of Bank any of its books and Records, and will furnish Bank any information regarding its business affairs and financial condition.

8.   Borrower will take all necessary steps to preserve its corporate existence and franchises and comply with all present and future Laws applicable to it in the operation of its business and all material agreements to which it is subject.

9.   Borrower will collect its accounts and sell its inventory, if any, only in the ordinary course of business.

10. Borrower will keep accurate and complete Records of its accounts, inventory, and equipment, consistent with sound business practices.

11. Borrower will give immediate notice to the Bank of:

    a.   any litigation or proceeding in which it is a party, if an adverse decision in the litigation or proceeding would require it to pay over more than $2,500 or deliver assets, the value of which exceeds such sum (whether or not the claim is considered to be covered by insurance); and

    b.   the institution of any other suit or proceeding involving it that might materially and adversely affect its operations, financial condition, property, or business.

12. Within five days after Bank's request, Borrower will furnish Bank with copies of federal income tax returns filed by Borrower.

13. Borrower will pay when due (or within applicable grace periods) all Indebtedness due third Persons, except when the amount is being contested in good faith by appropriate proceedings and with adequate reserves for the same being set aside on the books of Borrower. If Borrower defaults

in the payment of any principal (or installment of the same) of, or interest on, any such Indebtedness, Bank shall have the right, in its sole discretion, to pay the interest or principal for the account of Borrower or such Subsidiary and be reimbursed by Borrower on demand plus a 10% penalty payment fee.

14. Borrower will notify Bank immediately if it becomes aware of the occurrence of any event of default or of any fact, condition, or event that, with the giving of notice or passage of time, or both, could become an event of default, or of the failure of Borrower to observe any of its respective undertakings under this Agreement.

15. Borrower will notify Bank thirty days in advance of any change in the location of any of its places of business or of the establishment of any new, or the discontinuance of any existing, place of business.

16. Borrower will:

    a.   fund all its defined benefit pension plans in accordance with no less than the minimum funding standards required under ERISA;

    b.   furnish Bank, promptly after the filing of the same, with copies of all reports or other statements filed with the United States Department of Labor or the Internal Revenue Service with respect to all employee benefit plans; and

    c.   promptly advise Bank of any reportable event or prohibited transaction, as defined in ERISA, with respect to any employee benefit plan.

B.   <u>Negative Covenants</u>.

1.   Borrower will not change its name, enter into any merger, consolidation, reorganization or recapitalization, or reclassify its capital stock.

2.   Borrower will not sell, transfer, lease, or otherwise dispose of all, or (except in the ordinary course of business) any material part of, its assets.

3.   Borrower will not mortgage, pledge, grant, or promote to exist a security interest in or lien on any of its assets of any kind, now owned or later acquired, except for Permitted Liens.

4.   Borrower will not become liable, directly or indirectly, as guarantor or otherwise, for any obligation of any other Person, except for the endorsement of commercial paper for deposit or collection in the ordinary course of business.

5.   Borrower will not incur, create, assume, or permit to exist any Indebtedness except:

    a.   the Loan;

    b.   existing Indebtedness as set forth in Exhibit J;

    c.   trade Indebtedness incurred in the ordinary course of business;

    d.   contingent Indebtedness permitted by subparagraph 4 of this paragraph B;

    e.   Indebtedness secured by Permitted Liens; and

    f.   lease obligations permitted by subparagraph 10 of this paragraph B.

6.   Borrower will not declare or pay any dividends, or make any other payment or distribution on account of its capital stock without Bank's prior written consent.

7.   Borrower will not form any Subsidiary or make any investment in, or make any Loan in the nature of an investment to, a Person.

8.   Borrower will not make any Loan or advance to any officer, shareholder, director, or employee of Borrower or a Subsidiary, except temporary advances in the ordinary course of business, nor pay salary to executive and management personnel aggregating more than $500,000 per year.

9.   Borrower will not make payments on account of the purchase or lease of Consolidated Fixed Assets that, in the aggregate, in any fiscal year, commencing with the current fiscal year, will exceed the depreciation taken or to be taken with respect to Consolidated Fixed Assets during that year. As used in this paragraph, the term "lease" means a lease reflected on a consolidated balance sheet of Borrower or a lease that should be so reflected under generally accepted accounting principles.

10.   Borrower will not pay, in an aggregate amount in any fiscal year, commencing with the current fiscal year, lease obligations in excess of $15,000. As used in this subparagraph 10, the term "lease" means a lease that is not reflected on a consolidated balance sheet of Borrower and should not be so reflected under generally accepted accounting principles.

11.   Borrower will not purchase, or otherwise invest in or hold, securities, nonoperating real estate, or other nonoperating assets, except:

    a.   direct obligations of the United States of America;

    b.   the present investment in any such asset; and

    c.   operating assets that subsequently become nonoperating assets.

12.   Borrower will not issue, redeem, purchase, or retire any of its capital stock or grant or issue any warrant, right, or option pertaining to its capital stock, or other security convertible into any of the foregoing.

13.   Borrower will not prepay any Subordinated Indebtedness, Indebtedness for borrowed money, or Indebtedness secured by any of its assets (except the Obligations) or enter into or modify any agreement as a result of which the terms of payment of any of the foregoing Indebtedness are waived or modified.

14.   Borrower will not enter into any sale-leaseback transaction.

15.   Borrower will not acquire any stock in, or all or substantially all of the assets of, any Person.

16.   Borrower will not furnish Bank with any certificate or other document that will contain any untrue statement of material fact or that will omit to state a material fact necessary to make it not misleading in light of the circumstances under which it was furnished.

17.   Borrower will not directly or indirectly apply any part of the proceeds of the Loan to the purchasing or carrying of any "margin stock" within the meaning of Regulation U of the Board of Governors of the Federal Reserve System, or any regulations, interpretations, or rulings under the same.

SECTION SEVEN.
DEFAULT

A.   <u>Events of Default</u>. The occurrence of any one or more of the following events shall constitute an event of default under this Agreement:

1.   Borrower shall fail to pay when due any installment of principal or interest, or any fee or charge payable under this Agreement, and such failure shall continue for a period of two days.

2.   Borrower shall fail to observe or perform any other obligation to be observed or performed by it under this Agreement or under any of the Collateral Documents, and this failure shall continue for seven days after (a) notice of the failure from the Bank; or (b) the Borrower is notified of the

failure or should have been so notified pursuant to the provisions of subparagraph 14 of this paragraph A, whichever is earlier.

3. Borrower shall fail to pay any Indebtedness due to any third Persons, and this failure shall continue beyond any applicable grace period, or Borrower shall suffer to exist any other event of default under any agreement binding Borrower.

4. Any Financial Statement, representation, warranty, or certificate made or furnished by Borrower to Bank in connection with this Agreement, or as inducement to Bank to enter into this Agreement, or in any separate statement or document to be delivered under this Agreement to Bank, shall be false, incorrect, or incomplete when made.

5. Borrower shall admit its inability to pay its debts as they mature, or shall make an assignment for the benefit of its or any of its creditors.

6. Proceedings in bankruptcy, or for reorganization of Borrower, or for the readjustment of its respective debts, under the Bankruptcy Code, as amended, or any part of the same, or under any other Laws, whether state or federal, for the relief of debtors, now or later existing, shall be commenced against Borrower and shall not be discharged within fifteen days of their commencement, or any such proceeding shall be commenced by Borrower.

7. A receiver or trustee shall be appointed for Borrower or for any substantial part of its assets, or any proceedings shall be instituted for the dissolution or the full or partial liquidation of Borrower, and the receiver or trustee shall not be discharged within fifteen days of his or her appointment, or the proceedings shall not be discharged within fifteen days of their commencement, or Borrower shall discontinue business or materially change the nature of its business.

8. Borrower shall suffer final judgments for payment of money aggregating in excess of $15,000 and shall not discharge the same within a period of three days, unless, pending further proceedings, execution has not been commenced or, if commenced, has been effectively stayed.

9. A judgment creditor of Borrower shall obtain possession of any of the Collateral by any means, including, but not limited to, levy, distraint, replevin, or self-help.

10. Any obligee of Subordinated Indebtedness shall fail to comply with the subordination provisions of the instruments evidencing the Subordinated Indebtedness.

11. Bank believes, in its sole discretion, that there has been a material adverse change in the assets, liabilities, financial condition, or business of the Borrower.

B. Acceleration. Immediately, and without notice, on the occurrence of an event of default specified in subparagraphs A(1) through A(11) of this SECTION SEVEN, or at the option of Bank, but only on written notice to Borrower, or on the occurrence of any other event of default, all obligations, whether under this Agreement or otherwise, shall immediately become due and payable without further action of any kind.

C. Remedies. After any acceleration, as provided in paragraph B of this SECTION SEVEN, Bank shall have, in addition to the rights and remedies given to it by this Agreement, the Note, and the Collateral Documents, all those rights and remedies allowed by all applicable Laws, including, but not limited to, the Uniform Commercial Code as enacted in any jurisdiction in which any Collateral may be located. Without limiting the generality of the foregoing, Bank, immediately and without demand of performance and without other notice—except as specifically required by this Agreement or the Collateral Documents—for any demand whatsoever to Borrower, all of which are by this Agreement expressly made, and, without advertisement, may sell at public or private sale, or otherwise realized on, in the greater Denver, Colorado area or elsewhere, the whole, or from time to time, any part of the Collateral, or any interest that Borrower may have in it. After deducting from the proceeds of sale or other disposition of the Collateral all expenses, including all reasonable expenses for legal services, Bank shall apply the proceeds towards the satisfaction of the Obligation. Any remainder of the proceeds after satisfaction in full of the Obligation shall be distributed as required by applicable Laws. Notice of any sale or other disposition shall be given to Borrower at least three days before the time of any intended public sale or of the time after which any intended private sale or other disposition of the Collateral is to be made, which Borrower agrees shall be reasonable notice of the sale or other disposition. Borrower agrees to assemble, or cause to be assembled, at its own expense the Collateral at such place or places as Bank shall designate. At any such sale or other disposition, Bank, to the extent permissible under applicable Laws, may purchase the whole or any part of the Collateral, free from any right of redemption on the part of Borrower, which right is by this Agreement waived and released. Without limiting the generality of any of the rights and remedies conferred on Bank under this paragraph, Bank, to the full extent permitted by applicable Laws, may:

1.   enter on the premises of Borrower, exclude from the premises Borrower or any affiliate, and take immediate possession of the Collateral, either personally or by means of a receiver appointed by a court of competent jurisdiction;

2.   at Bank's option, use, operate, manage, and control the Collateral in any manner;

3.   collect and receive all rents, income, revenue, earnings, issues, and profits; and

4.   maintain, repair, renovate, alter, or remove the Collateral as Bank may determine in its discretion.

SECTION EIGHT.
CONSTRUCTION OF AGREEMENT

The provisions of this Agreement shall be in addition to those of any guaranty, pledge, security agreement, Note, or other evidence of liability held by Bank, all of which shall be construed as complementary to each other. Nothing contained in this Agreement shall prevent Bank from enforcing any or all other notes, guaranty, pledge, or security agreements in accordance with their respective terms.

SECTION NINE.
FURTHER ASSURANCE

From time to time, Borrower shall execute and deliver to Bank such additional documents and will provide such additional information as Bank may reasonably require to carry out the terms of this Agreement and be informed of Borrower's status and affairs.

SECTION TEN.
ENFORCEMENT AND WAIVER BY BANK

Bank shall have the right at all times to enforce the provisions of this Agreement and the Collateral Documents in strict accordance with their terms, notwithstanding any conduct or custom on the part of Bank in refraining from so doing at any time or times. The failure of Bank at any time or times to enforce its rights under such provisions, strictly in accordance with the same, shall not be construed as having created a custom in any way or manner contrary to specific provisions of this Agreement or as having in any way or manner modified or waived the same. All rights and remedies of Bank are cumulative and concurrent, and the exercise of one right or remedy shall not be deemed a waiver or release of any other right or remedy.

SECTION ELEVEN.
EXPENSES OF BANK

Borrower, on demand, will reimburse Bank for all expenses, including the fees and expenses of legal counsel for Bank, incurred by Bank in connection with the preparation, administration, amendment, modification, or enforcement of this Agreement and the Collateral Documents, and the collection or attempted collection of the Note.

SECTION TWELVE.
NOTICES

Any notices or consents required or permitted by this Agreement shall be in writing and shall be deemed delivered if delivered in person, or, if sent, by certified mail, postage prepaid, return receipt requested, as follows, unless the address is changed by written notice:

A.   <u>If to Borrower</u>: Tree Services, Inc., 6789 120th Street, Commerce City, CO 80022

B.   <u>If to Bank</u>: Big Bank of Colorado, 100 19th Street, Denver, CO 80202

SECTION THIRTEEN.
WAIVER AND RELEASE BY BORROWER

To the maximum extent permitted by applicable Laws, Borrower shall:

A.   waive (i) protest of all commercial paper at any time held by Bank on which Borrower is in any way liable; and (ii) notice of acceleration and of intention to accelerate, and notice and opportunity to be heard, after acceleration in the manner provided in SECTION SEVEN, paragraph B, before exercise by Bank of the remedies of self-help, set off, or of other summary procedures committed by any applicable Laws or by any agreement with Borrower, and, except when required by this Agreement or by any applicable Laws, notice of any other action taken by Bank; and

B.   release Bank and its officers, attorneys, agents, and employees from all claims for loss or damage caused by any act or omission on the part of any such Person.

SECTION FOURTEEN.
GOVERNING LAW

This Agreement shall be governed by, construed, and enforced in accordance with the Laws of Colorado.

SECTION FIFTEEN.
BINDING EFFECT

This Agreement shall inure to the benefit of, and shall be binding on, the respective successors and permitted assigns of the parties.

SECTION SIXTEEN.
ASSIGNMENT

Borrower has no right to assign any of its rights or obligations under this Agreement without the prior express, and written consent of Bank, which consent can be withheld in Bank's sole and absolute discretion.

SECTION SEVENTEEN.
ENTIRE AGREEMENT

This Agreement shall constitute the entire agreement between the parties and any prior understanding or representation of any kind preceding the date of this Agreement shall not be binding on either party except to the extent incorporated in this Agreement.

SECTION EIGHTEEN.
MODIFICATION OF AGREEMENT

Any modification of this Agreement or additional obligation assumed by either party in connection with this Agreement shall be binding only if evidenced in a writing signed by each party or an authorized representative of each party.

SECTION NINETEEN.
ATTORNEYS' FEES

If any action is filed in relation to this Agreement, the unsuccessful party in the action shall pay to the successful party, in addition to all sums that either party may be called on to pay, a reasonable sum for the successful party's attorneys' fees.

SECTION TWENTY.
HEADINGS

The titles to the sections and paragraphs of this Agreement are solely for the convenience of the parties and shall not be used to explain, modify, simplify, or aid in the interpretation of the provisions of this Agreement.

SECTION TWENTY-ONE.
SEVERABILITY

If any provision of this Agreement shall be held invalid under any applicable Laws, the invalidity shall not affect any other provision of this Agreement that can be given effect without the invalid provision, and, to this end, the provisions of this Agreement are severable.

SECTION TWENTY-TWO.
COUNTERPARTS

This Agreement may be executed in any number of counterparts, each of which shall be deemed to be an original, but all of which together shall constitute but one and the same instrument.

The parties have executed this Agreement the day and year first set forth above.

TREE SERVICES, INC.

By: /s/ Melissa Green
    Melissa Green, Chief Executive Officer

BIG BANK OF COLORADO

By: /s/ Andrea Westover
    Andrea Westover, President

Exhibit A
Note

Intentionally Omitted

(you can assume note is standard and contains no issues)

Exhibit B
Existing Liens

Lien on Borrower's equipment as a result of its Line of Credit with Bank of the Rockies

Exhibit C
Subordinated Indebtedness

None

Exhibit D
Pledge Agreement

Intentionally Omitted

(you can assume agreement is standard and contains no issues)

Exhibit E
Guaranty Agreement

Intentionally Omitted

(you can assume agreement is standard and contains no issues)

Exhibit F
States of Qualification to do Business

Colorado: 6789 120th Street, Commerce City, CO 80022

Nebraska: no local office

Wyoming: 1500 Dell Range Boulevard, Cheyenne, WY 82009

New Mexico: 300 South 1st Street, Raton, NM 87740

Exhibit G
Prior Names

None

Exhibit H
Pending Litigation and Legal Proceedings

All matters set forth below are as of June 15, 2018

Borrower has the following pending litigation:

Kris Ellis, a residential customer in Durango, Colorado, is suing Borrower claiming that as a result of Borrower's tree trimming all three of her more than 70-year-old elm trees have died. Borrower plans to contest the suit.

Borrower has the following threatened litigation:

Jason Plummer, a former employee of Borrower, has threatened, via a personal letter, to sue for wrongful termination.

Exhibit I
Non-Compliance with Applicable Laws

During the past twelve months, Borrower has been cited one time by each of A, D, and M counties for failing to have the proper permit before removing various trees that required Borrower to operate in public streets. Borrower paid the requisite fine associated with each permit violation. As of the date of this Agreement, there are no outstanding permit violations.

Exhibit J
Existing Indebtedness

In 2015, Borrower entered into a revolving line of credit with Bank of the Rockies. The line of credit permits borrowings of up to $750,000 for use by Borrower in its day-to-day operations. The line of credit is secured by Borrower's equipment.

Exhibit K
Material Contracts

Intentionally Omitted

(you can assume Borrower listed all material contracts as of June 15, 2018)

Exhibit L
Use of Loan Proceeds

Borrower shall only use the Loan proceeds to purchase new equipment, to refurbish or replace old equipment, to purchase any necessary supplies, materials, or ancillary products related to Borrower's primary business operations, and to meet any short-term liabilities or obligations related to Borrower's primary business operations.

3. Executive Employment Agreement

EXECUTIVE EMPLOYMENT AGREEMENT

This Executive Employment Agreement ("Agreement") is made and entered into effective as of February 1, 2008 ("Effective Date") by and between Tree Services, Inc. ("Company") and Melissa Green ("Executive").

RECITALS

A. The Company desires to employ Executive, and Executive desires to be employed by the Company.

B. The Company and Executive desire to enter into an agreement that sets forth the terms of the employment relationship.

Now, therefore, in consideration of the foregoing and the mutual promises set forth in this Agreement, and of other good and valuable consideration, the receipt and sufficiency of which is acknowledged, the Company and Executive agree as follows:

1. <u>Term of Employment</u>. The Company agrees to employ Executive, and Executive accepts such employment with the Company, in each case, on the terms and conditions set forth in this Agreement. Executive shall begin employment on February 1, 2008 (the "Employment Commencement Date"). The initial term of this Agreement shall commence on the Effective Date and shall expire on January 31, 2013 ("Initial Term"). After that Initial Term, the Agreement shall automatically renew for successive 60-month periods thereafter on the same terms and conditions as set forth in this Agreement, unless either party provides written notice of non-renewal to the other party no less than one hundred twenty (120) days prior to the end of the then-current Term (as defined below), or until the Agreement is otherwise terminated by the Company or Executive in accordance with the provisions of Section 4 (the duration of Executive's employment with the Company shall sometimes be referred to as the "Term").

2. <u>Duties and Responsibilities</u>. Beginning with the Employment Commencement Date and continuing during the Term, Executive agrees to serve as the Chief Executive Officer of the Company.

(a) In such capacity, Executive shall have such duties, authorities, and responsibilities as are commensurate with such position, including managing all aspects of the Company, and such other related duties and responsibilities as are customarily assigned to individuals serving in that position.

(b) Beginning with the Employment Commencement Date and continuing during the Term, Executive (i) will devote Executive's best efforts to the business and affairs of the Company; (ii) will exercise the highest degree of loyalty and the highest standards of conduct in the performance of Executive's duties; (iii) will not, except with the Company's written consent, engage in any other business activity, whether or not such business activity is pursued for gain, profit, or other pecuniary advantage; (iv) will not engage, directly or indirectly, in any activity that is competitive with the Company's business in any respect or make any preparations to engage in any competitive activities; and (v) will not take any action that deprives the Company of any business opportunities or otherwise act in a manner that conflicts with the best interests of the Company or that is detrimental to the business of the Company. Notwithstanding the foregoing, the Executive may (i) serve as an officer or director of or otherwise participate in educational, welfare, social, and civic organizations; (ii) deliver lectures or fulfill speaking engagements; (iii) manage personal investments; and (iv) with the prior consent of the Company, serve on for-profit boards, in each case so long as such activities are consistent with the Company's policies as in effect from time to time and do not materially interfere with the Executive's employment or responsibilities under this Agreement.

(c) During the Term, the Executive agrees to comply with Company's policies as in effect from time to time.

3. <u>Compensation and Benefits</u>. As remuneration for all services to be rendered by Executive during the Term, and as consideration for complying with the covenants in this Agreement, the Company shall pay and provide to Executive the following:

3.1 <u>Annual Base Salary</u>. Beginning with the Employment Commencement Date and continuing during the Term, the Company shall pay Executive on a salary basis. Executive's initial Base Salary (as defined below) will be in the amount of Two Hundred Seventy-Five Thousand Dollars ($275,000) on an annualized basis. The Company will review the Base Salary annually during the Term to determine, at the discretion of the Company and the board of directors of the Company ("Board"), whether the Base Salary should be adjusted and, if so, the amount of such adjustment and the time at which the adjustment should take effect. The term "Base Salary" as used in this Agreement shall refer to the Base Salary as in effect from time to time, including any adjustments.

3.2 <u>Annual Performance-Based Compensation</u>. The Company has established an annual incentive bonus program ("Annual Bonus"). For the duration of this Agreement, the Executive is eligible for an Annual Bonus, payable if, as, and when Annual Bonuses payable to other executive officers of Company are paid. The amount, if any, available to be paid to Executive and the time and form of payment of bonuses, will be determined and approved by the Board. During such time as Executive serves as Chief Executive Officer, the target amount of the Executive's Annual Bonus shall be equal to fifty percent (50%) of the Base Salary paid to Executive as of the last day of the previous fiscal year.

3.3 <u>Employee Benefit Plans</u>. Executive shall be eligible to participate in any employee benefit plans and programs to which employees of the Company are generally entitled to participate, commensurate with Executive's position with the Company and subject to the eligibility requirements and other terms and conditions of such plans and programs. The Company, in its sole discretion, may change, amend, or discontinue any of its employee benefit plans or programs at any time during Executive's employment with the Company, and nothing contained herein shall obligate the Company to institute, maintain, or refrain from changing, amending, or discontinuing any employee benefit plan or program.

3.4 <u>Paid Time Off</u>. During the Term, Executive shall be entitled to paid time off. Executive shall also be entitled to Company-designated holidays, but in no event, shall Executive have less than eight (8) weeks of paid time off per year.

3.5 <u>Business Expenses</u>. During the Term, the Company shall pay or reimburse the Executive for all reasonable business expenses incurred or paid by the Executive in the performance of her duties pursuant to this Agreement, upon presentation of expense statements or vouchers and such other information as the Company may require and in accordance with the generally applicable policies and procedures of the Company. Notwithstanding the foregoing, Executive is not required to provide documentation of business expenses that are less than $500, on an individual basis, to receive reimbursement.

3.6 <u>Travel Stipend</u>. During the Term, in the event that the Company requests or requires Executive to travel on Company business for greater than five (5) consecutive calendar days and Executive travels for greater than five (5) consecutive calendar days, then on each such occurrence Executive shall receive a travel stipend in the amount of $1,500 as additional compensation.

4. Termination.

4.1 Termination by Non-Renewal or Mutual Agreement. If either party gives notice of an intention not to renew the term of this Agreement pursuant to Section 1, Executive's employment shall terminate on the last day of the then-current Term. The Company and Executive may also agree to terminate Executive's employment at any time by mutual written agreement executed by Executive and a duly authorized officer of the Company. Upon termination of Executive's employment by non-renewal or by mutual written agreement, the Company's obligation to pay or provide Executive compensation and benefits under this Agreement shall terminate, except the Company shall pay or provide Executive: (i) that portion of Executive's Base Salary which is earned but unpaid through the termination date; (ii) that portion of Executive's paid time off (pursuant to Section 3.4) for the current fiscal year which is earned, but unused through the termination date; (iii) reimbursement of all expenses for which Executive is entitled to be reimbursed pursuant to Section 3.5, but for which Executive has not yet been reimbursed; (iv) payment of any travel stipend for which Executive is entitled pursuant to Section 3.6, but for which Executive has not yet been paid; and (v) vested benefits, if any, to which Executive may be entitled under the Company's employment benefit plans as of the date of termination (the foregoing subsections 4.1(i), (ii), (iii), (iv), and (v) shall be referred to collectively as the "Accrued Benefits"). In addition to the Accrued Benefits, the Company shall provide Executive with severance compensation in the form of salary continuation at the Base Salary rate in effect at the time of Executive's employment termination for a period of six (6) months. Subject to Section 4.11, the Company will pay the foregoing salary continuation severance compensation during the applicable severance period in accordance with the Company's customary payroll practices. All such payments shall be subject to all applicable payroll tax withholdings. Other than the foregoing, the Company will have no further obligations to Executive under this Agreement.

4.2 Termination Due to Death. If Executive dies during the Term, this Agreement shall terminate on the date of Executive's death. Upon the death of Executive, the Company's obligation to pay and provide to Executive (or Executive's estate or other legal successors) compensation and benefits under this Agreement shall immediately terminate, except the Company shall pay or provide Executive's estate or other legal successor the Accrued Benefits and the Company shall provide Executive's estate with severance compensation in the form of salary continuation at the Base Salary rate in effect at the time of Executive's death for a period of six (6) months. The Company will pay the foregoing salary continuation severance compensation to the Executive's estate (or legal successor) in one lump sum payment. Such payment shall be subject to all applicable payroll tax withholdings. Other than the foregoing, the Company shall have no further obligations to Executive (or Executive's estate or other legal successors) under this Agreement.

4.3 Termination Due to Disability. If Executive suffers a Disability (as defined below), the Company may terminate Executive's employment by providing written notice to Executive of the Company's termination because of Disability specifying in such notice the effective termination date and Executive's employment will terminate at the end of the day on the termination date specified in the Company's notice. For purposes of this Agreement, the term "Disability" means any of the following: (i) when Executive is deemed disabled and entitled to benefits in accordance with any Company-provided long-term disability insurance policy or plan, if any is applicable, covering Executive, (ii) the inability of Executive, because of injury, illness, disease, or bodily or mental infirmity, to perform, with or without reasonable accommodation, the essential functions of Executive's job for more than one hundred eighty (180) days during any period of three hundred sixty-five (365) days, or (iii) upon the written determination by a physician mutually selected by the Company and Executive that, because of an injury, illness, disease, or bodily or mental infirmity, Executive is unable to perform, with or without reasonable accommodation, the essential functions of Executive's job, and, as of the date of determination, such condition is reasonably expected to last for a period of more than one hundred eighty (180) days after the date of determination, based on the medical information reasonably available to such physician at the time of such determination. In connection with any determination under the foregoing subpart (iii), Executive: (a) consents to any examinations by any physician mutually selected by the Company and Executive; (b) agrees to furnish such medical information as may be requested by the Company or the selected physician; and (c) waives any applicable physician-patient privilege that may arise because of any such examination. Upon the termination of this Agreement because of Disability, the Company's obligation to pay and provide Executive compensation and benefits under this Agreement will immediately terminate, except the Company will pay or provide Executive the Accrued Benefits and the Company shall provide Executive with severance compensation in the form of salary continuation at the Base Salary rate in effect at the time of Executive's employment termination for a period of six (6) months. Subject to Section 4.11, the Company will pay the foregoing salary continuation severance compensation during the applicable severance period in accordance with the Company's customary payroll practices. All such payments shall be subject to all applicable payroll tax withholdings. Other than the foregoing, the Company will have no further obligations to Executive under this Agreement.

4.4 <u>Termination by the Company for Cause</u>. At any time during the Term, the Company may terminate this Agreement and Executive's employment with the Company for Cause (as defined below) by providing Executive with at least sixty (60) days prior written notice of the Company's termination for Cause specifying in such notice the termination date, which must be at least sixty (60) days from the date of the notice, and this Agreement and Executive's employment will terminate at the end of the day on the termination date specified in such notice. For purposes of this Agreement, "Cause" means the occurrence of one or more of the following events: (i) Executive's conviction for, or pleading no contest to, a felony, any crime involving moral turpitude, deceit, dishonesty, or fraud, or any crime that is injurious to the financial condition, reputation, or goodwill of the Company; (ii) Executive's misappropriation of any of the Company's property; (iii) Executive's engaging in any fraudulent or dishonest conduct in Executive's dealings with, or on behalf of, the Company; (iv) Executive's engaging in any illegal conduct, except for minor infractions such as minor traffic violations, in the performance of Executive's employment duties for the Company; (v) Executive's failure or refusal to follow the lawful and material instructions of the Company's Board (other than any such failure or refusal resulting from Executive's incapacity due to physical or mental illness), if such failure or refusal continues for a period of sixty (60) days after the Company provides Executive with written notice stating the instructions which Executive has failed or refused to follow; (vi) Executive's breach of Executive's obligations under this Agreement or any other agreement with the Company (provided that if the Company in good faith determines that the breach is curable, the Company shall give Executive notice of the breach and sixty (60) days in which to cure the breach); (vii) Executive's violation of any of the Company's written policies or procedures, including, without limitation, any Executive policies, business ethics policies, or code of conduct policies, and such violation, if curable as determined by the Company in good faith, remains uncured for a period of sixty (60) days after the Company provides Executive with written notice of such violation; (viii) Executive's engaging in any misconduct which is injurious to the financial condition, reputation, or goodwill of the Company (provided that if the Company in good faith determines that the misconduct is curable, the Company shall give Executive notice of the misconduct and sixty (60) days in which to cure the misconduct); (ix) Executive's gross or habitual neglect of Executive's material employment duties or responsibilities if such neglect continues at any time after the Company provides Executive with written notice of such gross or habitual neglect; or (x) Executive's misuse of alcohol or drugs which materially interferes with Executive's performance of Executive's duties for the Company or which is injurious to the reputation or goodwill of the Company. Upon termination of Executive's employment by the Company for Cause, the Company's obligation to pay or provide Executive compensation and benefits under this Agreement shall terminate, except the

Company shall pay or provide Executive the Accrued Benefits and the Company shall provide Executive with severance compensation in the form of salary continuation at the Base Salary rate in effect at the time of Executive's employment termination for a period of six (6) months. Subject to Section 4.11, the Company will pay the foregoing salary continuation severance compensation during the applicable severance period in accordance with the Company's customary payroll practices. All such payments shall be subject to all applicable payroll tax withholdings. Other than the foregoing, the Company shall have no further obligations to Executive under this Agreement.

4.5 <u>Termination by the Company without Cause</u>. At any time during the Term, the Company may terminate Executive's employment with the Company without Cause for any reason or no reason by providing Executive with at least one hundred twenty (120) days prior written notice of the Company's termination without Cause, specifying in such notice the effective termination date, which date shall be no less than one hundred twenty (120) days from the date of the notice, and Executive's employment with the Company shall terminate at the end of the day on the termination date specified in the Company's notice (or such other date as may be mutually agreed upon by the Company and Executive). Upon termination of Executive's employment by the Company without Cause, the Company's obligation to pay and provide Executive compensation and benefits under this Agreement shall immediately terminate, except: (i) the Company shall pay or provide Executive the Accrued Benefits; (ii) the Company shall provide Executive with severance compensation in the form of salary continuation at the Base Salary rate in effect at the time of Executive's employment termination for a period of twenty-four (24) months; (iii) the Company shall pay Executive an additional amount equal to twenty-four (24) times the monthly COBRA premium rate in effect for Executive's health plan coverage tier at the time of Executive's termination of employment (the "Insurance Payment"); and (iv) if an Annual Bonus would otherwise have been payable to Executive for the year of Executive's employment termination pursuant to Section 3.2, Executive shall receive the full amount of that Annual Bonus amount. Subject to Section 4.11, the Company will pay: (i) the foregoing salary continuation severance compensation during the applicable severance period in accordance with the Company's customary payroll practices, (ii) the Insurance Payment in a single lump sum payment within 30 days after the effective date of the Release Agreement under Section 4.11, and (iii) the full amount of the Annual Bonus, if any, on the date the Annual Bonus is otherwise payable under the terms set forth in Section 3.2. All such payments shall be subject to all applicable payroll tax withholdings. Other than the foregoing, the Company shall have no further obligations to Executive under this Agreement.

4.6 <u>Termination by Executive for Good Reason</u>. At any time during the Term, Executive may terminate Executive's employment with the Company by giving the Company written notice of termination for Good Reason (as defined below) specifying in such notice the basis for the Good Reason termination. For purposes of this Agreement, "Good Reason" means the occurrence of any of the following events without Executive's consent: (i) the Company demotes Executive or assigns Executive to duties that are inferior to and inconsistent with Executive's position, duties, and responsibilities immediately prior to such assignment; (ii) the Company breaches any term of this Agreement; (iii) the Company reduces Executive's Base Salary; or (iv) the Company eliminates or reduces the employee benefits provided to Executive; provided, however, the Company will have fifteen (15) days from its receipt of any written notice of the Good Reason termination in which to take corrective action to cure the Good Reason, and if the Company does not cure the Good Reason, the Good Reason termination will be effective at the end of the fifteenth (15th) day after the Company receives the written notice of Good Reason termination; and provided further, however, for Executive to exercise her right to terminate for Good Reason, Executive must provide written notice of termination for Good Reason within ninety (90) days after the occurrence of the event giving rise to the basis for the Good Reason termination. Upon Executive's termination of employment for Good Reason, the Company's obligation to pay or provide Executive compensation and benefits under this Agreement shall terminate, except: (i) the Company shall pay or provide Executive the Accrued Benefits; (ii) the Company shall provide Executive with severance compensation in the form of salary continuation at the Base Salary rate in effect at the time of Executive's employment termination for a period of twenty-four (24) months; and (iii) the Company shall pay Executive the "Insurance Payment. Subject to Section 4.11, the Company will pay: (i) the foregoing salary continuation severance compensation during the applicable severance period in accordance with the Company's customary payroll practices, and (ii) the Insurance Payment in a single lump sum payment within 30 days after the effective date of the Release Agreement under Section 4.11. All such payments shall be subject to all applicable payroll tax withholdings. Other than the foregoing, the Company shall have no further obligations to Executive under this Agreement.

4.7 <u>Termination by Executive without Good Reason</u>. At any time during the Term, Executive may terminate Executive's employment with the Company without Good Reason by giving the Company written notice of termination without Good Reason, specifying in such notice a termination date not less than ninety (90) calendar days after the giving of the notice (the "Executive's Notice Period"), and Executive's employment with the Company shall terminate at the end of the day on the last day of Executive's Notice Period. Upon termination of Executive's employment with the Company under this Section 4.7, the Company's obligation to pay Executive compensation and benefits under this Agreement shall immediately terminate, except the Company shall pay or provide Executive with the Accrued Benefits and the Company shall provide Executive with severance compensation in the form of salary continuation at the Base Salary rate in effect at the time of Executive's employment termination for a period of six (6) months. Subject to Section 4.11, the Company will pay the foregoing salary continuation severance compensation during the applicable severance period in accordance with the Company's customary payroll practices. All such payments shall be subject to all applicable payroll tax withholdings. Other than the foregoing, the Company shall have no further obligations to Executive under this Agreement.

4.8 <u>Termination Upon Change in Control</u>. In the event that the Company undergoes a Change in Control (as defined below), the Company shall provide the following payments to Executive on the date of the Change in Control:

(a) a lump sum amount equal to three (3) times Executive's Base Salary in effect as of the date of the Change in Control;

(b) a lump sum amount equal to two (2) times Executive's most recently paid Annual Bonus, but in no event less than two (2) times 30% of Executive's Base Salary in effect as of the date of the Change in Control; and

(c) a lump sum amount equal to the Insurance Payment.

A "Change of Control" shall mean, (i) one or more persons acquire beneficial ownership of the stock of the Company that, together with the stock held by such person or persons, constitutes more than 50% of the total voting power of the stock of the Company; provided, that, a Change in Control shall not occur if any person or persons owns more than 50% of the total voting power of the stock of the Company and acquires additional stock; (ii) a majority of the members of the Board are replaced during any twelve month period by directors whose appointment or election is not endorsed by a majority of the Board before the date of appointment or election; (iii) an asset assignment or asset sale of substantially all of the Company's assets; or (iv) a merger, consolidation, or reorganization of the Company.

4.9 <u>Notice of Termination</u>. Any termination of Executive's employment by the Company or by Executive (other than by reason of death) shall be communicated by a written Notice of Termination (as defined below) addressed to the other parties to this Agreement. A "Notice of Termination" shall mean a written notice stating that Executive's employment with the Company has been or will be terminated and the specific provisions of this Section 4 under which such termination is being effected.

4.10 Effect of Termination. In the event Executive's employment with the Company terminates for any reason (including, without limitation, pursuant to Sections 4.1–4.8 herein), Executive agrees and covenants that Executive will immediately resign and will be deemed to have resigned from, any and all positions Executive may hold with the Company or any of its subsidiaries or affiliates, whether now or hereafter existing. Notwithstanding the foregoing, if Executive's employment is terminated for any reason other than for Cause pursuant to Section 4.4, Executive shall have no obligation or requirement to resign from her position on the Board.

4.11 Severance Release. Executive acknowledges and agrees that the Company's payment of the severance and other compensation pursuant to Sections 4.1–4.8 shall be deemed to constitute a full settlement and discharge of any and all obligations of the Company to Executive arising out of this Agreement, Executive's employment with the Company, and the termination of Executive's employment with the Company. Executive further acknowledges and agrees that as a condition to receiving any of the severance and other compensation pursuant to Sections 4.1–4.8, Executive will execute, deliver to the Company, and not revoke a release agreement in a form prepared by, and mutually satisfactory to, the Company and Executive ("Release Agreement") pursuant to which Executive will release and waive, to the fullest extent permitted by law, all claims against the Company, its affiliates, and all of its and their present and former owners, officers, directors, members, shareholders, employees, agents, attorneys, insurers, representatives, employee benefit plans, and their fiduciaries, both individually and in their representative capacities, including, without limitation, all claims arising out of this Agreement, Executive's employment with the Company, and the termination of Executive's employment with the Company; provided, however, that the Release Agreement shall not affect or release (i) any claim for the Accrued Benefits, (ii) any rights to the severance and other compensation under Sections 4.1–4.8, as applicable; and (iii) any rights Executive may have with respect to vested benefits under any employee benefit plans or programs of the Company (except any severance plan). The severance and other compensation described in Sections 4.1–4.8 is in lieu of any severance benefits under any severance policy or plan the Company may have now or in the future, and Executive acknowledges that Executive is not entitled to any other severance benefits.

5. Restrictive Covenants.

5.1 Definitions. For purposes of this Agreement, the following terms have the following meanings:

(a) "Company's Customers" means: (i) any person or entity to whom the Company (or any of its subsidiaries or affiliates, now or hereafter existing) is selling or providing any products or services as of the date of termination of Executive's employment with the Company; and (ii) any person or entity to whom the Company (or any of its subsidiaries or affiliates, now or hereafter existing) sold or provided any products or services at any time during the six (6) months immediately preceding the termination of Executive's employment with the Company.

(b) "Competing Products or Services" means: (i) any products or services that are similar to or competitive with any of the products or services that the Company is developing, producing, offering, or providing as of the termination of Executive's employment with the Company; or (ii) any products or services that are competitive with the products or services that are being developed, produced, offered, sold, or provided by the Company as of termination of Executive's employment with the Company in that such competitive products or services would serve as a substitute for, and would displace or diminish a customer's need for, any of the Company's products or services.

(c) "Competitive Business" means any business that develops, produces, sells, or provides any Competing Products or Services or is competitive with the business of the Company.

(d) "Confidential Information" means any and all of the Company's (and its subsidiaries' or affiliates', now or hereafter existing) trade secrets, confidential and proprietary information, and all other non-public information and data of or about the Company (and its subsidiaries or affiliates) and its business, including, without limitation, lists of customers, information pertaining to customers, marketing plans and strategies, information pertaining to suppliers, information pertaining to prospective suppliers, pricing information, cost information, data compilations, research and development information, business plans, financial information, personnel information, information received from third parties that the Company has agreed to keep confidential, and information about prospective customers or prospective products and services, whether or not reduced to writing or other tangible medium of expression, including, without limitation, work product created by Executive in rendering services for the Company.

(e) "Prohibited Capacity" means: (i) in the same or similar capacity or function to that in which Executive worked for the Company at any time during the six (6) months immediately preceding the termination of Executive's employment with the Company; (ii) in any ownership capacity, except Executive may own, as a passive investment, shares of any class of securities regularly traded on a national stock exchange or other public market, (iii) in any capacity or function in which Executive likely would inevitably use or disclose the Company's trade secrets or Confidential Information; or (iv) in any other capacity or function in which Executive's knowledge of the Confidential Information would facilitate or assist Executive's work for the Competitive Business.

(f) "Restricted Geographic Area" means Denver, Colorado and anywhere within a thirty (30) mile radius of Denver, Colorado.

(g) "Restricted Time Period" means the period during Executive's employment with the Company and for twelve (12) months after the termination of Executive's employment for any reason.

5.2 <u>Non-Competition</u>. During the Restricted Time Period, Executive will not within the Restricted Geographic Area engage in (including, without limitation, being employed by, working for, or rendering services to) any Competitive Business in any Prohibited Capacity; provided, however, if the Competitive Business has multiple divisions, lines, or segments, some of which are not competitive with the business of the Company, nothing in this Agreement shall prohibit Executive from being employed by, working for, or assisting only that division, line, or segment of such Competitive Business that is not competitive with the business of the Company provided that Executive's work for such non-competitive division, line, or segment of the Competitive Business does not involve any Competing Products or Services.

5.3 <u>Customer Restrictions</u>.

(a) During the Restricted Time Period, Executive will not provide, sell, or market; attempt to provide, sell, or market; or assist any person or entity in the sale or provision of, any Competing Products or Services to any of the Company's Customers with respect to whom, at any time during the three (3) months immediately preceding the termination of Executive's employment with the Company, Executive had any sales or service contact on behalf of the Company, Executive had any business contact on behalf of the Company, Executive had any role (including without limitation any supervisory or managerial responsibility) on behalf of the Company in providing products or services, or Executive had access to, or gained knowledge of, any Confidential Information concerning the Company's business with such customer, or otherwise solicit or communicate with any such customers for the purposes of selling or providing any Competing Products or Services.

(b) During the Restricted Time Period, Executive will not provide, sell, or market; assist in the provision, selling, or marketing of; or attempt to provide, sell, or market any Competing Products or Services to any of the Company's Customers located in the Restricted Geographic Area or otherwise solicit or communicate with any of the Company's Customers located in the Restricted Geographic Area for the purpose of selling, marketing, or providing; assisting in the provision, selling, or marketing of; or attempting to sell, market, or provide any Competing Products or Services.

(c)   During the Restricted Time Period, Executive will not urge, induce, or seek to induce any of the Company's Customers to terminate their business with the Company or to cancel, reduce, limit, or in any manner interfere with the Company's Customers' business with the Company.

5.4   Non-Interference with Contractors and Vendors. During the Restricted Time Period, Executive will not urge, induce, or seek to induce any of the Company's independent contractors, subcontractors, distributors, brokers, consultants, sales representatives, vendors, suppliers, or any other person or entity with whom the Company has a business relationship to terminate their relationship with, or representation of, the Company or to cancel, withdraw, reduce, limit, or in any manner modify any such person's or entity's business with, or representation of, the Company.

5.5   Employee Restrictions. During the three (3) months after termination of Executive's employment for any reason, Executive will not solicit, recruit, hire, employ, attempt to hire or employ, or assist any person or entity in the recruitment or hiring of, any person who is an employee of the Company, or otherwise urge, induce or seek to induce any person to terminate his or her employment with the Company.

5.6   Non-Disparagement. During the Restricted Time Period, Executive will not make or publish any statements or comments that disparage or injure the reputation or goodwill of the Company or any of its officers, directors, or employees, including, but not limited to, making or publishing any comments or statements to the Company's customers, distributors, or employees that disparage the Company or its products or services or that otherwise injure or diminish the Company's relationship with such customers, distributors, or employees; provided, however, nothing herein shall prohibit Executive from providing any information that may be required or compelled by law or legal process.

5.7   Direct or Indirect Activities. Executive acknowledges and agrees that the covenants contained in this Section 5 prohibit Executive from engaging in certain activities directly or indirectly, whether on Executive's own behalf or on behalf of any other person or entity, and regardless of the capacity in which Executive is acting, including without limitation as an employee, independent contractor, owner, partner, officer, agent, consultant, or advisor.

5.8   Non-Disclosure of Confidential Information. During Executive's employment with the Company and thereafter, Executive will not use or disclose to others any of the Confidential Information, except (i) in the course of Executive's work for and on behalf of the Company, (ii) with the prior written consent of the Company, or (iii) as required by law or judicial process, provided Executive promptly notifies the Company in writing of any subpoena or other judicial request for disclosure involving Confidential Information or trade secrets, and cooperates with any effort by the Company to obtain a protective order preserving the confidentiality of the Confidential Information or trade secrets. Executive agrees that the Company owns the Confidential Information and Executive has no rights, title, or interest in any of the Confidential Information. Additionally, Executive will abide by the Company's policies protecting the Confidential Information, as such policies may exist from time to time. At the Company's request or upon termination of Executive's employment with the Company for any reason, Executive will immediately deliver to the Company any and all materials (including all copies and electronically stored data) containing any Confidential Information in Executive's possession, custody, or control. Upon termination of Executive's employment with the Company for any reason, Executive will, if requested by the Company, provide the Company with a signed written statement disclosing whether Executive has returned to the Company all materials (including all copies and electronically stored data) containing any Confidential Information previously in Executive's possession, custody, or control. Executive's confidentiality and non-disclosure obligations under this Agreement continue after the termination of Executive's employment with the Company for any reason. With respect to any particular trade secret information, Executive's confidentiality and non-disclosure obligations shall continue as long as such information constitutes a trade secret under applicable law. With respect to any particular Confidential Information that does not constitute a trade secret, Executive's confidentiality and non-disclosure obligations shall continue for a period of twelve (12) months from the termination of Executive's employment for any reason and shall not apply to information that becomes generally known to the public through no fault or action of Executive or others who were under confidentiality obligations with respect to such information. Executive acknowledges and agrees that Executive's obligations under this Section shall survive the expiration or termination of this Agreement and the cessation of Executive's employment with the Company for whatever reason. Executive further acknowledges and agrees that Executive's obligations under this Section shall be construed as independent covenants and that no breach of any contractual or legal duty by the Company shall be held sufficient to excuse or terminate Executive's obligations under this Section 5.8 or to preclude the Company from enforcing this Section 5.8.

5.9 <u>Survival of Restrictive Covenants</u>. Executive acknowledges and agrees that Executive's obligations under this Section 5 shall survive the expiration or termination of this Agreement and the cessation of Executive's service with the Company for whatever reason. Executive further acknowledges and agrees that Executive's restrictive covenant obligations under this Section 5 shall be construed as independent covenants and that no breach of any contractual or legal duty by the Company shall be held sufficient to excuse or terminate Executive's restrictive covenant obligations under this Section 5 or to preclude the Company from enforcing this Section 5.

5.10 <u>Extension</u>. In the event Executive violates any of the restrictive covenants contained in this Section 5, the duration of all restrictive covenants (and the Restricted Time Period) shall automatically be extended by the length of time during which Executive was in violation of any of the restrictive covenants.

5.11 <u>Severability; Reformation of Restrictions</u>. Although Executive and the Company consider the restrictions contained in this Section 5 to be reasonable, particularly given the competitive nature of the Company's business and Executive's position with the Company, Executive and the Company acknowledge and agree that: (i) if any covenant, subsection, portion, or clause of this Section 5 is determined to be unenforceable or invalid for any reason, such unenforceability or invalidity shall not affect the enforceability or validity of the remainder of the Agreement; and (ii) if any particular covenant, subsection, provision, or clause of this Section 5 is determined to be unreasonable or unenforceable for any reason, including, without limitation, the time period, geographic area, or scope of activity covered by any restrictive covenant, such covenant, subsection, provision, or clause shall automatically be deemed reformed such that the contested covenant, subsection, provision, or clause shall have the closest effect permitted by applicable law to the original form and shall be given effect and enforced as so reformed to whatever extent would be reasonable and enforceable under applicable law. Any court interpreting any restrictive covenant provision of this Agreement shall, if necessary, reform any such provision to make it enforceable under applicable law.

6.   <u>Company Property</u>. Executive acknowledges and agrees that all tangible materials, equipment, documents, copies of documents, data compilations (in whatever form), and electronically created or stored materials that Executive receives or makes in the course of her employment with the Company (or with the use of Company time, materials, facilities, or trade secrets or Confidential Information) are and shall remain the property of the Company. Upon the termination of Executive's service with the Company, or at the Company's request, Executive shall immediately deliver to the Company (i) any and all memoranda, notes, records, drawings, manuals, computer programs, documentation, diskettes, computer tapes, electronic data (in whatever form or media), and all

copies thereof, in Executive's possession or under Executive's control, whether prepared by Executive or others, containing any Confidential Information; and (ii) any and all property or equipment belonging to the Company, including, without limitation, keys, access cards, computers, files, and documents. Executive acknowledges and agrees that Executive's obligations under this Section shall survive the expiration or termination of this Agreement and the cessation of Executive's employment with the Company for whatever reason.

7.   Remedies. Executive acknowledges that a breach or threatened breach by Executive of Section 5 or Section 6 of this Agreement will give rise to irreparable injury to the Company and that money damages will not be adequate relief for such injury and, accordingly, Executive agrees that the Company shall be entitled to obtain equitable relief, including, but not limited to, temporary restraining orders, preliminary injunctions, or permanent injunctions, without having to post any bond or other security, to restrain or prohibit such breach or threatened breach, in addition to any other legal remedies which may be available, including the recovery of money damages. In addition to all other relief to which it shall be entitled, the prevailing party shall be entitled to recover from the non-prevailing party all litigation costs and attorneys' fees incurred by the prevailing party in any action or proceeding relating to Section 5 or Section 6 of this Agreement in which the prevailing party prevails in any respect, including, without limitation, any action in which the prevailing party seeks enforcement of Section 5 or Section 6 of this Agreement or seeks relief from the non-prevailing party's violation of Section 5 or Section 6 of this Agreement.

8.   Assignment.

8.1   Assignment by Company. The rights and obligations of the Company under this Agreement shall inure to the benefit of and be binding upon any and all successors and assigns of the Company, including without limitation by asset assignment, merger, consolidation, or other reorganization. As used in this Agreement, "Company" shall mean the Company as previously defined and any successor to its business or assets which assumes and agrees to perform this Agreement by operation of law, or otherwise.

8.2   Non-Assignment by Executive. The services to be provided by Executive to the Company under this Agreement are personal to Executive, and Executive's duties may not be assigned by Executive.

8.3   Notice. Any notice required or permitted under this Agreement shall be in writing and either delivered personally or sent by nationally recognized overnight courier, express mail, or certified or registered mail, postage prepaid, return receipt requested, at the following respective address unless the party notifies the other party in writing of a change of address:

If to the Company:

>   Tree Services, Inc.
>   6789 120th Street
>   Commerce City, CO 80022
>   Attention: Chief Financial Officer

If to Executive:

>   Melissa Green
>   1112 18th Street
>   Denver, CO 80202

A notice delivered personally shall be deemed delivered and effective as of the date of delivery. A notice sent by overnight courier or express mail shall be deemed delivered and effective the next business day after it is deposited with the postal authority or commercial carrier. A notice sent by certified or registered mail shall be deemed delivered and effective three (3) days after it is deposited with the postal authority.

9.   Miscellaneous Provisions

9.1   Entire Agreement. This Agreement constitutes the entire agreement of the parties with respect to the subjects addressed herein, and supersedes any prior agreements, understandings, or representations, oral or written, on the subjects addressed herein.

9.2   Modification. This Agreement shall not be varied, altered, modified, canceled, changed, or in any way amended except by (i) mutual agreement of the parties in a written instrument executed by Executive and a duly authorized officer or member of the Board or (ii) reformation by a court as provided in Section 5.11.

9.3   Tax Withholding. The Company may withhold from any compensation or benefits payable under this Agreement all federal, state, city, or other taxes as may be required pursuant to any law or governmental regulation or ruling.

9.4   Contractual Rights to Benefits. Any benefits payable under this Agreement shall be paid solely from the general assets of the Company. Neither Executive nor Executive's estate shall have interest in any specific assets of the Company under the terms of this Agreement. This Agreement shall not be considered to create an escrow account, trust fund, or other funding arrangement of any kind between Executive and the Company. Nothing herein contained shall require or be deemed to require, or prohibit or be deemed to prohibit, the Company to segregate, earmark, or otherwise set aside any funds or other assets, in trust or otherwise, to provide for any payments to be made or required hereunder.

9.5   No Waiver. Failure to insist upon strict compliance with any of the terms, covenants, or conditions of this Agreement shall not be deemed a waiver of such term, covenant, or condition, nor shall any waiver or relinquishment of any right or power hereunder at any one or more times be deemed a waiver or relinquishment of such right or power at any other time or times.

9.6   Governing Law; Choice of Forum. To the extent not preempted by federal law, the provisions of this Agreement shall be construed and enforced in accordance with the laws of the State of Colorado, notwithstanding any states' choice-of-law or conflicts-of-law rules to the contrary. The Company and Executive further acknowledge and agree that this Agreement is intended, among other things, to supplement the provisions of the Uniform Trade Secrets Act, as amended from time to time, and the duties Executive owes to the Company under the common law, including, but not limited to, the duty of loyalty. The parties agree that any legal action relating to this Agreement shall be commenced and maintained exclusively before any appropriate state court of record in the City and County of Denver, Colorado, or in the United States District Court for the District of Colorado, and the parties submit to the personal jurisdiction and venue of such courts and waive any right to challenge or otherwise object to personal jurisdiction or venue in any action commenced or maintained in such courts.

9.7   No Conflicting Agreements. Executive represents and warrants to the Company that: (i) Executive's employment by the Company and the performance of Executive's employment duties will not constitute a breach of any agreements to which Executive is a party, including without limitation any employment or non-competition agreement with any former employer; and (ii) Executive has not provided and will not provide to the Company, and will not use or disclose during the performance of Executive's employment services for the Company, any documents, materials, or information of any third party subject to any legally enforceable restrictions or obligations as to confidentiality or secrecy.

9.8   Compliance with Section 409A of the Code. The intent of the parties is that payments and benefits under this Agreement comply with Section 409A of the Internal Revenue Code ("Code Section 409A"), to the extent subject thereto, and, accordingly, to the maximum extent permitted, this Agreement shall be interpreted and be administered to be in compliance therewith.

Notwithstanding anything contained herein to the contrary, to the extent required in order to avoid accelerated taxation or tax penalties under Code Section 409A, Executive shall not be considered to have terminated employment with the Company for purposes of this Agreement until Executive would be considered to have incurred a "separation from service" from the Company within the meaning of Code Section 409A. Any payments described in this Agreement that are due within the "short-term deferral period" (as defined in Code Section 409A) shall not be treated as deferred compensation unless applicable law requires otherwise. Each amount to be paid or benefit to be provided to Executive pursuant to this Agreement that constitutes deferred compensation subject to Code Section 409A shall be construed as a separate identified payment for purposes of Code Section 409A. Notwithstanding anything to the contrary in this Agreement, to the extent that any payments to be made in connection with Executive's separation from service would result in the imposition of any individual excise tax and late interest charges imposed under Code Section 409A, the payment shall instead be made on the first business day after the earlier of (i) the date that is six (6) months following such separation from service or (ii) the date of Executive's death.

9.9 <u>Construction</u>. This Agreement is the result of negotiations between the parties, and neither party shall be deemed to be the drafter of this Agreement. The language of this Agreement shall in all cases be construed as a whole, according to its fair meaning, and not strictly for or against either party. This Agreement shall be interpreted and construed without any presumption or inference based upon or against the party causing this Agreement to be drafted.

9.10 <u>Voluntary Agreement</u>. Executive acknowledges: (i) Executive has read this Agreement; (ii) Executive has been given ample time to consider this Agreement; (iii) Executive has been given the opportunity to consult with Executive's own attorney or other advisors if Executive so chooses; and (iv) Executive is entering into this Agreement knowingly and voluntarily intending to be legally bound.

9.11 <u>Counterparts</u>. This Agreement may be executed in one (1) or more counterparts, each of which shall be deemed to be an original, but all of which together will constitute one and the same Agreement. Signatures transmitted by facsimile or other electronic means shall be effective the same as original signatures for execution of this Agreement.

IN WITNESS WHEREOF, Executive and Company have executed this Agreement on the Effective Date.

EXECUTIVE

<u>/s/ Melissa Green</u>
Melissa Green
Chief Executive Officer

TREE SERVICES, INC.

<u>/s/ Thomas Shrub</u>
Thomas Shrub
Chief Financial Officer

4. Equity Incentive Plan

TREE SERVICES, INC.
2013 EQUITY INCENTIVE PLAN

1. Purpose; Eligibility.

1.1   General Purpose. The name of this plan is the Tree Services, Inc. 2013 Equity Incentive Plan (the "Plan"). The purposes of the Plan are to (a) enable Tree Services, Inc., a Colorado corporation (the "Company"), to attract and retain the types of Employees, Consultants and Directors who will contribute to the Company's long range success; (b) provide incentives that align the interests of Employees, Consultants and Directors with those of the shareholders of the Company; and (c) promote the success of the Company's business.

1.2   Eligible Award Recipients. The persons eligible to receive Awards are the Employees, Consultants and Directors of the Company and its Affiliates.

1.3   Available Awards. Awards that may be granted under the Plan include: (a) Incentive Stock Options, and (b) Non-qualified Stock Options.

2. Definitions.

"Affiliate" means a corporation or other entity that, directly or through one or more intermediaries, controls, is controlled by or is under common control with, the Company.

"Applicable Laws" means the requirements related to or implicated by the administration of the Plan under applicable state corporate law, United States federal and state securities laws, the Code and the applicable laws of any foreign country or jurisdiction where Awards are granted under the Plan.

"Award" means any right granted under the Plan, including an Incentive Stock Option or a Non-qualified Stock Option.

"Award Agreement" means a written agreement, contract, certificate or other instrument or document evidencing the terms and conditions of an individual Award granted under the Plan which may, in the discretion of the Company, be transmitted electronically to any Participant. Each Award Agreement shall be subject to the terms and conditions of the Plan.

"Board" means the Board of Directors of the Company, as constituted at any time.

"Cause" means, unless the applicable Award Agreement provides otherwise:

With respect to any Employee or Consultant:

(a) If the Employee or Consultant is a party to an employment or service agreement with the Company or an Affiliate and such agreement provides for a definition of Cause, the definition contained therein; or

(b) If no such agreement exists, or if such agreement does not define Cause: (i) failure to perform such duties as are reasonably requested by the Board; (ii) material breach of any agreement with the Company or an Affiliate, or a material violation of the Company's or an Affiliate's code of conduct or other written policy; (iii) commission of, or plea of guilty or no contest to, a felony or a crime involving moral turpitude or the commission of any other act involving willful malfeasance or material fiduciary breach with respect to the Company or an Affiliate; (iv) use of illegal drugs or abuse of alcohol that materially impairs the Participant's ability to perform his or her duties to the Company or an Affiliate; or (v) gross negligence or willful misconduct with respect to the Company or an Affiliate.

With respect to any Director, a determination by a majority of the disinterested Board members that the Director has engaged in any of the following:

(a) malfeasance in office; or

(b) gross misconduct or neglect.

The Committee, in its absolute discretion, shall determine the effect of all matters and questions relating to whether a Participant has been discharged for Cause.

• "Change in Control" means:

(a) One Person (or more than one Person acting as a group) acquires ownership of stock of the Company that, together with the stock held by such Person or group, constitutes more than 50% of the total fair market value or total voting power of the stock of the Company; provided, that, a Change in Control shall not occur if any Person (or more than one Person acting as a group) owns more than 50% of the total fair market value or total voting power of the Company's stock and acquires additional stock;

(b) One Person (or more than one Person acting as a group) acquires (or has acquired during the twelve-month period ending on the date of the most recent acquisition) ownership of the Company's stock possessing 20% or more of the total voting power of the stock of the Company;

(c) A majority of the members of the Board are replaced during any twelve-month period by directors whose appointment or election are not endorsed by all of the Board before the date of appointment or election; or

(d) One Person (or more than one Person acting as a group), acquires (or has acquired during the twelve-month period ending on the date of the most recent acquisition) assets from the Company that have a total gross fair market value equal to or more than 30% of the total gross fair market value of all of the assets of the Company immediately before such acquisition(s).

"Code" means the Internal Revenue Code of 1986, as it may be amended from time to time. Any reference to a section of the Code shall be deemed to include a reference to any regulations promulgated thereunder.

"Committee" means a committee of one or more members of the Board appointed by the Board to administer the Plan in accordance with Section 3.4 and 3.5.

"Common Stock" means the common stock, $0.01 par value per share, of the Company.

"Company" means Tree Services, Inc. a Colorado corporation, and any successor thereto.

"Consultant" means any individual who is engaged by the Company or any Affiliate to render consulting or advisory services, whether or not compensated for such services.

"Continuous Service" means that the Participant's service with the Company or an Affiliate, whether as an Employee, Consultant or Director, is not interrupted or terminated. The Participant's Continuous Service shall not be deemed to have terminated merely because of a change in the capacity in which the Participant renders service to the Company or an Affiliate as an Employee, Consultant or Director or a change in the entity for which the Participant renders such service, provided that there is no interruption or termination of the Participant's Continuous Service; provided further that if any Award is subject to Section 409A of the Code, this sentence shall only be given effect to the extent consistent with Section 409A of the Code. For example, a change in status from an Employee of the Company to a Director of an Affiliate will not constitute an interruption of Continuous Service. The Committee or its delegate, in its sole discretion, may determine whether Continuous Service shall be considered interrupted in the case of any leave of absence approved by that party, including sick leave, military leave or any other personal or family leave of absence.

"Detrimental Activity" means any of the following: (i) unauthorized disclosure of any confidential or proprietary information of the Company or any of its Affiliates; (ii) any activity that would be grounds to terminate the Participant's employment or service with the Company or any of its Affiliates for Cause; (iii) the breach of any non-competition, non-solicitation, non-disparagement or other agreement containing restrictive covenants, with the Company or its Affiliates; (iv) fraud or conduct contributing to any financial restatements or irregularities, as determined by the Committee in its sole discretion; or (v) any other conduct or act determined to be materially injurious, detrimental or prejudicial to any interest of the Company or any of its Affiliates, as determined by the Committee in its sole discretion.

"Director" means a member of the Board.

"Disability" means that the Participant is unable to engage in any substantial gainful activity by reason of any medically determinable physical or mental impairment; provided, however, for purposes of determining the term of an Incentive Stock Option pursuant to Section 6.9 hereof, the term Disability shall have the meaning ascribed to it under Section 22(e)(3) of the Code. The determination of whether an individual has a Disability shall be determined under procedures established by the Committee. Except in situations where the Committee is determining Disability for purposes of the term of an Incentive Stock Option pursuant to Section 6.9 hereof within the meaning of Section 22(e)(3) of the Code, the Committee may rely on any determination that a Participant is disabled for purposes of benefits under any long-term disability plan maintained by the Company or any Affiliate in which a Participant participates.

"Disqualifying Disposition" has the meaning set forth in Section 13.9.

"Effective Date" shall mean the date as of which this Plan is adopted by the Board.

"Employee" means any person, including an officer or Director, employed by the Company or an Affiliate; provided, that, for purposes of determining eligibility to receive Incentive Stock Options, an Employee shall mean an employee of the Company or a parent or subsidiary corporation within the meaning of Section 424 of the Code. Mere service as a Director or payment of a director's fee by the Company or an Affiliate shall not be sufficient to constitute "employment" by the Company or an Affiliate.

"Exchange Act" means the Securities Exchange Act of 1934, as amended, and any successor thereto.

"Fair Market Value" means, on a given date, (i) if there is a public market for the shares of Common Stock on such date, the closing price of the shares as reported on such date on the principal national securities exchange on which the shares are listed or, if no sales of shares have been reported on any national securities exchange, then the immediately preceding date on which sales of the shares have been so reported or quoted, and (ii) if there is no public market for the shares of Common Stock on such date, then the fair market value shall be determined by the Committee in good faith after taking into consideration all factors which it deems appropriate, including, without limitation, Sections 409A and 422 of the Code.

"Grant Date" means the date on which the Committee adopts a resolution, or takes other appropriate action, expressly granting an Award to a Participant that specifies the key terms and conditions of the Award or, if a later date is set forth in such resolution, then such date as is set forth in such resolution.

"Incentive Stock Option" means an Option intended to qualify as an incentive stock option within the meaning of Section 422 of the Code.

"Non-qualified Stock Option" means an Option that by its terms does not qualify or is not intended to qualify as an Incentive Stock Option.

"Option" means an Incentive Stock Option or a Non-qualified Stock Option granted pursuant to the Plan.

"Optionholder" means a person to whom an Option is granted pursuant to the Plan or, if applicable, such other person who holds an outstanding Option.

"Option Exercise Price" means the price at which a share of Common Stock may be purchased upon the exercise of an Option.

"Participant" means an eligible person to whom an Award is granted pursuant to the Plan or, if applicable, such other person who holds an outstanding Award.

"Permitted Transferee" means: (a) a member of the Optionholder's immediate family (child, stepchild, grandchild, parent, stepparent, grandparent, spouse, former spouse, sibling, niece, nephew, mother-in-law, father-in-law, son-in-law, daughter-in-law, brother-in-law, or sister-in-law, including adoptive relationships), any person sharing the Optionholder's household (other than a tenant or employee), a trust in which these persons have more than 50% of the beneficial interest, a foundation in which these persons (or the Optionholder) control the management of assets, and any other entity in which these persons (or the Optionholder) own more than 50% of the voting interests; or (b) such other transferees as may be permitted by the Committee in its sole discretion.

"Person" means any individual, entity or group (within the meaning of Section 13(d)(3) or 14(d)(2) of the Exchange Act).

"Plan" means this Tree Services, Inc. 2013 Equity Incentive Plan, as amended or as amended and restated from time to time.

"Ten Percent Shareholder" means a person who owns (or is deemed to own pursuant to Section 424(d) of the Code) stock possessing more than 10% of the total combined voting power of all classes of stock of the Company or of any of its Affiliates.

3. Administration.

3.1   Authority of Committee. The Plan shall be administered by the Committee or, in the Board's sole discretion, by the Board. Subject to the terms of the Plan, the Committee's charter and Applicable Laws, and in addition to other express powers and authorization conferred by the Plan, the Committee shall have the authority:

(a)   to construe and interpret the Plan and apply its provisions;

(b)   to promulgate, amend and rescind rules and regulations relating to the administration of the Plan;

(c)   to authorize any person to execute, on behalf of the Company, any instrument required to carry out the purposes of the Plan;

(d)   to delegate its authority to one or more officers of the Company;

(e)   to determine when Awards are to be granted under the Plan and the applicable Grant Date;

(f)   from time to time to select, subject to the limitations set forth in this Plan, those Participants to whom Awards shall be granted;

(g)   to determine the number of shares of Common Stock to be made subject to each Award;

(h)   to determine whether each Option is to be an Incentive Stock Option or a Non-qualified Stock Option;

(i)   to prescribe the terms and conditions of each Award, including, without limitation, the exercise price and medium of payment and vesting provisions, and to specify the provisions of the Award Agreement relating to such grant;

(j)   to amend any outstanding Awards, including for the purpose of modifying the time or manner of vesting, or the term of any outstanding Award; provided, however, that if any such amendment impairs a Participant's rights or increases a Participant's obligations under his or her Award or creates or increases a Participant's federal income tax liability with respect to an Award, such amendment shall also be subject to the Participant's consent;

(k)   to determine the duration and purpose of leaves of absences which may be granted to a Participant without constituting termination of their employment for purposes of the Plan, which periods shall be no shorter than 180 days;

(l)   to make decisions with respect to outstanding Awards that may become necessary upon a change in corporate control or an event that triggers anti-dilution adjustments;

(m) to interpret, administer, reconcile any inconsistency in, correct any defect in or supply any omission in the Plan and any instrument or agreement relating to, or Award granted under, the Plan; and

(n)   to exercise discretion to make any and all other determinations which it deems to be necessary or advisable for the administration of the Plan.

3.2   Acquisitions and Other Transactions. The Committee may, from time to time, assume outstanding awards granted by another entity, whether in connection with an acquisition of such other entity or otherwise, by either (i) granting an Award under the Plan in replacement of or in substitution for the award assumed by the Company, or (ii) treating the assumed award as if it had been granted under the Plan if the terms of such assumed award could be applied to an Award granted under the Plan. Such assumed award shall be permissible if the holder of the assumed award would have been eligible to be granted an Award hereunder if the other entity had applied the rules of this Plan to such grant. The Committee may also grant Awards under the Plan in settlement of or in substitution for outstanding awards or obligations to grant future awards in connection with the Company or an Affiliate acquiring another entity, an interest in another entity or an additional interest in an Affiliate whether by merger, stock purchase, asset purchase or other form of transaction.

3.3   Committee Decisions Final. All decisions made by the Committee pursuant to the provisions of the Plan shall be final and binding on the Company and the Participants, unless such decisions are determined by a court having jurisdiction to be arbitrary and capricious.

3.4   Delegation. The Committee, or if no Committee has been appointed, the Board, may delegate administration of the Plan to a committee or committees of one or more members of the Board, and the term "Committee" shall apply to any person or persons to whom such authority has been delegated. The Committee shall have the power to delegate to a subcommittee any of the administrative powers the Committee is authorized to exercise (and references in this Plan to the Board or the Committee shall thereafter be to the committee or subcommittee), subject, however, to such resolutions, not inconsistent with the provisions of the Plan, as may be adopted from time to time by the Board. The Board may abolish the Committee at any time and revest in the Board the administration of the Plan. The members of the Committee shall be appointed by and serve at the pleasure of the Board. From time to time, the Board may increase or decrease the size of the Committee, add additional members to, remove members (with or without cause) from, appoint new members in substitution therefor, and fill vacancies, however caused, in the Committee. The Committee shall act pursuant to a vote of the majority of its members or, in the case of a Committee comprised of only two members, the unanimous consent of its members, whether present or not, or by the written consent of the majority of its members and minutes shall be kept of all of its meetings and copies thereof shall be provided to the Board. Subject to the limitations prescribed by the Plan and the Board, the Committee may establish and follow such rules and regulations for the conduct of its business as it may determine to be advisable.

3.5   Committee Composition. Except as otherwise determined by the Board, the Committee shall consist solely of two or more Directors appointed to the Committee from time to time by the Board, with one such member being the Chief Executive Officer of the Company provided such person is a Director.

3.6   Indemnification. In addition to such other rights of indemnification as they may have as Directors or members of the Committee, and to the extent allowed by Applicable Laws, the Committee shall be indemnified by the Company against all expenses, including attorney's fees, actually incurred in connection with any action, suit or proceeding or in connection with any appeal therein, to which the Committee may be party by reason of any action taken or failure to act under or in connection with the Plan or any Award granted under the Plan, and against all amounts paid by the Committee in settlement thereof (provided, however, that the settlement has been approved by the Company, which approval shall not be unreasonably withheld) or paid by the Committee in satisfaction of a judgment in any such action, suit or proceeding, except in relation to matters as to which it shall be adjudged in such action, suit or proceeding that such Committee did not act in good faith and in a manner which such person reasonably believed to be in the best interests of the Company, or in the case of a criminal proceeding, had no reason to believe that the conduct complained of was unlawful; provided, however, that within 60 days after institution of any such action, suit or proceeding, such Committee shall, in writing, offer the Company the opportunity at its own expense to handle and defend such action, suit or proceeding.

4.   Shares Subject to the Plan.

4.1   Subject to adjustment in accordance with Section 10, a total of 1,000,000 shares of Common Stock shall be available for the grant of Awards under the Plan; provided that, no more than 250,000 shares of Common Stock may be granted as Incentive Stock Options. During the terms of the Awards, the Company shall keep available at all times the number of shares of Common Stock required to satisfy such Awards.

4.2   Shares of Common Stock available for distribution under the Plan may consist, in whole or in part, of authorized and unissued shares or treasury shares.

4.3   Any shares of Common Stock subject to an Award that is canceled, forfeited or expires prior to exercise or realization, either in full or in part, shall again become available for issuance under the Plan. Notwithstanding anything to the contrary contained herein: shares subject to an Award under the Plan shall not again be made available for issuance or delivery under the Plan if such shares are (a) shares tendered in payment of an Option or (b) shares delivered or withheld by the Company to satisfy any tax withholding obligation.

4.4   If the Committee authorizes the assumption of awards pursuant to Section 3.2 or Section 11.1 hereof, the assumption will reduce the number of shares available for issuance under the Plan in the same manner as if the assumed awards had been granted under the Plan.

5.   Eligibility.

5.1   Eligibility for Specific Awards. Incentive Stock Options may be granted to Employees only. Awards other than Incentive Stock Options may be granted to Employees, Consultants and Directors.

5.2   Ten Percent Shareholders. A Ten Percent Shareholder shall not be granted an Incentive Stock Option unless the Option Exercise Price is at least 110% of the Fair Market Value of the Common Stock at the Grant Date and the Option is not exercisable after the expiration of five years from the Grant Date.

6. Option Provisions.

Each Option granted under the Plan shall be evidenced by an Award Agreement. Each Option so granted shall be subject to the conditions set forth in this Section 6, and to such other conditions not inconsistent with the Plan as may be reflected in the applicable Award Agreement. All Options shall be separately designated Incentive Stock Options or Non-qualified Stock Options at the time of grant, and, if certificates are issued, a separate certificate or certificates will be issued for shares of Common Stock purchased on exercise of each type of Option. Notwithstanding the foregoing, the Company shall have no liability to any Participant or any other person if an Option designated as an Incentive Stock Option fails to qualify as such at any time or if an Option is determined to constitute "nonqualified deferred compensation" within the meaning of Section 409A of the Code and the terms of such Option do not satisfy the requirements of Section 409A of the Code. The provisions of separate Options need not be identical, but each Option shall include (through incorporation of provisions hereof by reference in the Option or otherwise) the substance of each of the following provisions:

6.1   Term. Subject to the provisions of Section 5.2 regarding Ten Percent Shareholders, no Incentive Stock Option shall be exercisable after the expiration of 20 years from the Grant Date. The term of a Non-qualified Stock Option granted under the Plan shall be determined by the Committee; provided, however, no Non-qualified Stock Option shall be exercisable after the expiration of 20 years from the Grant Date.

6.2   Exercise Price of an Incentive Stock Option. Subject to the provisions of Section 5.2 regarding Ten Percent Shareholders, the Option Exercise Price of each Incentive Stock Option shall be not less than 100% of the Fair Market Value of the Common Stock subject to the Option on the Grant Date. Notwithstanding the foregoing, an Incentive Stock Option may be granted with an Option Exercise Price lower than that set forth in the preceding sentence if such Option is granted pursuant to an assumption or substitution for another option in a manner satisfying the provisions of Section 424(a) of the Code.

6.3   Exercise Price of a Non-qualified Stock Option. The Option Exercise Price of each Non-qualified Stock Option shall be not less than 100% of the Fair Market Value of the Common Stock subject to the Option on the Grant Date. Notwithstanding the foregoing, a Non-qualified Stock Option may be granted with an Option Exercise Price lower than that set forth in the preceding sentence if such Option is granted pursuant to an assumption or substitution for another option in a manner satisfying the provisions of Section 409A of the Code.

6.4   Method of Exercise. The Option Exercise Price shall be paid, to the extent permitted by Applicable Laws, either (a) in cash or by certified or bank check at the time the Option is exercised or (b) in the discretion of the Committee, upon such terms as the Committee shall approve: (i) by delivery to the Company of other shares of Common Stock, duly endorsed for transfer to the Company, with a Fair Market Value on the date of delivery equal to the Option Exercise Price (or portion thereof) due for the number of shares being acquired; (ii) by a "net exercise" procedure effected by withholding the minimum number of shares of Common Stock otherwise issuable in respect of an Option that are needed to pay the Option Exercise Price; (iii) by any combination of the foregoing methods; or (iv) in any other form of legal consideration that may be acceptable to the Committee. Unless otherwise specifically provided in the Option, the Option Exercise Price that is paid by delivery to the Company of other Common Stock acquired, directly or indirectly from the Company, shall be paid only by shares of Common Stock that have been held for more than six months (or such longer or shorter period of time required to avoid a charge to earnings for financial accounting purposes).

6.5   Transferability of an Incentive Stock Option. An Incentive Stock Option shall not be transferable except by will or by the laws of descent and distribution and shall be exercisable during the lifetime of the Optionholder only by the Optionholder. Notwithstanding the foregoing, the Optionholder may, by delivering written notice to the Company, in a form satisfactory to the Company, designate a third party who, in the event of the death of the Optionholder, shall thereafter be entitled to exercise the Option.

6.6 <u>Transferability of a Non-qualified Stock Option</u>. A Non-qualified Stock Option may, in the sole discretion of the Committee, be transferable to a Permitted Transferee, upon written approval by the Committee to the extent provided in the Award Agreement. If the Non-qualified Stock Option does not provide for transferability, then the Non-qualified Stock Option shall not be transferable except by will or by the laws of descent and distribution and shall be exercisable during the lifetime of the Optionholder only by the Optionholder. Notwithstanding the foregoing, the Optionholder may, by delivering written notice to the Company, in a form satisfactory to the Company, designate a third party who, in the event of the death of the Optionholder, shall thereafter be entitled to exercise the Option.

6.7 <u>Vesting of Options</u>. Each Option may, but need not, vest and therefore become exercisable in periodic installments that may, but need not, be equal. The Option may be subject to such other terms and conditions on the time or times when it may be exercised (which may be based on performance or other criteria) as the Committee may deem appropriate. The vesting provisions of individual Options may vary. No Option may be exercised for a fraction of a share of Common Stock. The Committee may, but shall not be required to, provide for an acceleration of vesting and exercisability in the terms of any Award Agreement upon the occurrence of a specified event.

6.8 <u>Termination of Continuous Service</u>. Unless otherwise provided in an Award Agreement or in an employment agreement the terms of which have been approved by the Committee, in the event an Optionholder's Continuous Service terminates (other than upon the Optionholder's death or Disability), the Optionholder may exercise his or her Option (to the extent that the Optionholder was entitled to exercise such Option as of the date of termination) but only within such period of time ending on the earlier of (a) the date 12 months following the termination of the Optionholder's Continuous Service or (b) the expiration of the term of the Option as set forth in the Award Agreement; provided that, if the termination of Continuous Service is by the Company for Cause, all outstanding Options (whether or not vested) shall immediately terminate and cease to be exercisable. If, after termination, the Optionholder does not exercise his or her Option within the time specified in the Award Agreement, the Option shall terminate.

6.9 <u>Disability of Optionholder</u>. Unless otherwise provided in an Award Agreement, in the event that an Optionholder's Continuous Service terminates as a result of the Optionholder's Disability, the Optionholder may exercise his or her Option (to the extent that the Optionholder was entitled to exercise such Option as of the date of termination), but only within such period of time ending on the earlier of (a) the date 24 months following such termination or (b) the expiration of the term of the Option as set forth in the Award Agreement. If, after termination, the Optionholder does not exercise his or her Option within the time specified herein or in the Award Agreement, the Option shall terminate.

6.10 <u>Death of Optionholder</u>. Unless otherwise provided in an Award Agreement, in the event an Optionholder's Continuous Service terminates as a result of the Optionholder's death, then the Option may be exercised (to the extent the Optionholder was entitled to exercise such Option as of the date of death) by the Optionholder's estate, by a person who acquired the right to exercise the Option by bequest or inheritance or by a person designated to exercise the Option upon the Optionholder's death, but only within the period ending on the earlier of (a) the date 24 months following the date of death or (b) the expiration of the term of such Option as set forth in the Award Agreement. If, after the Optionholder's death, the Option is not exercised within the time specified herein or in the Award Agreement, the Option shall terminate.

6.11   Incentive Stock Option $100,000 Limitation. To the extent that the aggregate Fair Market Value (determined at the time of grant) of Common Stock with respect to which Incentive Stock Options are exercisable for the first time by any Optionholder during any calendar year (under all plans of the Company and its Affiliates) exceeds $100,000, the Options or portions thereof which exceed such limit (according to the order in which they were granted) shall be treated as Non-qualified Stock Options.

6.12   Detrimental Activity. Unless otherwise provided in an Award Agreement, all outstanding Options (whether or not vested) shall immediately terminate and cease to be exercisable on the date on which an Optionholder engages in Detrimental Activity.

7.   Securities Law Compliance.

7.1   Securities Registration. No Awards shall be granted under the Plan and no shares of Common Stock shall be issued and delivered upon the exercise of Options granted under the Plan unless and until the Company or the Participant or both have complied with all applicable federal and state registration, listing and qualification requirements and all other requirements of law or of any regulatory agencies having jurisdiction.

7.2   Representations; Legends. The Committee may, as a condition to the grant of any Award or the exercise of any Option under the Plan, require a Participant to (i) represent in writing that the shares of Common Stock received in connection with such Award are being acquired for investment and not with a view to distribution and (ii) make such other representations and warranties as are deemed appropriate by counsel to the Company. Each certificate representing shares of Common Stock acquired under the Plan shall bear a legend in such form as the Company deems appropriate.

8.   Use of Proceeds from Stock.

Proceeds from the sale of Common Stock pursuant to Awards, or upon exercise thereof, shall constitute general funds of the Company.

9.   Miscellaneous.

9.1   Acceleration of Exercisability and Vesting. The Committee shall have the power to accelerate the time at which an Award may first be exercised or the time during which an Award or any part thereof will vest in accordance with the Plan, notwithstanding the provisions in the Award stating the time at which it may first be exercised or the time during which it will vest.

9.2   Shareholder Rights. Except as provided in the Plan or an Award Agreement, no Participant shall be deemed to be the holder of, or to have any of the rights of a holder with respect to, any shares of Common Stock subject to an Award unless and until such Participant has satisfied all requirements for exercise or settlement of the Award pursuant to its terms and no adjustment shall be made for dividends (ordinary or extraordinary, whether in cash, securities or other property) or distributions of other rights for which the record date is prior to the date such Common Stock certificate is issued, except as provided in Section 10 hereof.

9.3   No Employment or Other Service Rights. Nothing in the Plan or any instrument executed or Award granted pursuant thereto shall confer upon any Participant any right to continue to serve the Company or an Affiliate in the capacity in effect at the time the Award was granted or shall affect the right of the Company or an Affiliate to terminate (a) the employment of an Employee with or without notice and with or without Cause or (b) the service of a Director pursuant to the Bylaws of the Company or an Affiliate, and any applicable provisions of the corporate law of the state in which the Company or the Affiliate is incorporated, as the case may be.

9.4   Transfer; Approved Leave of Absence. For purposes of the Plan, no termination of employment by an Employee shall be deemed to result from either (a) a transfer of employment to the Company from an Affiliate or from the Company to an Affiliate, or from one Affiliate to another, or (b) an approved leave of absence for military service or sickness, or for any other purpose approved by the Company, if the Employee's right to reemployment is guaranteed either by a statute or by contract or under the policy pursuant to which the leave of absence was granted or if the Committee otherwise so provides in writing, in either case, except to the extent inconsistent with Section 409A of the Code if the applicable Award is subject thereto.

9.5   Withholding Obligations. To the extent provided by the terms of an Award Agreement and subject to the discretion of the Committee, the Participant may satisfy any federal, state or local tax withholding obligation relating to the exercise or acquisition of Common Stock under an Award by any of the following means (in addition to the Company's right to withhold from any compensation paid to the Participant by the Company) or by a combination of such means: (a) tendering a cash payment; (b) authorizing the Company to withhold shares of Common Stock from the shares of Common Stock otherwise issuable to the Participant as a result of the exercise or acquisition of Common Stock under the Award, provided, however, that no shares of Common Stock are withheld with a value exceeding the minimum amount of tax required to be withheld by law; or (c) delivering to the Company previously owned and unencumbered shares of Common Stock of the Company.

10. Adjustments Upon Changes in Stock.

In the event of changes in the outstanding Common Stock or in the capital structure of the Company by reason of any stock or extraordinary cash dividend, stock split, reverse stock split, an extraordinary corporate transaction such as any recapitalization, reorganization, merger, consolidation, combination, exchange, or other relevant change in capitalization occurring after the Grant Date of any Award, Awards granted under the Plan and any Award Agreements, the exercise price of Options and the maximum number of shares of Common Stock subject to Awards stated in Section 4 will be equitably adjusted or substituted, as to the number, price or kind of a share of Common Stock or other consideration subject to such Awards to the extent necessary to preserve the economic intent of such Award. In the case of adjustments made pursuant to this Section 10, unless the Committee specifically determines that such adjustment is in the best interests of the Company or its Affiliates, the Committee shall, in the case of Incentive Stock Options, ensure that any adjustments under this Section 10 will not constitute a modification, extension or renewal of the Incentive Stock Options within the meaning of Section 424(h)(3) of the Code and in the case of Non-qualified Stock Options, ensure that any adjustments under this Section 10 will not constitute a modification of such Non-qualified Stock Options within the meaning of Section 409A of the Code.

11. Effect of Change in Control.

11.1   In the event of a Change in Control, all Awards shall automatically accelerate and vest and all restrictions shall lapse with respect to all or any portion of any Award.

11.2   The obligations of the Company under the Plan shall be binding upon any successor corporation or organization resulting from the merger, consolidation or other reorganization of the Company, or upon any successor corporation or organization succeeding to all or substantially all of the assets and business of the Company and its Affiliates, taken as a whole.

12. Amendment of the Plan and Awards.

12.1   Amendment of the Plan. The Board at any time, and from time to time, may amend or terminate the Plan. However, except as provided in Section 10 relating to adjustments upon changes in Common Stock and Section 12.3, no amendment shall be effective unless approved by the shareholders of the Company to the extent shareholder approval is necessary to satisfy any Applicable Laws. At the time of such amendment, the Board shall determine, upon advice from counsel, whether such amendment will be contingent on shareholder approval.

12.2   Shareholder Approval. The Board may, in its sole discretion, submit any other amendment to the Plan for shareholder approval.

12.3   Contemplated Amendments. It is expressly contemplated that the Board may amend the Plan in any respect the Board deems necessary or advisable to provide eligible Employees, Consultants and Directors with the maximum benefits provided or to be provided under the provisions of the Code and the regulations promulgated thereunder relating to Incentive Stock Options or to the nonqualified deferred compensation provisions of Section 409A of the Code or to bring the Plan or Awards granted under it into compliance therewith.

12.4   No Impairment of Rights. Rights under any Award granted before amendment of the Plan shall not be impaired by any amendment of the Plan unless (a) the Company requests the consent of the Participant and (b) the Participant consents in writing.

12.5   Amendment of Awards. The Committee at any time, and from time to time, may amend the terms of any one or more Awards; provided, however, that the Committee may not affect any amendment which would otherwise constitute an impairment of the rights under any Award unless (a) the Company requests the consent of the Participant and (b) the Participant consents in writing.

13. General Provisions.

13.1   Clawback; Forfeiture. Notwithstanding anything to the contrary contained herein, the Committee may, in its sole discretion, provide in an Award Agreement or otherwise that the Committee may cancel such Award if the Participant has engaged in or engages in any Detrimental Activity. The Committee may, in its sole discretion, also provide in an Award Agreement or otherwise that (i) if the Participant has engaged in or engages in Detrimental Activity, the Participant will forfeit any gain realized on the vesting, exercise or settlement of any Award, and must repay the gain to the Company and (ii) if the Participant receives any amount in excess of what the Participant should have received under the terms of the Award for any reason (including, without limitation, by reason of a financial restatement, mistake in calculations or other administrative error), then the Participant shall be required to repay any such excess amount to the Company. Without limiting the foregoing, all Awards shall be subject to reduction, cancellation, forfeiture or recoupment to the extent necessary to comply with Applicable Laws.

13.2   Sub-plans. The Committee may from time to time establish sub-plans under the Plan for purposes of satisfying blue sky, securities, tax or other laws of various jurisdictions in which the Company intends to grant Awards. Any sub-plans shall contain such limitations and other terms and conditions as the Committee determines are necessary or desirable. All sub-plans shall be deemed a part of the Plan, but each sub-plan shall apply only to the Participants in the jurisdiction for which the sub-plan was designed.

13.3   Unfunded Plan. The Plan shall be unfunded. Neither the Company, the Board nor the Committee shall be required to establish any special or separate fund or to segregate any assets to assure the performance of its obligations under the Plan.

13.4   Recapitalizations. Each Award Agreement shall contain provisions required to reflect the provisions of Section 10.

13.5   Delivery. Upon exercise of a right granted under this Plan, the Company shall issue Common Stock or pay any amounts due within a reasonable period of time thereafter. Subject to any statutory or regulatory obligations the Company may otherwise have, for purposes of this Plan, 30 days shall be considered a reasonable period of time.

13.6   No Fractional Shares. No fractional shares of Common Stock shall be issued or delivered pursuant to the Plan. The Committee shall determine whether cash, additional Awards or other securities or property shall be issued or paid in lieu of fractional shares of Common Stock or whether any fractional shares should be rounded, forfeited or otherwise eliminated.

13.7   Other Provisions. The Award Agreements authorized under the Plan may contain such other provisions not inconsistent with this Plan, including, without limitation, restrictions upon the exercise of the Awards, as the Committee may deem advisable.

13.8   Section 409A. The Plan is intended to comply with Section 409A of the Code to the extent subject thereto, and, accordingly, to the maximum extent permitted, the Plan shall be interpreted and administered to be in compliance therewith. Any payments described in the Plan that are due within the "short-term deferral period" as defined in Section 409A of the Code shall not be treated as deferred compensation unless Applicable Laws require otherwise. Notwithstanding anything to the contrary in the Plan, to the extent required to avoid accelerated taxation and tax penalties under Section 409A of the Code, amounts that would otherwise be payable and benefits that would otherwise be provided pursuant to the Plan during the six (6) month period immediately following the Participant's termination of Continuous Service shall instead be paid on the first payroll date after the six-month anniversary of the Participant's separation from service (or the Participant's death, if earlier). Notwithstanding the foregoing, neither the Company nor the Committee shall have any obligation to take any action to prevent the assessment of any additional tax or penalty on any Participant under Section 409A of the Code and neither the Company nor the Committee will have any liability to any Participant for such tax or penalty.

13.9   Disqualifying Dispositions. Any Participant who shall make a "disposition" (as defined in Section 424 of the Code) of all or any portion of shares of Common Stock acquired upon exercise of an Incentive Stock Option within two years from the Grant Date of such Incentive Stock Option or within one year after the issuance of the shares of Common Stock acquired upon exercise of such Incentive Stock Option (a "Disqualifying Disposition") shall be required to immediately advise the Company in writing as to the occurrence of the sale and the price realized upon the sale of such shares of Common Stock.

13.10   Beneficiary Designation. Each Participant under the Plan may from time to time name any beneficiary or beneficiaries by whom any right under the Plan is to be exercised in case of such Participant's death. Each designation will revoke all prior designations by the same Participant, shall be in a form reasonably prescribed by the Committee and shall be effective only when filed by the Participant in writing with the Company during the Participant's lifetime.

13.11   Expenses. The costs of administering the Plan shall be paid by the Company.

13.12   Severability. If any of the provisions of the Plan or any Award Agreement is held to be invalid, illegal or unenforceable, whether in whole or in part, such provision shall be deemed modified to the extent, but only to the extent, of such invalidity, illegality or unenforceability and the remaining provisions shall not be affected thereby.

13.13   Plan Headings. The headings in the Plan are for purposes of convenience only and are not intended to define or limit the construction of the provisions hereof.

13.14   Non-Uniform Treatment. The Committee's determinations under the Plan need not be uniform and may be made by it selectively among persons who are eligible to receive, or actually receive, Awards. Without limiting the generality of the foregoing, the Committee shall be entitled to make non-uniform and selective determinations, amendments and adjustments, and to enter into non-uniform and selective Award Agreements.

14. Termination or Suspension of the Plan.

The Board may suspend or terminate the Plan at any time. No Awards may be granted under the Plan while the Plan is suspended or after it is terminated.

15. Choice of Law.

The law of the State of Colorado shall govern all questions concerning the construction, validity and interpretation of this Plan, without regard to such state's conflict of law rules.

As adopted by the Board of Directors of Tree Services, Inc. on March 10, 2013.

As approved by the shareholders of Tree Services, Inc. on March 11, 2013.

5.   **Customer Relationship Management Software License Agreement**

Customer Relationship Management Software License Agreement

This Customer Relationship Management Software License Agreement (the "Agreement"), effective as of June 10, 2017 (the "Effective Date"), is by and between CRM Suiteware, Inc., a Delaware corporation with offices located at 10000 Technology Road, Westminster, CO 80003 ("Licensor") and Tree Services, Inc., a Colorado corporation with offices located at 6789 120th Street, Commerce City, CO 80022 ("Licensee"). Licensor and Licensee may be referred to herein collectively as the "Parties" or individually as a "Party."

Recitals

A.   Licensor desires to license the Software described in Exhibit A and attached hereto to Licensee; and

B.   Licensee desires to obtain a license to use the Software for its internal business purposes, subject to the terms and conditions of this Agreement.

NOW, THEREFORE, in consideration of the mutual covenants, terms, and conditions set forth herein, and for other good and valuable consideration, the Parties agree as follows:

1.   Definitions.

(a)   "Authorized User" means an employee or contractor of Licensee who Licensee permits to access and use the Software and Documentation pursuant to Licensee's license hereunder.

(b)   "Documentation" means Licensor's user manuals, handbooks, and installation guides relating to the Software provided by Licensor to Licensee either electronically or in hard copy form or end user documentation relating to the Software available at www.crmsuiteware.com.

(c)   "Software" means the product described in Exhibit A in object code format, including any Updates provided to Licensee pursuant to this Agreement.

(d)   "Updates" means any updates, bug fixes, patches, or other error corrections to the Software that Licensor generally makes available free of charge to all licensees of the Software.

2.   License.

(a)   <u>License Grant</u>. Subject to and conditioned on Licensee's payment of the Fees set forth in Section 5 and compliance with all the terms and conditions of this Agreement, Licensor hereby grants Licensee a non-exclusive, non-sublicensable, and non-transferable (except in compliance with Section 12(g)) license during the Term (as defined in Section 11(a)) to: (i) use the Software solely for Licensee's internal business purposes up to the number of Authorized Users set forth in Exhibit A; and (ii) use and make a reasonable number of copies of the Documentation solely for Licensee's internal business purposes in connection with Licensee's use of the Software. The total number of Authorized Users will not exceed the number set forth in Exhibit A, except as expressly agreed to in writing by the Parties and subject to any appropriate adjustment of the Fees payable hereunder. Licensee may make one copy of the Software, with Licensor's prior written consent, solely for back-up, disaster recovery, and testing purposes. Any such copy of the Software: (x) remains Licensor's exclusive property; (y) is subject to the terms and conditions of this Agreement; and (z) must include all copyright or other proprietary rights notices contained in the original.

(b)   <u>Use Restrictions</u>. Licensee shall not use the Software or Documentation for any purposes beyond the scope of the license granted in this Agreement. Without limiting the foregoing and except as otherwise expressly set forth in this Agreement, Licensee shall not at any time, directly or indirectly: (i) copy, modify, or create derivative works of the Software or the Documentation, in whole or in part; (ii) rent, lease, lend, sell, sublicense, assign, distribute, publish, transfer, or otherwise make available the Software or the Documentation; (iii) reverse engineer, disassemble, decompile, decode, adapt, or otherwise attempt to derive or gain access to the source code of the Software, in whole or in part; (iv) remove any proprietary notices from the Software or the Documentation; or (v) use the Software in any manner or for any purpose that infringes, misappropriates, or otherwise violates any intellectual property right or other right of any person, or that violates any applicable law.

(c) <u>Reservation of Rights</u>. Licensor reserves all rights not expressly granted to Licensee in this Agreement. Except for the limited rights and licenses expressly granted under this Agreement, nothing in this Agreement grants, by implication, waiver, estoppel, or otherwise, to Licensee or any third party any intellectual property rights or other right, title, or interest in or to the Software.

(d) <u>Delivery</u>. Licensor shall deliver the Software electronically, on tangible media, or by other means, as determined in Licensor's sole discretion, to Licensee within ten days following the Effective Date. Risk of loss of any tangible media on which the Software is delivered will pass to Licensee on delivery to carrier.

3. Licensee Responsibilities.

(a) <u>General</u>. Licensee is responsible and liable for all uses of the Software and Documentation resulting from access provided by Licensee, directly or indirectly, whether such access or use is permitted by or in violation of this Agreement. Without limiting the generality of the foregoing, Licensee is responsible for all acts and omissions of Authorized Users (or any unauthorized user if Licensee had knowledge of such unauthorized user), and any act or omission by an Authorized User (or any unauthorized user if Licensee had knowledge of such unauthorized user) that would constitute a breach of this Agreement if taken by Licensee will be deemed a breach of this Agreement by Licensee. Licensee shall take reasonable efforts to make all Authorized Users aware of this Agreement's provisions as applicable to such Authorized User's use of the Software, and shall cause Authorized Users to comply with such provisions.

4. Support.

Licensor shall provide Licensee with the support services described from time to time on Licensor's website located at www.crmsuiteware.com for sixty days following the Effective Date and thereafter, solely if Licensee purchases additional support services.

5. Fees and Payment.

(a) <u>Fees</u>. Licensee shall pay Licensor the fees ("Fees") set forth in Exhibit A without offset or deduction. Licensee shall make all payments hereunder in US dollars on or before the due date set forth in Exhibit A. If Licensee fails to make any payment when due, in addition to all other remedies that may be available: (i) Licensor may charge interest on the past due amount at the rate of 1.5% per month calculated daily and compounded monthly or, if lower, the highest rate permitted under applicable law; (ii) Licensee shall reimburse Licensor for all costs incurred by Licensor in collecting any late payments or interest, including attorneys' fees, court costs, and collection agency fees; and (iii) if such failure continues for three days following written notice thereof, Licensor may prohibit access to the Software until all past due amounts and interest thereon have been paid in full, without incurring any obligation or liability to Licensee or any other person by reason of such prohibition of access to the Software.

(b) <u>Taxes</u>. All Fees and other amounts payable by Licensee under this Agreement are exclusive of taxes and similar assessments. Licensee is responsible for all sales, use, and excise taxes, and any other similar taxes, duties, and charges of any kind imposed by any federal, state, or local governmental or regulatory authority on any amounts payable by Licensee hereunder, other than any taxes imposed on Licensor's income.

(c) <u>Auditing Rights and Required Records</u>. Licensee agrees to maintain complete and accurate records in accordance with generally accepted accounting principles during the Term and for a period of five years after the termination or expiration of this Agreement with respect to the matters necessary for accurately determining amounts due hereunder. Licensor may, at its own expense, on reasonable prior notice, periodically inspect and audit Licensee's records with respect to the matters covered by this Agreement, provided that if such inspection and audit reveals that Licensee has underpaid Licensor with respect to any amounts due and payable during the Term, Licensee shall promptly pay the amounts necessary to rectify such underpayment, together with interest in accordance with Section 5(a). Licensee shall pay for the costs of the audit if the audit determines that Licensee underpaid for any month. Such inspection and auditing rights will extend throughout the Term of this Agreement and continue for a period of five years after the termination or expiration of this Agreement.

6. Confidential Information.

From time to time during the Term, either Party may disclose or make available to the other Party information about its business affairs, products, confidential intellectual property, trade secrets, third-party confidential information, and other sensitive or proprietary information, whether orally or in written, electronic, or other form or media, and whether or not marked, designated or otherwise identified as "confidential" (collectively, "Confidential Information"). Confidential Information does not include information that at the time of disclosure is: (a) in the public domain; (b) known to the receiving Party at the time of disclosure; (c) rightfully obtained by the receiving Party on a non-confidential basis from a third party; or (d) independently developed by the receiving Party. The receiving Party shall not disclose the disclosing Party's Confidential Information to any person or entity, except to the receiving Party's employees who have a need to know the Confidential Information for the receiving Party to exercise its rights or perform its obligations hereunder. Notwithstanding the foregoing, each Party may disclose Confidential Information to the limited extent required (i) in order to comply with the order of a court or other governmental body, or as otherwise necessary to comply with applicable law, provided that the Party making the disclosure pursuant to the order shall first have given written notice to the other Party and make a reasonable effort to obtain a protective order; or (ii) to establish a Party's rights under this Agreement, including to make required court filings. On the expiration or termination of this Agreement, the receiving Party shall promptly return to the disclosing Party all copies, whether in written, electronic, or other form or media, of the disclosing Party's Confidential Information, or destroy all such copies and certify in writing to the disclosing Party that such Confidential Information has been destroyed. The Licensee's obligations of non-disclosure with regard to Licensor's Confidential Information are effective as of the Effective Date and will expire five years from the date first disclosed to the Licensee, and the Licensor's obligations of non-disclosure with regard to Licensee's Confidential Information are effective as of the Effective Date and will expire one year from the date first disclosed to the Licensor; provided, however, with respect to any Confidential Information that constitutes a trade secret (as determined under applicable law), such obligations of non-disclosure will survive the termination or expiration of this Agreement for as long as such Confidential Information remains subject to trade secret protection under applicable law.

7. Intellectual Property Ownership; Feedback.

(a) <u>Intellectual Property Ownership</u>. Licensee acknowledges that, as between Licensee and Licensor, Licensor owns all right, title, and interest, including all intellectual property rights, in and to the Software and Documentation.

(b) <u>Feedback</u>. If Licensee or any of its employees or contractors sends or transmits any communications or materials to Licensor by mail, email, telephone, or otherwise, suggesting or recommending changes to the Software or Documentation, including without limitation, new features or functionality relating thereto, or any comments, questions, suggestions, or the like ("Feedback"), Licensor is free to use such Feedback irrespective of any other obligation or limitation between the Parties governing such Feedback. Licensee hereby assigns to Licensor on Licensee's behalf, and on behalf of its employees, contractors and agents, all right, title, and interest in, and Licensor is free to use, without any attribution or compensation to any party, any ideas, know-how, concepts, techniques, or other intellectual property rights contained in the Feedback, for any purpose whatsoever, although Licensor is not required to use any Feedback.

8. Limited Warranties and Warranty Disclaimer.

(a) Licensor warrants that: (i) the Software will perform materially as described in the specifications available at www.crmsuiteware.com for a period of one hundred twenty days following the Effective Date; and (ii) at the time of delivery the Software does not contain any virus or other malicious code.

(b) The warranties set forth in Section 8(a) do not apply and become null and void if Licensee breaches any provision of this Agreement, or if Licensee, any Authorized User (or any unauthorized user if Licensee had knowledge of such unauthorized user), or any other person provided access to the Software by Licensee or any Authorized User, whether or not in violation of this Agreement: (i) installs or uses the Software on or in connection with any hardware or software not specified in the Documentation or expressly authorized by Licensor in writing; (ii) modifies or damages the Software; or (iii) misuses the Software, including any use of the Software other than as specified in the Documentation.

(c) If, during the period specified in Section 8(a), any Software fails to comply with the warranty in Section 8(a), and such failure is not excluded from warranty pursuant to Section 8(b), Licensor shall, subject to Licensee's promptly notifying Licensor in writing of such failure, at its sole option, either: (i) repair or replace the Software, provided that Licensee provides Licensor with all information Licensor requests to resolve the reported failure, including sufficient information to enable the Licensor to recreate such failure; or (ii) refund the Fees paid for such Software, subject to Licensee's ceasing all use of and, if requested by Licensor, returning to Licensor all copies of the Software. If Licensor repairs or replaces the Software, the warranty will continue to run from the Effective Date and not from Licensee's receipt of the repair or replacement Software. The remedies set forth in this Section 8(c) are Licensee's sole remedies and Licensor's sole liability under the limited warranty set forth in Section 8(a).

(d) EXCEPT FOR THE LIMITED WARRANTY SET FORTH IN SECTION 8(a), THE SOFTWARE AND DOCUMENTATION ARE PROVIDED "AS IS" AND LICENSOR HEREBY DISCLAIMS ALL WARRANTIES, WHETHER EXPRESS, IMPLIED, STATUTORY, OR OTHERWISE. LICENSOR SPECIFICALLY DISCLAIMS ALL IMPLIED WARRANTIES OF MERCHANTABILITY, FITNESS FOR A PARTICULAR PURPOSE, TITLE, AND NON-INFRINGEMENT, AND ALL WARRANTIES ARISING FROM COURSE OF DEALING, USAGE, OR TRADE PRACTICE. EXCEPT FOR THE LIMITED WARRANTY SET FORTH IN SECTION 8(a), LICENSOR MAKES NO WARRANTY OF ANY KIND THAT THE SOFTWARE AND DOCUMENTATION, OR ANY PRODUCTS OR RESULTS OF THE USE THEREOF, WILL MEET LICENSEE'S OR ANY OTHER PERSON'S REQUIREMENTS, OPERATE WITHOUT INTERRUPTION, ACHIEVE ANY INTENDED RESULT, BE COMPATIBLE OR WORK WITH ANY SOFTWARE, SYSTEM OR OTHER SERVICES, OR BE SECURE, ACCURATE, COMPLETE, FREE OF HARMFUL CODE, OR ERROR FREE.

9. Indemnification.

(a) <u>Licensor Indemnification</u>.

(i) Licensor shall indemnify, defend, and hold harmless Licensee from and against any and all losses, damages, liabilities, and costs ("Losses") incurred by Licensee resulting from any third-party claim, suit, action, or proceeding ("Third-Party Claim") that the Software or Documentation, or any use of the Software or Documentation in accordance with this Agreement, infringes or misappropriates such third party's US intellectual property rights, provided that Licensee promptly notifies Licensor in writing of the claim, cooperates with Licensor, and allows Licensor sole authority to control the defense and settlement of such claim.

(ii) If such a claim is made or appears possible, Licensee agrees to permit Licensor, at Licensor's sole discretion, to (A) modify or replace the Software or Documentation, or component or part thereof, to make it non-infringing, or (B) obtain the right for Licensee to continue use. If Licensor determines that none of these alternatives is reasonably available, Licensor may terminate this Agreement in its entirety or with respect to the affected component or part, effective immediately on written notice to Licensee.

(iii) This Section 9(a) will not apply to the extent that the alleged infringement arises from: (A) use of the Software in combination with data, software, hardware, equipment, or technology not provided by Licensor or authorized by Licensor in writing; (B) modifications to the Software not made by Licensor; or (C) use of any version other than the most current version of the Software or Documentation delivered to Licensee.

(b) <u>Licensee Indemnification</u>. Licensee shall indemnify, hold harmless, and, at Licensor's option, defend Licensor from and against any Losses resulting from any Third-Party Claim based on Licensee's, or any Authorized User's (or any unauthorized user if Licensee had knowledge of such unauthorized user): (i) negligence or willful misconduct; (ii) use of the Software or Documentation in a manner not authorized or contemplated by this Agreement; (iii) use of the Software in combination with data, software, hardware, equipment or technology not provided by Licensor or authorized by Licensor in writing; (iv) modifications to the Software not made by Licensor; or (v) use of any version other than the most current version of the Software or Documentation delivered to Licensee, provided that Licensee may not settle any Third-Party Claim against Licensor unless such settlement completely and forever releases Licensor from all liability with respect to such Third-Party Claim or unless Licensor consents to such settlement in Licensor's sole and absolute discretion, and further provided that Licensor will have the right, at its option, to defend itself against any such Third-Party Claim or to participate in the defense thereof by counsel of its own choice and Licensee shall pay the reasonably costs and expenses of Licensor's counsel.

(c) <u>Sole Remedy</u>. THIS SECTION 9 SETS FORTH LICENSEE'S SOLE REMEDIES AND LICENSOR'S SOLE LIABILITY AND OBLIGATION FOR ANY ACTUAL, THREATENED, OR ALLEGED CLAIMS THAT THE SOFTWARE OR DOCUMENTATION INFRINGES, MISAPPROPRIATES, OR OTHERWISE VIOLATES ANY INTELLECTUAL PROPERTY RIGHTS OF ANY THIRD PARTY. IN NO EVENT WILL LICENSOR'S LIABILITY UNDER THIS SECTION 9 EXCEED $25,000.

10. Limitations of Liability.

IN NO EVENT WILL LICENSOR BE LIABLE UNDER OR IN CONNECTION WITH THIS AGREEMENT UNDER ANY LEGAL OR EQUITABLE THEORY, INCLUDING BREACH OF CONTRACT, TORT INCLUDING NEGLIGENCE, STRICT LIABILITY, AND OTHERWISE, FOR ANY: (a) CONSEQUENTIAL, INCIDENTAL, INDIRECT, EXEMPLARY, SPECIAL, ENHANCED, OR PUNITIVE DAMAGES; (b) INCREASED COSTS, DIMINUTION IN VALUE OR LOST BUSINESS, PRODUCTION, REVENUES, OR PROFITS; (c) LOSS OF GOODWILL OR

REPUTATION; (d) USE, INABILITY TO USE, LOSS, INTERRUPTION, DELAY OR RECOVERY OF ANY DATA, OR BREACH OF DATA OR SYSTEM SECURITY; OR (e) COST OF REPLACEMENT GOODS OR SERVICES, IN EACH CASE REGARDLESS OF WHETHER LICENSOR WAS ADVISED OF THE POSSIBILITY OF SUCH LOSSES OR DAMAGES OR SUCH LOSSES OR DAMAGES WERE OTHERWISE FORESEEABLE. IN NO EVENT WILL LICENSOR'S AGGREGATE LIABILITY ARISING OUT OF OR RELATED TO THIS AGREEMENT UNDER ANY LEGAL OR EQUITABLE THEORY, INCLUDING BREACH OF CONTRACT, TORT INCLUDING NEGLIGENCE, STRICT LIABILITY, AND OTHERWISE EXCEED ONE TIMES THE TOTAL AMOUNTS PAID TO LICENSOR UNDER THIS AGREEMENT IN THE TWELVE MONTH PERIOD PRECEDING THE EVENT GIVING RISE TO THE CLAIM OR $25,000, WHICHEVER IS LESS.

11. Term and Termination.

(a) <u>Term</u>. The initial term of this Agreement begins on the Effective Date and, unless terminated earlier pursuant to any of the Agreement's express provisions, will continue in effect until five years from such date (the "Initial Term"). This Agreement will automatically renew for up to five additional successive five year terms unless earlier terminated pursuant to this Agreement's express provisions or Licensee gives Licensor written notice of non-renewal at least one hundred twenty days prior to the expiration of the then-current term or Licensor gives Licensee written notice of non-renewal at least sixty days prior to the expiration of the then-current term (each a "Renewal Term" and together with the Initial Term, the "Term").

(b) <u>Termination</u>. In addition to any other express termination right set forth in this Agreement:

(i) Licensor may terminate this Agreement, effective on written notice to Licensee, if Licensee: (A) fails to pay any amount when due hereunder, and such failure continues for more than three days after Licensor's delivery of written notice thereof; or (B) breaches any of its obligations under Section 2(b) or Section 6;

(ii) Licensor may terminate this Agreement, effective on written notice to the Licensee if Licensee breaches this Agreement, and such breach: (A) is incapable of cure; or (B) being capable of cure, remains uncured 30 days after the Licensor provides Licensee with written notice of such breach;

(iii) Licensee may terminate this Agreement, effective on written notice to the Licensor if Licensor materially breaches this Agreement, and such breach: (A) is incapable of cure; or (B) being capable of cure, remains uncured 30 days after the Licensee provides Licensor with written notice of such breach; or

(iv) either Party may terminate this Agreement, effective immediately upon written notice to the other Party, if the other Party: (A) becomes insolvent or is generally unable to pay, or fails to pay, its debts as they become due; (B) files or has filed against it, a petition for voluntary or involuntary bankruptcy or otherwise becomes subject, voluntarily or involuntarily, to any proceeding under any domestic or foreign bankruptcy or insolvency law; (C) makes or seeks to make a general assignment for the benefit of its creditors; or (D) applies for or has appointed a receiver, trustee, custodian, or similar agent appointed by order of any court of competent jurisdiction to take charge of or sell any material portion of its property or business.

(c) <u>Effect of Expiration or Termination</u>. Upon expiration or earlier termination of this Agreement, the license granted hereunder will also terminate, and, without limiting Licensee's obligations under Section 6, Licensee shall cease using and delete, destroy, or return all copies of the Software and Documentation and certify in writing to the Licensor that the Software and Documentation have been deleted or destroyed. No expiration or termination will affect Licensee's obligation to pay all Fees that may have become due before such expiration or termination, or entitle Licensee to any refund.

(d) Survival. This Section 11(d) and Sections 1, 5, 6, 7, 8(d), 9, 10, and 12 survive any termination or expiration of this Agreement. No other provisions of this Agreement survive the expiration or earlier termination of this Agreement.

12. Miscellaneous.

(a) Entire Agreement. This Agreement, together with any other documents incorporated herein by reference and all related Exhibits, constitutes the sole and entire agreement of the Parties with respect to the subject matter of this Agreement and supersedes all prior and contemporaneous understandings, agreements, and representations and warranties, both written and oral, with respect to such subject matter. In the event of any inconsistency between the statements made in the body of this Agreement, the related Exhibits, and any other documents incorporated herein by reference, the following order of precedence governs: (a) first, this Agreement, excluding its Exhibits; (b) second, the Exhibits to this Agreement as of the Effective Date; and (c) third, any other documents incorporated herein by reference.

(b) Notices. All notices, requests, consents, claims, demands, waivers, and other communications hereunder (each, a "Notice") must be in writing and addressed to the Parties at the addresses set forth on the first page of this Agreement (or to such other address that may be designated by the Party giving Notice from time to time in accordance with this Section). All Notices must be delivered by personal delivery, nationally recognized overnight courier (with all fees pre-paid), facsimile, or email (with confirmation of transmission) or certified or registered mail (in each case, return receipt requested, postage pre-paid). Except as otherwise provided in this Agreement, a Notice is effective only: (i) upon receipt by the receiving Party, and (ii) if the Party giving the Notice has complied with the requirements of this Section.

(c) Force Majeure. In no event shall Licensor be liable to Licensee, or be deemed to have breached this Agreement, for any failure or delay in performing its obligations under this Agreement, if and to the extent such failure or delay is caused by any circumstances beyond Licensor's reasonable control, including but not limited to acts of God, flood, fire, earthquake, explosion, war, terrorism, invasion, riot or other civil unrest, strikes, labor stoppages or slowdowns or other industrial disturbances, or passage of law or any action taken by a governmental or public authority, including imposing an embargo.

(d) Amendment and Modification; Waiver. No amendment to or modification of this Agreement is effective unless it is in writing and signed by an authorized representative of each Party. No waiver by any Party of any of the provisions hereof will be effective unless explicitly set forth in writing and signed by the Party so waiving. Except as otherwise set forth in this Agreement, (i) no failure to exercise, or delay in exercising, any rights, remedy, power, or privilege arising from this Agreement will operate or be construed as a waiver thereof and (ii) no single or partial exercise of any right, remedy, power, or privilege hereunder will preclude any other or further exercise thereof or the exercise of any other right, remedy, power, or privilege.

(e) Severability. If any provision of this Agreement is invalid, illegal, or unenforceable in any jurisdiction, such invalidity, illegality, or unenforceability will not affect any other term or provision of this Agreement or invalidate or render unenforceable such term or provision in any other jurisdiction. Upon such determination that any term or other provision is invalid, illegal, or unenforceable, the Parties hereto shall negotiate in good faith to modify this Agreement so as to effect the original intent of the Parties as closely as possible in a mutually acceptable manner in order that the transactions contemplated hereby be consummated as originally contemplated to the greatest extent possible.

(f)   <u>Governing Law; Submission to Jurisdiction</u>. This Agreement is governed by and construed in accordance with the internal laws of the State of Colorado without giving effect to any choice or conflict of law provision or rule that would require or permit the application of the laws of any jurisdiction other than those of the State of Colorado. Any legal suit, action, or proceeding arising out of or related to this Agreement or the licenses granted hereunder will be instituted exclusively in the federal courts of the United States or the courts of the State of Colorado in each case located in the city of Denver and County of Denver, and each Party irrevocably submits to the exclusive jurisdiction of such courts in any such suit, action, or proceeding.

(g)   <u>Assignment</u>. Licensee may not assign or transfer any of its rights or delegate any of its obligations hereunder, in each case whether voluntarily, involuntarily, by operation of law or otherwise, without the prior written consent of Licensor, which consent may be withheld, conditioned, or delayed in Licensor's sole discretion. Any purported assignment, transfer, or delegation in violation of this Section is null and void. No assignment, transfer, or delegation will relieve the assigning or delegating Party of any of its obligations hereunder. This Agreement is binding upon and inures to the benefit of the Parties hereto and their respective permitted successors and assigns.

(h)   <u>Export Regulation</u>. The Software may be subject to US export control laws, including the Export Control Reform Act and its associated regulations. Licensee shall not, directly or indirectly, export, re-export, or release the Software to, or make the Software accessible from, any jurisdiction or country to which export, re-export, or release is prohibited by law, rule, or regulation. Licensee shall comply with all applicable federal laws, regulations, and rules, and complete all required undertakings (including obtaining any necessary export license or other governmental approval), prior to exporting, re-exporting, releasing, or otherwise making the Software available outside the US.

(i)   <u>US Government Rights</u>. Each of the Documentation and the Software is a "commercial item" as that term is defined at 48 C.F.R. § 2.101, consisting of "commercial computer software" and "commercial computer software documentation" as such terms are used in 48 C.F.R. § 12.212. Accordingly, if Licensee is an agency of the US Government or any contractor therefor, Licensee only receives those rights with respect to the Software and Documentation as are granted to all other end users under license, in accordance with (a) 48 C.F.R. § 227.7201 through 48 C.F.R. § 227.7204, with respect to the Department of Defense and their contractors, or (b) 48 C.F.R. § 12.212, with respect to all other US Government licensees and their contractors.

(j)   <u>Equitable Relief</u>. Each Party acknowledges and agrees that a breach or threatened breach by such Party of any of its obligations under Section 6 or, in the case of Licensee, Section 2(b), would cause the other Party irreparable harm for which monetary damages would not be an adequate remedy and agrees that, in the event of such breach or threatened breach, the other Party will be entitled to equitable relief, including a restraining order, an injunction, specific performance, and any other relief that may be available from any court, without any requirement to post a bond or other security, or to prove actual damages or that monetary damages are not an adequate remedy. Such remedies are not exclusive and are in addition to all other remedies that may be available at law, in equity, or otherwise.

(k)   <u>Counterparts</u>. This Agreement may be executed in counterparts, each of which is deemed an original, but all of which together are deemed to be one and the same agreement.

IN WITNESS WHEREOF, the Parties hereto have executed this Agreement as of the Effective Date.

CRM SUITEWARE, INC.

By: /s/ Jamie L. Bauer

    Jamie L. Bauer
    General Counsel

TREE SERVICES, INC.

By: /s/ Melissa Green

    Melissa Green
    Chief Executive Officer

EXHIBIT A

Capitalized terms used but not defined in this Exhibit A have the meaning given to those terms in the Agreement.

1. <u>Description Of Software</u>: CRM Suiteware for Services Industry, Version 10.2, which includes the following functionality and modules: customer data tool, customer interaction tool, business information access and reporting tool, sales automation tool, lead tracking tool, contracts flow management tool, customer support tool, and reporting and data analytics tool.

2. <u>Fees</u>: The following sets forth the fees for licensing and utilizing the CRM Suiteware for Services Industry package (as described above) for the Initial Term:

Initial Installation Charge:	$5,500
Initial Training Charge (for all 7 Authorized Users):	$3,200
Hourly Training Charge:	$35.00/hour
Monthly Fee, If Paid Monthly (charged per Authorized User):	$75.00/user ($525/month)
Monthly Fee, If Paid Annually (charged per Authorized User):	$65.00/user ($5,460/year)

Licensor reserves the right, in its sole and absolute discretion, to increase the Monthly Fee, whether paid on a monthly or annual basis, for each successive Renewal Term and the Hourly Training Charge at any time 6 months after the Effective Date.

Licensee is required to pay the Monthly Fee, if paid monthly, on or before the first business day of each calendar month. Licensee is required to pay the Monthly Fee, if paid yearly, on or before June 1, or the next business day thereafter, for each year of the Initial Term and any Renewal Term. Notwithstanding the foregoing, if Licensee opts to pay the Monthly Fee paid annually for the first year of the Initial Term, such payment is due on or before June 10, 2017, the commencement date of the Initial Term.

3. <u>Authorized Users</u>: Up to 7 Authorized Users.

APPENDIX D

INDEMNIFICATION PROVISION

ARTICLE 10
INDEMNIFICATION

10.1 Indemnification of Buyer by Selling Shareholders. Subject to the other terms, conditions, and limitations contained in this Article 10, the Selling Shareholders shall jointly and severally defend, indemnify and hold harmless Buyer and its Affiliates (including the Target) and their respective officers, directors, shareholders, employees, agents, and Representatives (the "Buyer Indemnitees") from and against, and shall pay and reimburse each of them for, any and all Losses incurred or sustained by, or imposed upon, the Buyer Indemnitees based upon, arising out of, with respect to, or by reason of the following:

(a)   any inaccuracy in or breach of any of the representations or warranties of the Target contained in this Agreement or in any certificate or instrument delivered by or on behalf of the Target pursuant to this Agreement (other than with respect to Section 3.22 (Taxes), it being understood that the sole remedy for any inaccuracy or breach of Section 3.22 shall be pursuant to Article 8), as of the date such representation or warranty was made or as if such representation and warranty was made on and as of the Closing Date (except for representations and warranties that expressly relate to a specified date, the inaccuracy in or breach of which will be determined by reference to such specified date);

(b)   any breach or non-fulfillment of any covenant, agreement, or obligation to be performed by the Target pursuant to this Agreement (other than any breach or violation of, or failure to fully perform, any covenant, agreement, undertaking, or obligation in Article 8 (Taxes), it being understood that the sole remedy for any such breach, violation, or failure shall be pursuant to Article 8);

(c)   any claim made by any Selling Shareholder relating to such Person's rights with respect to the Merger Consideration, or the calculations and determinations set forth on Exhibit N regarding such Merger Consideration;

(d)   any Transaction Expenses or Indebtedness of Target outstanding as of the Closing to the extent not paid or satisfied by the Target at or prior to the Closing, or if paid by Buyer or Merger Sub at or prior to the Closing, to the extent not deducted in the determination of the Closing Merger Consideration.

10.2 Indemnification of Selling Shareholders by Buyer. Subject to the other terms, conditions, and limitations contained in this Article 10, the Buyer shall defend, indemnify, and hold harmless the Selling Shareholders and their Affiliates and Representatives (the "Selling Shareholder Indemnitees") from and against, and shall pay and reimburse each of them for, any and all Losses incurred or sustained by, or imposed upon, the Selling Shareholder Indemnitees based upon, arising out of, with respect to, or by reason of the following:

(a)   any inaccuracy in or breach of any of the representations or warranties of the Buyer and Merger Sub contained in this Agreement or in any certificate or instrument delivered by or on behalf of the Buyer or Merger Sub pursuant to this Agreement, as of the date such representation or warranty was made or as if such representation and warranty was made on and as of the Closing Date (except for representations and warranties that expressly relate to a specified date, the inaccuracy in or breach of which will be determined by reference to such specified date); or

(b) any breach or non-fulfillment of any covenant, agreement, or obligation to be performed by the Buyer or Merger Sub pursuant to this Agreement (other than any breach or violation of, or failure to fully perform, any covenant, agreement, undertaking, or obligation in Article 8 (Taxes), it being understood that the sole remedy for any such breach, violation, or failure shall be pursuant to Article 8).

10.3 Limitations. The indemnification provided for in Sections 10.1 and 10.2 shall be subject to the following limitations:

(a) Selling Shareholders shall not be liable to the Buyer Indemnitees for indemnification under Section 10.1(a) until the aggregate amount of all Losses in respect of indemnification under Section 10.1(a) exceeds two hundred thousand dollars ($200,000) (the "Selling Shareholder Basket"), in which event the Selling Shareholders shall be required to pay or be liable for all such Losses from the first dollar. The aggregate amount of all Losses for which the Selling Shareholders shall be liable pursuant to 10.1(a) shall not exceed the Total Purchase Price (the "Selling Shareholders Cap").

(b) Buyer shall not be liable to the Selling Shareholder Indemnitees for indemnification under Section 10.2(a) until the aggregate amount of all Losses in respect of indemnification under Section 10.2(a) exceeds five hundred thousand dollars ($500,000) (the "Buyer Basket"), in which event the Buyer shall be required to pay or be liable for all such Losses from the first dollar. The aggregate amount of all Losses for which Buyer shall be liable pursuant to Section 10.2(a) shall not exceed one million five hundred thousand dollars ($1,500,000) (the "Buyer Cap").

(c) Notwithstanding the foregoing, the limitations set forth in Sections 10.3(a) and (b) shall not apply to Losses based upon, arising out of, with respect to, or by reason of any inaccuracy in or breach of any representation or warranty in Section 3.1 (Organization and Qualification of Target), 3.2 (Power and Authority of Target), 3.5 (Capitalization of Target), Section 3.20 (Employee Benefit Matters of Target), 3.23 (Brokers), Section 4.1 (Organization and Authority of Buyer and Merger Sub), and Section 4.6 (Brokers).

(d) For purposes of this Article 10, any inaccuracy in or breach of any representation or warranty shall be determined without regard to any materiality, Material Adverse Effect, or other similar qualification contained in or otherwise applicable to such representation or warranty.

Section 10.4 Claim Procedures. The party making a claim under this Article 10 is referred to as the "Indemnified Party" and the party against who such claims are asserted under this Article 10 is referred to as the "Indemnifying Party".

(a) Third Party Claims. If any Indemnified Party receives notice of the assertion or commencement of any Action made or brought by any Person who is not a party to this Agreement or an Affiliate of a party to this Agreement or a Representative of the foregoing (a "Third Party Claim") against such Indemnified Party with respect to which the Indemnifying Party is obligated to provide indemnification under this Agreement, the Indemnified Party shall give the Indemnifying Party reasonably prompt written notice thereof, but in any event not later than thirty (30) calendar days after receipt of such notice of such Third Party Claim. The failure to give such prompt written notice shall not, however, relieve the Indemnifying Party of its indemnification obligations, except and only to the extent that the Indemnifying Party forfeits rights or defenses by reason of such failure. Such notice by the Indemnified Party shall describe the Third Party Claim in reasonable detail, shall include copies of all material written evidence thereof, and shall indicate the estimated amount, if reasonably practicable, of the Loss that has been or may be sustained by the Indemnified Party. The Indemnifying Party shall have the right to participate in, or by giving written notice to the Indemnified Party, to assume the defense of any Third Party Claim at the Indemnifying Party's expense and by the Indemnifying Party's own counsel, and the Indemnified Party shall cooperate in good faith in such defense; provided, that if the Indemnifying Party is a Selling Shareholder, such

Indemnifying Party shall not have the right to defend or direct the defense of any such Third Party Claim that (x) is asserted directly by or on behalf of a Person that is a supplier or customer of the Target, or (y) seeks an injunction or other equitable relief against the Indemnified Parties. In the event that the Indemnifying Party assumes the defense of any Third Party Claim, subject to Section 10.4(b), it shall have the right to take such action as it deems necessary to avoid, dispute, defend, appeal, or make counterclaims pertaining to any such Third Party Claim in the name and on behalf of the Indemnified Party. The Indemnified Party shall have the right to participate in the defense of any Third Party Claim with counsel selected by it subject to the Indemnifying Party's right to control the defense thereof. The fees and disbursements of such counsel shall be at the expense of the Indemnified Party. If the Indemnifying Party elects not to compromise or defend such Third Party Claim, fails to promptly notify the Indemnified Party in writing of its election to defend as provided in this Agreement, or fails to diligently prosecute the defense of such Third Party Claim, the Indemnified Party may, subject to Section 10.4(b), pay, compromise, or defend such Third Party Claim and seek indemnification for any and all Losses based upon, arising from, or relating to such Third Party Claim. Stockholder Representative and Buyer shall cooperate with each other in all reasonable respects in connection with the defense of any Third Party Claim, including making available records relating to such Third Party Claim and furnishing, without expense (other than reimbursement of actual out-of-pocket expenses) to the defending party, management employees of the non-defending party as may be reasonably necessary for the preparation of the defense of such Third Party Claim.

(b) Settlement of Third Party Claims. Notwithstanding any other provision of this Agreement, the Indemnifying Party shall not enter into settlement of any Third Party Claim without the prior written consent of the Indemnified Party, except as provided in this Section 10.4(b). If a firm offer is made to settle a Third Party Claim without leading to liability or the creation of a financial or other obligation on the part of the Indemnified Party and provides, in customary form, for the unconditional release of each Indemnified Party from all liabilities and obligations in connection with such Third Party Claim and the Indemnifying Party desires to accept and agree to such offer, the Indemnifying Party shall give written notice to that effect to the Indemnified Party. If the Indemnified Party fails to consent to such firm offer within ten (10) days after its receipt of such notice, the Indemnified Party may continue to contest or defend such Third Party Claim and in such event, the maximum liability of the Indemnifying Party as to such Third Party Claim shall not exceed the amount of such settlement offer. If the Indemnified Party fails to consent to such firm offer and also fails to assume defense of such Third Party Claim, the Indemnifying Party may settle the Third Party Claim upon the terms set forth in such firm offer to settle such Third Party Claim. If the Indemnified Party has assumed the defense pursuant to Section 10.4(a), it shall not agree to any settlement without the written consent of the Indemnifying Party (which consent shall not be unreasonably withheld or delayed).

(c) Direct Claims. Any Action by an Indemnified Party on account of a Loss which does not result from a Third Party Claim (a "Direct Claim") shall be asserted by the Indemnified Party giving the Indemnifying Party reasonably prompt written notice thereof, but in any event not later than thirty (30) days after the Indemnified Party becomes aware of such Direct Claim. The failure to give such prompt written notice shall not, however, relieve the Indemnifying Party of its indemnification obligations, except and only to the extent that the Indemnifying Party forfeits rights or defenses by reason of such failure. Such notice by the Indemnified Party shall describe the Direct Claim in reasonable detail, shall include copies of all material written evidence thereof, and shall indicate the estimated amount, if reasonably practicable, of the Loss that has been or may be sustained by the Indemnified Party. The Indemnifying Party shall have thirty (30) days after its receipt of such notice to respond in writing to such Direct Claim. The Indemnified Party shall allow the Indemnifying Party and its professional advisors to investigate the matter or circumstance alleged

to give rise to the Direct Claim, and whether and to what extent any amount is payable in respect of the Direct Claim and the Indemnified Party shall assist the Indemnifying Party's investigation by giving such information and assistance (including access to the Target's premises and personnel and the right to examine and copy any accounts, documents or records) as the Indemnifying Party or any of its professional advisors may reasonably request. If the Indemnifying Party does not so respond within such thirty (30) day period, the Indemnifying Party shall be deemed to have rejected such claim, in which case the Indemnified Party shall be free to pursue such remedies as may be available to the Indemnified Party on the terms and subject to the provisions of this Agreement.

(d) Tax Claims. Notwithstanding any other provision of this Agreement, the control of any claim, assertion, event, or proceeding in respect of Taxes of the Target (including, but not limited to, any such claim in respect of a breach of the representations and warranties in Section 3.22 or any breach or violation of or failure to fully perform any covenant, agreement, undertaking or obligation in Article 8) shall be governed exclusively by Article 8.

Section 10.5 Payments; Indemnification Escrow Fund.

(a) Once a Loss is agreed to by the Indemnifying Party or finally adjudicated to be payable pursuant to this Article 10, the Indemnifying Party shall satisfy its obligations within fifteen (15) Business Days of such final, non-appealable adjudication by wire transfer of immediately available funds. The parties hereto agree that should an Indemnifying Party not make full payment of any such obligation within such fifteen (15) Business Day period, any amount payable shall accrue interest from and including the date of agreement of the Indemnifying Party or final, non-appealable adjudication to and excluding the date such payment has been made at a rate per annum equal to ten percent (10%). Such interest shall be calculated daily on the basis of a 365 day year and the actual number of days elapsed, without compounding.

(b) Any Losses payable to a Buyer Indemnitee pursuant to this Article 10 shall be satisfied (i) from the Indemnification Escrow Fund; and (ii) to the extent the amount of Losses exceeds the amount available in the Indemnification Escrow Fund, from the Selling Shareholders, jointly and severally.

(c) Upon the termination of the Indemnification Escrow Fund pursuant to the terms of the Escrow Agreement, the Escrow Agent shall pay any amounts remaining in the Indemnification Escrow Fund to the Selling Shareholders as set forth in the Escrow Agreement.

10.6 Characterization of Payments. For tax purposes, all of the parties to this Agreement agree to treat any indemnification payment under this Article 10 as an adjustment to the Total Purchase Price, unless otherwise required by Law.

10.7 Effect of Insurance and Other Recoveries.

(a) All Losses for which Indemnified Parties would otherwise be entitled to indemnification under this Article 10 shall be reduced by the amount of insurance proceeds, indemnity payments, and other third-party recoveries actually received by the Indemnified Parties, net of reasonable costs and expenses incurred by the Indemnified Party in such recovery, with respect to the Losses incurred by such Indemnified Parties.

(b) In the event the Indemnified Parties are entitled to any insurance proceeds, indemnity payments, or any third-party recoveries with respect to any Losses (or any of the circumstances giving rise to Losses) for which such Indemnified Parties are entitled to indemnification pursuant to this Article 10, the Indemnified Parties will attempt to obtain, receive, or realize such proceeds, benefits, payments, or recoveries or may demand that the Indemnifying Party attempt to obtain, receive, or realize such proceeds, benefits, payments, or recoveries on behalf of Indemnified Parties at Indemnified Parties' reasonable cost and expense.

(c) In the event that any of the insurance proceeds, indemnity payments, or other third-party recoveries not previously taken into account are obtained by the Indemnified Parties subsequent to receipt by such Indemnified Parties of any indemnification payment under this Agreement with respect to Claims to which such insurance proceeds, indemnity payments, or other third-party recoveries relate, refunds shall be made to the Indemnifying Parties by the Indemnified Parties of the relevant portion of such recovery, net of reasonable costs or expenses incurred by the Indemnified Party in such recovery.

(d) All such payments or recoveries received pursuant to this Section 10.7 shall be reduced by any and all expenses, costs, or other fees incurred by the Indemnified Parties, including any loss or erosion of insurance coverage, increase in insurance premiums, or the reasonable costs and expenses of outside counsel, accountants, and other advisors to such Indemnified Parties, all as determined in Indemnified Parties reasonable discretion.

10.8 Exclusive Remedy. The Indemnified Parties acknowledge and agree that, from and after the Closing Date, their sole and exclusive monetary remedy with respect to any and all Claims relating to the subject matter of this Agreement shall be pursuant to the indemnification provisions set forth in this Article 10. Notwithstanding the foregoing, nothing in this Agreement shall be deemed to constitute a waiver of any injunctive or other equitable remedies or any tort claims of, or causes of action arising from any intentionally fraudulent misrepresentations, willful breaches, or deceit.

10.9 Survival Period. Subject to the limitations and other provisions of this Agreement, the representations and warranties contained in this Agreement (other than any representations or warranties contained in Section 3.22 (Taxes, which are subject to Article 8) shall survive the Closing and shall remain in full force and effect until the date that is thirty-six (36) months from the Closing Date, provided that the representations and warranties in sections (a) 3.1 (Organization and Qualification of Target), 3.2 (Power and Authority of Target), 3.5 (Capitalization of Target), 3.23 (Brokers), 4.1 (Organization and Authority of Buyer and Merger Sub), and 4.6 (Brokers) shall survive indefinitely, (b) 3.17 (Environmental Matters of Target) shall survive for a period of twenty (20) years after Closing, and (c) 3.20 (Employee Benefit Matters of Target) shall survive for the full period of all applicable statutes of limitations (giving effect to any waiver, mitigation, or extension thereof) plus 120 days. All covenants and agreements of the Target and the Selling Shareholders contained in this Agreement (other than any covenants or agreements contained in Article 8 (Tax Matters) which are subject to Article 8) shall survive the Closing indefinitely or for the period explicitly specified therein. Notwithstanding the foregoing, any Claims asserted in good faith with reasonable specificity and in writing by notice from the Indemnified Party to the Indemnifying Parties prior to the expiration date of the applicable survival period shall not be barred by the expiration of the relevant representation or warranty and such Claims shall survive until finally resolved.

APPENDIX E

ANCILLARY INFORMATION

Tree Services, Inc.

Tree Services, Inc. Contact Information

> 6789 120th Street
> Commerce City, CO 80602
> (303) 555-5555
> www.tsi.com

Tree Services, Inc. Founders

> Melissa Green
> Thomas Shrub
> Susan Brown

Tree Services, Inc. Primary Shareholders

> Melissa Green, 39.22%
> Thomas Shrub, 39.22%
> Susan Brown, 19.61%

Tree Services, Inc. Executive Officers

> Melissa Green, Chief Executive Officer
> Thomas Shrub, Chief Financial Officer
> Susan Brown, Senior Vice President—Marketing
> Timothy Han, Senior Vice President & Secretary

Tree Services, Inc. Board of Directors

> Melissa Green, Chairperson
> Thomas Shrub
> Jonathon Nixon
> Erin Mooney
> Rolland Brown

Tree Services, Inc. Outside Legal Counsel

> Williams & Rader, LLC
> 1400 29th Street, Suite 2201
> Denver, CO 80205
> Sasha Williams, Partner and primary contact

Tree Services, Inc. Commercial Lender (Term Loan)

> Big Bank of Colorado
> 100 19th Street
> Denver, CO 80202

Tree Services, Inc. Commercial Lender (Line of Credit)

> Bank of the Rockies
> 1800 19th Street
> Denver, CO 80203

Tree Services, Inc. Outside Accountant

> Dunton & Teller, LLC
> 1300 East 18th Avenue
> Denver, CO 80202
> Madison Schopp, primary contact

Dutch Elm Company

Dutch Elm Company Contact Information

> Dutch Elm Company
> 10000 Patrick Lane
> Las Vegas, NV 89118
> (702) 555-5555
> www.dec.com

Dutch Elm Company Founders

> Fred Wilcox
> Bernard Thompson
> Margaret Fine

Dutch Elm Company Primary Shareholders

> Fred Wilcox, 40.86%
> Bernard Thompson, 27.31%
> Margaret Fine, 22.80%

Dutch Elm Company Executive Officers

> Fred Wilcox, Chief Executive Officer & President
> Bernard Thompson, Chief Operating Officer
> Margaret Fine, Chief Financial Officer
> Michelle Smith, Senior Vice President of Sales & Marketing
> Robert Lawson, Senior Vice President & Secretary

Dutch Elm Company Board of Directors

> Fred Wilcox, Chairman
> Bernard Thompson
> Margaret Fine
> William Carlton
> Lisa Montgomery

Dutch Elm Company Outside Legal Counsel

> McClelland, Springer & Combelic, PC
> 5555 Rampart Ridge Road, Suite 55
> Las Vegas, NV 89117
> Greg Combelic, Partner and primary contact

INDEX

References are to Pages
